The renewal of radicalism

Manchester University Press

The renewal of radicalism

Politics, identity and ideology in England, 1867–1924

MATTHEW KIDD

Manchester University Press

Copyright © Matthew Kidd 2020

The right of Matthew Kidd to be identified as the author of this work has been asserted by him in accordance with the Copyright, Designs and Patents Act 1988.

Published by Manchester University Press
Altrincham Street, Manchester M1 7JA

www.manchesteruniversitypress.co.uk

British Library Cataloguing-in-Publication Data
A catalogue record for this book is available from the British Library

ISBN 978 1 5261 4072 2   hardback

First published 2020

The publisher has no responsibility for the persistence or accuracy of URLs for any external or third-party internet websites referred to in this book, and does not guarantee that any content on such websites is, or will remain, accurate or appropriate.

Typeset by Newgen Publishing UK

Contents

List of figures	vi
List of abbreviations	vii
Acknowledgements	ix
Introduction	1
1 Radicalism, class and populism	28
2 Charles Bradlaugh and the constitution	55
3 Radicalism, socialism and labourism	80
4 Splits in the progressive party	105
5 Labour and the nationalisation of politics	128
6 Labourism, class and populism	152
7 Labourism and the challenge of war	176
8 Old radicalism and the new social order	201
Conclusion	225
Bibliography	232
Index	246

Figures

1. 'A Contrast!', 1874 (Northamptonshire Central Library; NCL, 198–781/9/1874, NEE) — 43
2. 'Rather more than he can swallow', *The Wyvern*, 25 May 1894 (University of Leicester Special Collections; LUSC, MS81 76, GOR) — 99
3. 'The Profiteer', *The Labour Outlook*, 31 March 1920 (British Library of Political and Economic Science; LSE, ILP/6/20/15, ILP PEA) — 209

Abbreviations

Parties, unions and organisations

BLEA	Bristol and District Trades' Council Labour Electoral Association
BSP	British Socialist Party
BSS	Bristol Socialist Society
CPGB	Communist Party of Great Britain
ILP	Independent Labour Party
LAHU	Leicester Amalgamated Hosiery Union
LHA	Labour History Archive and Study Centre, Manchester
LRA	Liberal and Radical Association
LRC	Labour Representation Committee
NALRWU	National Agricultural Labourers' and Rural Workers' Union
NUBSO	National Union of Boot and Shoe Operatives
NUBSRF	National Union of Boot and Shoe Rivetters and Finishers
PLP	Parliamentary Labour Party
SDF	Social Democratic Federation

Abbreviations used only in references

AR	annual reports
BILP	Independent Labour Party, Bristol branch
BLP	Bristol Labour Party
BRO	Bristol Records Office
BTC	Bristol Trades' Council
C	correspondence
CR	conference reports
GC	general correspondence
GOR	political memorabilia collection of Archibald Gorrie, Leicester
LP	Labour Party

LRO	Record Office for Leicestershire
LSE	British Library of Political and Economic Science, London (known as 'LSE Library')
LUSC	University of Leicester Special Collections
M	minutes
MEA	municipal election addresses
MR	monthly reports
MRC	Modern Records Centre
NCL	Northamptonshire Central Library
NEE	Northampton election ephemera
NFRO	Norfolk Record Office
NHRO	Northamptonshire Record Office
PEA	parliamentary election addresses
TC	Trades Councils

Acknowledgements

I would like to thank all those friends, family members and colleagues who have supported me through the writing of this book. In particular, I would like to thank Raen for her patience and understanding, Mum and Pove for their hospitality, Nan for everything, Jessie for her companionship and Christine for the books. I am also grateful to many people, in various capacities, for making this book possible. Above all, I would like to thank Sascha Auerbach and Dean Blackburn for their expert guidance and encouragement over the last eight years. My appreciation also goes to Chris Wrigley, Jon Lawrence, Luke Finley, Manchester University Press, Darren Treadwell at the People's History Museum and the hardworking staff at the libraries, archives and institutions that facilitated the research for this book.

Introduction

Throughout the 1920s, Labour candidates and activists promised voters that if Labour was returned to office, they would begin to build a new social order. In their view, Labour's position on the key issues of the day stood in stark contrast to those of their major rivals, the Conservatives and the Liberals. Unlike the old established parties of the past, Labour was a forward-looking party with a bold vision for the future.

But party activists also claimed that Labour had its roots in a much older political tradition. In their speeches and writings, Labour activists positioned their party as the rightful heir to a working-class radical tradition whose members had been at the forefront of campaigns for political and social reform in the mid- to late nineteenth century. Having emerged from this political tradition, Labour, it was argued, was best placed to put its historic ideals into effect.

This book contends that the emergence of labour politics in towns and cities across the East Midlands, East Anglia and the South West of England represented the renewal of the working-class radical tradition. In the mid- to late Victorian period, working-class radicals formed lively political subcultures in Bristol, Leicester, Lincoln, Northampton and Norwich. With a distinctive set of discursive practices and a unique vision of the social order, working-class radicals sustained local political subcultures that were distinct from, and sometimes opposed to, mainstream liberalism. They also articulated a coherent ideology and a highly expansive workerist notion of democracy that led them into conflict with classical liberals and proponents of populist forms of radicalism.

During the 1880s and 1890s, working-class radicals played a pivotal role in building local labour parties that would eventually affiliate to the national Labour Party, formed as the Labour Representation Committee (LRC) in 1900. They also began to display an increasing interest in using the state to remedy social ills such as unemployment, long working hours and poverty in old age. But while the transition from radical politics to labour politics represented an important organisational development, it did not reflect a substantive change in the way activists thought and spoke about themselves or the social order. Even as they formed new political organisations, labourists remained committed to the discursive strategies and ideological assumptions of their working-class radical predecessors.

Continuity, populism and class

Establishing lines of continuity between working-class radicalism and later forms of labour politics challenges conventional understandings of English political history. The three-stage model of British political development suggests that social and economic developments in the final decades of the nineteenth century forced radicals to renounce their loyalty to the cross-class Liberal Party and embrace alternative frameworks for understanding the socio-political order.[1] Those swept up in the socialist revival of the 1880s began to advocate (among other things) the collective ownership of the means of production and direct labour representation on local and national governing bodies. The latter demand struck a chord with those who had come to describe themselves as labour activists, many of whom rejected the impractical doctrines of the socialists but supported the principle of labour (or trade union) representation. How to achieve this goal was a matter of heated debate within labour and socialist circles, but this did not stop activists from improvising at a local level. In some constituencies, socialist parties stood their own candidates in parliamentary and municipal elections. In others, socialists and labourists worked together to stand candidates in opposition to the Conservative and Liberal parties. And in others, labourists worked with the Liberal and Conservative parties to achieve their objectives, much to the chagrin of their socialist counterparts.

As this brief overview suggests, the business of achieving labour representation at the end of the nineteenth century was a complex affair. It was also a largely futile exercise. However, for proponents of the stagist interpretation, this is not the crucial issue. What is crucial is the fact that activists put the question of labour representation on the table at all, for it signified a decisive shift in the way workers thought about politics and society. In short, workers' political activity had increasingly come to revolve around the question of class. The formation of the LRC in 1900, renamed the Labour Party in 1906, was yet another sign of the rise of 'class politics'. Founded and largely funded by the trade unions, the Labour Party, which was set up to vocalise the concerns of the trade union movement, was the political embodiment of a new form of politics. The evolution of a class-based party from a trade union pressure group to a party of government, a feat that Labour accomplished in a little under twenty-five years, symbolised the decline of populist politics and, with it, the demise of the Liberal Party.

The stagist narrative thus draws attention to major discontinuities in popular politics during the nineteenth and early twentieth centuries, and stresses the importance of class as a determinant of political allegiance. But since the 1980s this once-dominant view has come under sustained attack from a diverse range of scholars who, to varying degrees, have embraced the 'linguistic turn' in the humanities and social sciences.[2] Taken as a collective body of work, their studies have helped to dethrone the concept of class from its position as the main explanatory framework for understanding British politics before the First World War. The work of Gareth Stedman Jones and Patrick Joyce in particular has shed light on the importance of non-class identities in nineteenth-century England and questioned the extent to which material factors dictate the nature and pace of political change.[3] The work of Eugenio Biagini and Alastair Reid has challenged the discontinuous narrative of political change by suggesting that the revival of socialism and the emergence of labour politics in the 1880s and 1890s represented the recomposition of the 'popular radical' tradition rather than the beginning of a new phase in Britain's political development.[4] 'Popular' is the crucial word here, for Biagini and Reid contend that radicalism was a 'plebeian' or cross-class movement of 'the people', a group that included artisans, small tradesmen, organised workers and, in some places, gentlemen rather than the movement of a single class.[5] The work of Patrick Joyce, though differing from that of Biagini and Reid in its focus on the questions of identity and belonging, has also suggested that radicals generally avoided a language of class in favour of terms and phrases that denoted inclusiveness, reconciliation, fellowship and extra-economic categorisation.[6] In this view, popular radicalism was a populist movement that survived the tumultuous final years of the nineteenth century and continued to shape the tone of progressive politics until at least 1914.

There appears to be little middle ground between the two interpretations discussed so far. Whereas the stagist interpretation emphasises discontinuity and the rise of class politics, the 'continuity thesis' emphasises continuity and the survival of non-class politics. The aim of this book is to demonstrate that this dichotomy is unnecessary. Drawing on five local case studies, it suggests that a persuasive argument for continuity can be made without having to abandon class as a tool of historical analysis. It attempts to show that labour activists remained committed to the discursive practices and core ideological beliefs of their radical predecessors even as they formed new political organisations. But it argues that their radical predecessors were *working-class* radicals rather than *populist* radicals. The distinction is not merely semantic. Differences between the two iterations of radicalism reveal themselves in several ways, not least in the way they spoke about the socio-political order and used certain terms, phrases and concepts. Where populist radicals saw the basic division in society as between 'the idle' and 'the industrious', working-class radicals framed their understandings of the social order in a language of class. Populist radicals tended to emphasise the benefits that political and social reform would bring to the community, while working-class radicals were more concerned with furthering the interests of the working class. And whereas populist radicals spoke of 'the people' as an intermediary social group situated between the idle rich and the idle poor, working-class radicals tended to use the term side by side with and sometimes as an alternative description for the working class (or classes).

The working-class radical tradition left an indelible mark on the political labour movement. Using the term 'populist' to describe the character of this tradition would only serve to conceal the complexities that characterised its relationships with other political and intellectual forces. It would also conceal the very real tensions that existed between radicals and liberals in the mid- to late nineteenth century. The existence of such tensions has not gone unnoticed. Since the early 1990s, the work of Antony Taylor, Mark Bevir and Jon Lawrence, among others, has brought to light the persistence of a vibrant and semi-independent radical subculture that existed outside the sphere of mainstream liberalism.[7] These studies have helped to show that the distinctions between radicalism and liberalism were far more pronounced and complex than scholars had previously acknowledged. Still, they have only gone so far in challenging the continuity thesis. For example, they have tended to focus on the continuities between radicalism and socialist politics rather than the continuities between radicalism and labour politics.[8] This is perhaps understandable given that socialists were often the most vocal, disruptive and, for some, interesting political actors at the time. It is important, though, not to overstate the numerical strength and political impact of the socialist movement. While the boundaries between socialism and labourism were far from clear-cut, socialist organisations such as the Social Democratic Federation (SDF) and the Independent Labour Party (ILP) were always small minorities within the wider labour movement.

Moreover, these studies have only briefly considered the tensions that existed *within* the radical movement. Uncovering such tensions contributes to our understanding of later developments in British politics. For one thing, it makes it easier to account for the emergence of a class-based and class-orientated Labour Party without having to abandon either an emphasis on class or an emphasis on continuity. While the creation of the Labour Party represented an important development in British politics, locating it as part of an older tradition in which class had served as a defining element makes it possible to understand the workerist tone of its early rhetoric. In addition, seeing local labour parties as successors to the working-class radical movements of the nineteenth century helps to explain the dynamics of progressive politics in the Edwardian era. For instance, it becomes easier to explain the nature of the relationship between local Liberal Associations and their Labour counterparts after 1900. In many towns and cities across urban Britain, progressive politics was often divided between a cross-class Liberal Party and an overwhelmingly working-class (and less electorally successful) labour movement. As in the Victorian period, activists on both sides of the progressive divide agreed on a broad range of issues, but there were also numerous questions, both strategic and ideological, on which they disagreed. Interpreting these developments as the outcome of a rise of 'class politics' would involve ignoring the similar relationship that had existed between organised liberalism and the radical movement in the mid- to late nineteenth century. And seeing Liberal and Labour activists as joint heirs of a populist 'radical liberal' tradition would mean overlooking the ideological and class-based tensions that so often characterised their relationship during the Edwardian period. It is only by seeing local LRCs or 'labour parties' as the descendants of a decidedly working-class radical tradition that we can fully explain both their character and their attitudes to the Liberal Party in the years before the First World War.

Exposing tensions in the Victorian radical movement goes some way towards reinstating the concept of class in discussions about British political history. Class-based terminology was an ever-present feature of both working-class radical and labourist discourse between 1867 and 1924. The tendency for some scholars to minimise the prevalence of class vocabulary in political discourse may have arisen because they have been looking for a conception of class that connotes conflict.[9] This is somewhat understandable given that an adversarial notion of class has informed so many studies of British history. Articulated most famously by E. P. Thompson, this notion suggests that:

> Class happens when some men, as a result of common experiences (inherited or shared), feel and articulate the identity of their interests as between themselves, and *as against* other men whose interests are different from (and *usually opposed to*) theirs.[10]

In the towns and cities that form the basis of this book, working-class radicals and their labourist successors articulated a rather different conception of class. While they were committed trade unionists who proudly described themselves as members of the working class, they refuted accusations that they recognised or hoped to instigate a class war. And while they adopted a class-centred approach to politics and worked to place working-class representatives on local and national governing bodies, they did so to fix perceived defects in the political and industrial system rather than to subvert the existing social order. Resembling in many ways the 'introverted and defensive' sense of class that Ross McKibbin has identified among workers in the interwar period, though devoid of its 'defeatist and fatalistic' qualities, this was a shared tradition in which a language of class was strong but a language of class opposition was not.[11]

Radical strongholds

This book uses case studies of five English towns and cities to reveal continuities between working-class radicalism and twentieth-century Labour politics. Focusing on Bristol, Leicester, Lincoln, Northampton and Norwich addresses the geographical imbalance of previous scholarship on the topic. With a few notable exceptions, the historiography of progressive politics in pre-war England has tended to focus on constituencies in London, the North and the West Midlands.[12] Given the electoral importance of these regions for the Liberal and Labour parties, this is somewhat understandable. However, as Duncan Tanner showed, there were other important seats in England that needed to be won if the Liberals and, later, the Labour Party wished to form stable governments.[13] As the first study of its kind to integrate these case studies and examine them in parallel, this book provides a necessary corrective to a historiography that has often prioritised political heartlands or electoral anomalies.

On any conventional map, the area covered in this book stretches from Bristol in the South West via Leicester, Northampton and Lincoln in the East Midlands to Norwich in East Anglia. Despite their economic differences, these towns and cities shared a reputation as centres of religious and political radicalism. They also shared a broadly similar political trajectory. Between the mid- to late nineteenth century and the First World War, they were widely considered to be electoral strongholds of the Liberal Party, though divisions between radicals and liberals sometimes allowed Conservative candidates to win a plurality of votes. During the 1880s and 1890s, the Liberals began to face electoral challenges from their left flank, but the advance of socialism and labourism was uneven before the First World War. At the 1923 general election, though, the Labour Party captured seats in all five towns and cities, and, while it lost some of them a year later after the fall of the first Labour government, they tended to fall into the hands of the Conservatives rather than the once-dominant Liberals.

It would be misleading to stress the typicality of these towns and cities. As a wealth of studies have shown, Britain's socio-economic structure was regionally diverse during this period. Its political culture was fragmented, and local peculiarities, contexts, pressures and traditions exerted an influence on electoral outcomes well into the 1920s. Many of the concerns of working-class radicals and labourists were also local in nature. Radical dissatisfaction with organised liberalism was essentially dissatisfaction with *local* Liberal Associations, and the emergence of local labour politics was often the product of *localised* political or industrial disagreements. While the establishment of a national Labour Party in 1900 served to impose a semblance of unity on these disparate political forces, there remained in effect hundreds of labour parties, 'all with similarities but all distinctive within their own geographical context'.[14]

By mapping the organisational trajectory of labour politics from its origins in the working-class radical movements of the 1870s through to its consolidation and triumph in the interwar period, this book sheds light on some aspects of the 'nationalisation' phenomena. Intentionally or not, the Labour Party made a strong contribution to a process through which 'highly localized and territorialized politics' gave way to 'national electoral alignments and oppositions'.[15] The presence of a small body of Labour MPs in the House of Commons provided local activists with an example to follow, and party head office began to act as a co-ordinating centre that drew together and offered guidance to previously disconnected local activists. In short, the party, its MPs and its leading spokespersons acted as poles of attraction towards which local activists could navigate. This imposed a degree of order on 'unofficial' forms of politics and, to some extent, served to standardise labourist discourse. While they may have disagreed with its tactics or seen little need to replicate its model at a local level, local activists considered Labour to be a party that was distinct from others and, therefore, worthy of sympathy if not active support. While this may seem like a modest change, it laid the basis for the growth of the party in interwar period.

Still, the growth of the party did not fundamentally alter the identities and ideologies of local activists. This is one of the reasons why in-depth local studies are so valuable. One of the aims of this book is to suggest that developments at the local level may have more accurately reflected changes in the way people spoke about politics, identity and ideology. Examining political discourse at this level reveals much about the way in which widely used terms, phrases and concepts took on different meanings in different contexts, and suggests that discursive tussles over meaning could be initiated by localised statements and developments. Take, for example, the following hypothetical scenario, which closely mirrors an incident that will be discussed in Chapter 2. A prospective election candidate for a two-member constituency informs a group of voters that he is a staunch 'radical liberal' in politics. At subsequent meetings, he refers to himself as a 'working-man's candidate' and declares his opposition to both the Conservatives and the aristocratic wing of the Liberal Party. His speeches, reported in the largely unsympathetic provincial press, initiate a heated discussion in local political circles. Populist radicals rally around the candidate and announce that he represents the true spirit of liberalism. Working-class radicals also rally around the candidate but prefer to emphasise his working-class credentials and his promise to represent the 'working classes'. Radicals of different stripes then engage in a discussion about the true meaning of radicalism, and debate whether radicals should prioritise the claims of one section of the community over all others. Liberals, sensing the electoral implications of these divisions, accuse the candidate of stirring up class hatred and of deliberately seeking to disrupt the harmony of the radical–liberal alliance. Conservatives, keen to take advantage of radical–liberal disunity, accept the candidate's claim that he represents the true voice of liberalism, safe in the knowledge that by doing so, they will be strengthening their own appeal to voters who feel little sympathy with the candidate's 'extreme' views.

Untangling debates of this kind brings to light some of the complexities at the heart of popular politics. As the above example suggests, verbal contests over meaning were conducted as much at the constituency level as at the national, parliamentary level. Rather than simply adopting the views of high-level thinkers or politicians, local-level political actors played an active role in constructing and reconstructing the meaning of the terms and phrases that made up the language of politics. They engaged in contests over the meaning and significance of historical stories, traditions or myths and often referred to dramatic episodes in English history such as the Peasants' Revolt, the English Civil War, the Peterloo Massacre, Chartism, and, in exalted moments, the destruction of the golden age of Anglo-Saxon democracy and the imposition of the 'Norman Yoke'.[16] In an attempt to gain legitimacy, they also weaved stories about local rebellions, such as the 1831 reform riots in Bristol, the anti-enclosure Kett's Rebellion in Norfolk in 1549, and the firm support afforded to the Puritan and parliamentary cause by Northamptonians during the Civil War, into their political appeals.

By constructing a narrative of popular rebellion against injustice, labour and socialist activists sought to demonstrate that the roots of their political visions lay deep in English history.[17] It is also likely that activists incorporated historical stories into their propaganda for electoral purposes. Keir Hardie, the 'father of the Labour Party', seemed well aware of the importance of sending the right message to voters, advising a Norwich-based activist in 1898 that he should replace sketches of foreign radicals in a forthcoming article with 'home patriots' such as 'the Levellors [sic] of the Cromwellian period' and 'the Radicals + Chartists'.[18] Still, even if there were strategic reasons for retelling these stories, labourists and socialists clearly demonstrated a strong affinity with the ideas and assumptions on which they were based. In short, they genuinely believed that the examples set by certain historical figures and traditions remained relevant in the modern era.

Rethinking radicalism

Examining the content and tone of the discussions described above helps to identify the building blocks of political ideologies. Building on the work of political theorist Michael Freeden, this book takes the novel step of applying the conceptual approach to ideologies to the chaotic world of local politics.[19] This involves approaching ideologies as assemblages of concepts, the meanings of which are determined by their position in an ideology's internal 'morphology'. When the structure of an ideology is perceived in spatial terms, it takes the form of a concentric circle with 'core' concepts at the centre, 'adjacent' concepts in the next band and 'peripheral' concepts on the outer edge. At the centre of any ideology is a group of core concepts that, if removed from their central position, significantly alter the nature of an ideology. They are surrounded by a set of adjacent concepts that help to anchor the concepts at the core and limit the potentially infinite meanings that individuals could assign to them. Concepts in the periphery band, which take the form of specific practices, institutions, events or policy proposals, help to link core and adjacent concepts to their temporal and spatial context.[20]

For Freeden, it is the relationship between core, adjacent and peripheral concepts that gives them and their parent ideologies their distinctive meanings. The example of classical liberalism, which was arguably the dominant ideology in Britain during the mid- to late nineteenth century, can be used to illustrate this point. While liberals were not alone in emphasising liberty, individualism and progress, they offered an interpretation of these concepts that differed from that of their rivals. This was because these concepts were located at the core of liberalism's morphology and positioned in close proximity to adjacent concepts such as democracy, equality and rights of property. The precise location and arrangement of these concepts, and the mutually influential relationship between them, generated a particular version of liberalism that led its proponents to advocate policies that encouraged moral improvement through self-help, thrift and individual exertion.

Seeing ideologies as distinct configurations of political concepts makes it easier to establish their uniqueness. For example, it allows us to see that the demand for the nationalisation of the railways is not necessarily evidence of a socialist perspective. Between 1867 and 1924, this demand was put forward by individuals from across the ideological spectrum, from socialists and labourists through to liberals and even conservatives. However, they favoured the proposal for different reasons. Whereas socialists saw nationalisation as a stepping-stone to a future socialist commonwealth, labourists tended to focus on the immediate, material benefits that nationalisation would bring to railway workers. To understand why this was the case, it is useful to look beyond political demands to the conceptual framework upon which these demands were based.

By exploring the ways in which 'ordinary' political activists articulated their understanding of political concepts, this book challenges the idea that ideology is primarily constructed and disseminated by high-level theorists or politicians. Very often, assessments of the Labour Party's political thought have been skewed towards those who have written or spoken in a theoretical way, which, for Jose Harris, has involved narrowing the focus to a 'tiny group of people ... who have functioned as "academic" theorists'.[21] But as Michael Freeden has argued:

> Political thought is to be found at any level of political action, on different levels of sophistication. It is not necessarily identical with the coherent speculation of a number of isolated men regarded as having inherent worth and significant bearing on political life.[22]

By extending Freeden's analysis to the local level, it becomes clear that local political activists, whether or not they read a wide selection of political or philosophical works, made a strong contribution to the ideological landscape by refracting national-level messages through a local lens and by engaging in 'less sophisticated and more open' debates about the meaning of a concept or ideology.[23] Debates of this kind were vitally important in the development of the Labour Party, as it was local activists who, in the words of Matthew Worley, 'most perceptibly encompassed Labour's actual and projected identity' and who 'propagated and articulated Labour policy' to the public.[24]

An exploration of these debates yields the conclusion that radicalism was a conceptually coherent ideology that should be treated separately from liberalism. Far from lacking 'any clear ideological basis', as Royden Harrison once argued, radicals offered a clear ideological vision and put forward a consistent set of demands that included the peaceful expansion of the franchise, a more equitable distribution of political representation and power, the protection and extension of workers' political and industrial rights, and the reform or dismantling of institutions, such as the House of Lords, which subverted the 'true' nature of the English (or British) constitution.[25] These demands rested on a firm ideological basis, and by constructing a conceptual framework for radical ideology we can more fully understand their nature and tone.

Political scientists have paid little attention to radicalism as an ideology.[26] Freeden, for example, has drawn upon Eugenio Biagini's work and suggested that radicalism was a member of the liberal ideological family rather than an ideology in its own right. But while the boundaries between radicalism and liberalism were certainly blurred and though conceptual overlaps did occur, it is possible to make a strong case for the distinctiveness of the radical morphology. Radicals were above all guided by the concepts of democracy, liberty, individuality, progress and rationality. These core concepts were situated at the heart of the radical worldview and were present in all known varieties of the ideology. They were surrounded by a set of adjacent concepts that included equality, the general interest and rights, as well as a set of 'marginal' concepts, including the state, whose importance to the ideological core was 'intellectually and emotionally insubstantial'. To prevent these concepts from existing at an abstract level with little relevance to the real world, radicalism, like all ideologies, contained a set of 'perimeter' concepts, including (male) adult suffrage, triennial Parliaments, vote by ballot, Irish Home Rule, equal electoral districts, and reform or abolition of the House of Lords.[27]

The relationship between radicalism's core, adjacent and peripheral concepts generated a highly expansive notion of democracy. Democracy, as Freeden has noted, is 'heavily packed with past associations, debates and prejudices stretching back to antiquity'.[28] But because of its proximity to liberty, long understood in the English 'idea environment' to mean non-constraint and the absence of impediments to making choices, and individuality, widely understood as the sovereignty of the individual, radicals saw democracy as a form of self-government in which all adult males should exercise power through democratically elected representatives. The radical notion of democracy was coloured by a belief in the essential rationality of human beings and the assumption that at least half the population had the capacity to determine their own future. All these concepts were tied to the concept of progress, which in general terms means the movement from a less desirable state to a more desirable state but which for radicals meant gradual social and political progress along democratic lines. As radicals liked to remind their listeners and readers, 'radicalism' in its literal sense means 'to the root', which explains why they dedicated themselves to identifying defects in the existing order and seeking to resolve them as speedily as possible.

While democracy's adjacent position in liberalism often served to temper the democratic inclinations of its proponents, the presence of democracy in the radical core explains why radicals played such a prominent role in campaigns to democratise liberal politics and the political system. Discussions about historical events could help to tease out the differences between radical and liberal notions of democracy. One such debate about 'democratic principles' was conducted through the pages of the *Leicester Pioneer*, an ecumenical progressive journal that evolved into a mouthpiece for the Labour Party. In a discussion about Oliver Cromwell in 1902, one writer described the Lord Protector as a great benefactor of 'the common people' and 'a man of peace' who was 'driven to be a man of war'. In this view, the fall of the English republic was the result of 'treachery and dissension in the ranks of the people', a sign, perhaps, that the writer subscribed to a tempered view of democracy. This contrasted with the view of another writer who believed that Cromwell had acted like a 'prince or peer of the realm' in crushing Gerrard Winstanley and the Diggers, who had attempted to establish 'a true commonwealth'. Cromwell was also a despot who was guilty of violating the cardinal principle that 'in a democracy the people should govern themselves'. Rather than idealising men like Cromwell, reformers should idealise 'the people, the common, labouring, uncomplaining people, who bear the burdens of the world'.[29]

This exchange gives some indication of radicalism's adjacent concepts. Though it is not possible to provide a complete list of such concepts, it seems uncontroversial to state that equality exerted a strong influence on the radical core. As in classical forms of liberalism, equality was understood to mean equality before the law and equal civil and religious rights rather than equality of outcome. But unlike liberals, and because of its proximity to the core concept of democracy and liberty, radicals believed that equality also meant equal political rights and the right of all adult males, regardless of their educational or social worth and with certain exceptions, to participate in the government of their country. In fact, rights could be considered an adjacent concept in its own right, as its role in protecting and prioritising the concepts of democracy, liberty and equality convinced radicals to demand the right to vote, the right to secrecy when voting and the right to nominate their own representatives. The general or common interest, or the assumption that human beings are social animals that thrive in communities of interdependent individuals, was also one of radicalism's adjacent concepts, which explains why radicals argued that their proposals for reform would accrue benefits to all members of society and prevent disruption to the social order by allowing voters to vent their anger through constitutional channels.

As political concepts are always located in specific historical and geographical contexts, their meanings are inevitably shaped by prevailing beliefs and attitudes, institutions, events, ideas, policy proposals, ethical systems, technologies and influential theories.[30] Some of the cultural constraints that influenced the articulation of radicalism may have already become apparent. Candidates for peripheral status in radical morphology during the late nineteenth century include the empire; patriotism; national self-determination; reform or abolition of the House of Lords; nationalisation of the land, mines and railways; old-age pensions; and free trade. Restrictive assumptions about work, place, gender, race, ethnicity and nationality also served to mould male activists' understanding of these concepts. As the following chapters will demonstrate, radicals rarely spoke about democracy, liberty or equality in an abstract sense; they spoke of 'the rights of Englishmen' rather than 'the rights of man'.

The constitution, one of the most important cultural influences on political discourse during this period, was also a peripheral concept in radical morphology.[31] Contrary to the claims of their critics, radicals were zealous constitutionalists who sought to bring the political system into line with the 'true' principles of the constitution.[32] For radicals, the English constitution guaranteed equality before the law, the liberty of the individual, political authority rooted in consent, limited and responsible government, and the sovereignty of the people through their representatives.[33] As Robert Saunders has noted, this highly democratic (and Anglocentric) reading of the constitution served as an 'ideal standard against which particular laws and governments could be held to account'.[34]

Because of the conceptual connections between democracy, liberty, progress, rights and equality, radicals saw themselves as part of the long struggle to protect the constitutional rights of the English people against infringements by tyrants and oppressors. As Jonathan Parry has shown, liberals also articulated a constitutionalist language of patriotism and a progressive account of England's past, emphasising the country's 'constitutional distinctness' and insisting that reform was a crucial part of a native political tradition.[35] By binding patriotism to constitutionalism, radicals and liberals could claim that the 'particular British genius for reform', and the constitution that this genius produced, enabled them to achieve their objectives without resorting to the kind of violence found in countries such as France. Still, while there were similarities between radical and liberal forms of constitutionalism, patriotic celebrations of the constitution 'sat on top of numerous local variations and contests'.[36] And for working-class radicals who offered a class-based reading of the constitution, one of the evils of the system of government that contravened the constitution was the continued absence of working men from the House of Commons.

The origins of labourism

Contests over the meaning of the constitution revealed differences not only between radicals and liberals, but also between populist radicals and working-class radicals. To some extent, these differences can be accounted for by seeing class and trade unionism as adjacent concepts in working-class radicalism and absent from populist radicalism. These concepts shaped working-class radical interpretations of democracy, which led activists to portray the struggle for political representation as a struggle of the working class against the intransigent upper classes and the ambivalent middle classes. The concepts helped to broaden the meaning of rights to include those of an industrial as well as a political nature, which encouraged working-class radicals to view liberty as the freedom to join a trade union as well as the right to vote. Class and trade unionism also informed working-class radical understandings of 'the general interest', which became subservient to class-orientated priorities. While liberals and populist radicals tended to emphasise the good of society as a whole, working-class radicals drew special attention to the concerns of the working classes.

Appending the prefix 'working-class' to 'radicalism' may bother those who do not believe that ideologies can be crudely associated with one social group. This is quite right, and it is not the intention of this book to claim that working-class radicalism was the sole preserve of those who fit the description of 'working class'. The focus of this book is on the languages of radicalism, and, to paraphrase Gareth Stedman Jones, an analysis of radical ideology must start from what radicals actually said and the terms in which they addressed each other and their opponents.[37] The term 'working-class radicalism' is simply used as a way of showing that groups of mainly male manual workers, many of whom were involved in trade unions, friendly societies and similar organisations, tended to articulate a version of radicalism that differed from the populist variant offered by tradesmen, professionals and employers in the towns discussed in this book.[38]

By demonstrating that working-class radicals could subvert the dominant meanings of political concepts, this book challenges the idea that they were non-ideological creatures who were only capable of regurgitating 'middle-class' views.[39] In fact, they were also capable of modifying their views in response to political and intellectual developments. Inspired by the formation of socialist organisations, the demands of the 'new' trade unions, research into the conditions of the poor, and a broader acceptance of the doctrine of scientific and cultural evolution in the 1880s and 1890s, working-class radicals began to display an increasing interest in using the state to remedy social ills. This represented the emergence of the state as an adjacent concept in working-class radical ideology, a shift that served to alter the meaning of democracy, liberty, equality and other component concepts. It also added a collectivist gloss to working-class radical programmes, which began to include demands such as the municipalisation of local monopolies and public works schemes for the unemployed.[40]

For the sake of clarity, this book uses the term 'labourism' to describe this collectivist form of working-class radicalism. But except for the addition of the state, all working-class radical core and adjacent concepts were preserved in labourism. Because of the interrelationship between democracy, liberty, rationality and other concepts, labourists continued to favour a form of self-government in which adult males could exercise power through their representatives. And because of the presence of class and trade unionism in its adjacent band, labourists interpreted these concepts through the lens of class. They associated the principle of democracy with the struggle of the working classes for a fair share of representation and believed that increasing the number of labour representatives on local and national governing bodies would help to achieve this goal. They interpreted rights, liberty and equality in class terms, laying stress on the rights of labour and the liberties of trade unions. And like their predecessors, labourists claimed to be staunch defenders of the constitution who wished to reform or abolish institutions that subverted its foundational principles.[41] In essence, labourism was working-class radicalism in an updated form.

This is not the first book to use the term labourism. In the 1960s, new leftists such as John Saville, Ralph Miliband, Tom Nairn and Perry Anderson used the term pejoratively to describe the spirit of the

Labour Party. For Miliband, labourism was a theory and practice that involved an advancement of 'concrete demands for immediate advantage to the working class and organised labour', a refusal to work for 'a fundamentally different kind of society' and a 'very weak concern' for socialist objectives.[42] In this view, labourism evolved in response to the peculiarities of Britain's political and industrial development, which, for Perry Anderson, had invested the working-class movement with a 'coagulated conservatism', a 'philistinism' towards ideas, a 'mystagogy' towards institutions, an 'intense consciousness of separate identity' and an unwillingness to 'set and impose goals for society as whole'.[43]

Subsequent work helped to broaden the debate on the Labour Party's ideology. For Geoffrey Foote, labourism was a set of assumptions rather than an ideology, which allowed Labour to distinguish itself from other parties while successfully accommodating a diversity of opinion within its ranks.[44] For Ross McKibbin the early party lacked any 'ideological exactness', while for Gareth Stedman Jones it acted as a 'vacant centre' that could inhabit groups 'possessing different and sometimes incompatible political languages of widely varying provenance'.[45] Other scholars, such as Martin Pugh and Duncan Tanner, have sought to challenge the idea that Labour leaders were indifferent to theory by drawing attention to intellectual strands, including 'popular radicalism', 'Radical Liberalism', Fabianism and 'Tory-socialism', which exerted an influence on the party in its formative years.[46] After all, as Jose Harris has pointed out, the party's roots lay not only in trade unionism and democratic socialism, but also in:

> Radical republicanism and pro-Gladstonian Lib-Labism, Marxism and municipal reformism, positivism and idealism, Nonconformist and incarnationalist Christianity, anti-modernist mediaevalism and the quest for advanced 'scientific' modernity.[47]

This serves as a useful reminder that Labour has always been a broad church. It also highlights the futility in attempting to attach a single ideological label to a national political party. As Duncan Tanner's magisterial study of the pre-war Labour Party showed, there were pronounced local and regional variations in the strength of ideological groupings within the party, and the 'precise nature and meaning of ideologies or of class consciousness' tended to differ from place to place.[48] With this in mind, and as a way of addressing the geographical imbalance of previous scholarship on the topic, this book uses local case studies to identify the major currents of thought that influenced the intellectual development of local labour parties in their formative years.

As the following chapters will show, labourism was the dominant ideology among Labour Party activists and sympathisers in these localities. But the aim of this book is not to merely restate the case made by new left thinkers. Rather, it is to suggest that the conceptual approach to ideology can yield a more robust interpretation of what labourism was. Using such an approach calls into question the idea that by exhibiting a propensity for pragmatism and compromise, labourists were essentially non-ideological. For Henry Pelling, for example, many of those who worked for the party before the First World War were free of any commitment to ideas or programme because they simply wanted to 'defend themselves at Westminster against legislation or judge-made law which they regarded as hostile to the principles of unionism'.[49] But surely the very act of deciding to enter the political arena, to establish a party independent of both the Liberals and the Conservatives, and to seek direct as opposed to indirect representation in the House of Commons rests on a set of assumptions about, for example, 'the principles of unionism' and the ability of ordinary voters to seek redress for their grievances through parliamentary action?[50] This may seem like a fairly obvious point to make, but it is one that serves to demonstrate how the attitudes of ordinary voters and activists have been deemed non-ideological simply because they have not been codified in an official programme or statement of principles.

Labourism, like all ideologies, was not dependent for its existence on isolated thinkers or intellectuals. In fact, as political thought is to be found at all levels of political action, it may even be more appropriate to look to the local level to find exemplars of labourist ideology. Though there are numerous candidates who meet this criterion, William Hornidge stands out as particularly strong example. Hornidge worked in every major centre of the boot and shoe industry before settling in Northampton in 1889. He quickly worked his way through the ranks of the National Union of Boot and Shoe Operatives (NUBSO), becoming its general secretary in 1899, a position he held until his death ten years later. He was a self-described collectivist who disparaged the socialist 'quest for visionary reforms' and its recognition of the class war. He was a pragmatist who allied himself to the Liberal Party in the 1890s and urged the newly formed Labour Party to accept assistance from those 'closest to them in thought'. But despite his hostility to socialism and his tendency towards organised liberalism, Hornidge articulated a class-based rather than a populist vision of politics. He worked with the Liberal Party to 'get out of it all he could for the good of Labour' and favoured a 'pure and simple' Labour Party that would contain 'workers' rather than 'middle-class men'. As a 1901 article in the *Leicester Pioneer* made clear:

> [Hornidge] is a fighter certainly; but not a noisy one. He may be an agitator; but not a stirrer up of needless strife ... He is conciliatory so far as conciliation may tend to obtain the results he desires. He has a very considerable programme for the betterment of the wage-earner; but believes he can best obtain it by taking that which is within reach at the moment; still looking onward with unsatisfied ideals; yet seeing that more can be got easily, and with increased speed, by claim, continuous effort, than by violence more restive spirits might prefer – violence of speech even, that might at any time ... lead to immense disaster.[51]

A trade unionist inspired by the slogan of 'defence not defiance', Hornidge was the archetypal labourist of the late nineteenth and early twentieth centuries.

Tracing the radical thread

The book is organised chronologically into eight chapters, each of which addresses a different historical theme, moment or development in English politics during the period 1867–1924. This structure serves the purpose of the book, which is to construct a narrative of continuity between older and newer political traditions. This is not to suggest that the transition from working-class radicalism to labourism was painless. As we shall see, there were moments when alternate paths of development presented themselves to working-class radical activists. At these moments, a change in circumstances, such as an electoral victory rather than defeat, could have disrupted this narrative and brought down the book's central argument. Consequently, each chapter considers paths of development that do not fit neatly into the book's dominant narrative and that, while essentially subplots to the main story, demonstrate that paths of political and ideological development are not teleological processes.

The narrative begins after the passage of the 1867 Reform Act, an Act that enfranchised a substantial portion of the male working-class population. The purpose of the first two chapters is to emphasise the vibrancy of a working-class radical tradition and its distinctness from both mainstream liberalism and populist forms of radicalism in the two decades after the Act's passage. The first chapter uses newspaper reports and election ephemera to explore the attempts of working-class radicals to challenge, either electorally or non-electorally, the unrepresentative nature of local Liberal Associations. It suggests that working-class radicals engaged in these activities because they formulated their understanding of the socio-political order through the lens of class. It also elaborates on the conceptual framework of radical ideology and its populist and working-class variants.

The exploration of late-nineteenth-century radicalism continues in the second chapter, which focuses on the campaign to elect the atheist Charles Bradlaugh to Parliament. One of the most controversial political and legal struggles of the Victorian era, this campaign has long been considered a broad-based populist movement in which social and political tensions were largely absent. This chapter, though, suggests that the campaign is better understood as an uneasy and fragile alliance of two mutually suspicious sections. By offering contrasting perspectives on the nature and importance of 'the Bradlaugh case' and on the 'true' meaning of the constitution, radicals and liberals served to reveal the important differences that separated the two traditions. The chapter also uses newspaper reports and election songs, poems and posters to uncover subtle differences in the way working-class and populist radicals handled certain political concepts and articulated their understanding of the social order. Establishing the existence of such tensions helps to account for the tone, strategy and ideological basis of 'newer' forms of politics that had begun to emerge in Bradlaugh's final years.

The third chapter considers how working-class radicals responded to debates about the role of the state in the final years of the nineteenth century. During this period, 'collectivism', a term often used synonymously with 'socialism', became a hotly debated topic in political and intellectual circles, and activists across England engaged in fierce debates about the merits and feasibility of using state power to alleviate social problems. Working-class radicals were not absent from these discussions. Those who established socialist societies lamented the moderation of their former allies and claimed that they were the true heirs of the radical legacy. Working-class radicals who came to describe themselves as 'labour' activists also embraced the collectivist spirit of the times. But, as this chapter suggests, while they came to see the state as an effective tool for alleviating social distress, they remained stubbornly attached to their old ways of thinking about democracy, liberty, progress and other concepts at the core of working-class radical ideology. The emergence of local labour parties in the 1880s and 1890s and the conceptual mutation of working-class radical ideology into labourism represented the renewal rather than the displacement of older traditions.

The fourth chapter examines some of the key electoral battlegrounds where intra-progressive divisions contributed to the defeat or near defeat of Liberal candidates in 1895. While these election and by-election contests have been relatively neglected in the historiography, they help to reveal the fractured nature of the radical tradition in the years prior to the formation of the national Labour Party. Drawing on correspondence, trade union records, newspaper reports, songs, handbills and election addresses, this chapter suggests that there was an essential continuity in the way labourists thought and spoke about the socio-political order. This chapter also suggests that teasing out the differences between labourism, liberalism, conservatism, socialism and 'constructive' forms of radicalism in the 1890s makes it easier to explain the tone of popular politics in early twentieth century. Identifying the connection between working-class radicalism and labourism makes the foundation of the Labour Party seem less like a birth of a new epoch or the continuation of a populist 'radical liberalism' and more like the renewal of a 'class-conscious' radical tradition.

The fifth chapter examines the extent to which the Labour Party contributed to the nationalisation of British political culture in the period before the First World War. With a focus on local labour newspapers, trade union records and correspondence between local activists and Labour head office, this chapter suggests that the party, its MPs and its leading spokespersons acted as poles of attraction towards which labourists and sympathetic socialist activists could navigate. It also argues that the existence of a national party promoted the idea that Labour head office would act as a co-ordinating centre that could draw together previously unconnected trade unionists and socialists. Finally, the chapter argues that many of those who supported the Labour Party in the Edwardian period, as well as those who sympathised with the party while remaining outside of it, retained a strong sense of loyalty to the discursive and ideological frameworks of older radical traditions.

The sixth chapter examines the way in which Labour activists articulated their understanding of the working class prior to the First World War. It shows that Labour activists' definition of the working class, as well as their conception of the social order, owed a great deal to older notions of class relations. It does so by interrogating the way in which activists interacted with women, the unemployed, non-manual workers, foreigners, agricultural labourers, 'the poor' and others who had historically been excluded from labourist definitions of the working class. The aim of this chapter is to show that long-held and restrictive assumptions about gender, place, work, nationality and race were hard to shake off even in the face of social and political change.

The seventh chapter considers the extent to which the First World War contributed to the post-war realignment of progressive politics. With notable exceptions, scholars have largely agreed that certain developments during the war years, including splits in the Liberal Party, the expansion of the wartime state and the growth of trade unionism, provided the necessary framework for a political realignment in which Labour replaced the Liberals as the dominant force on the British left. This chapter offers a fresh perspective on this debate by examining the ideological evolution of Labour activists in towns and cities at the forefront of this realignment. Drawing on trade union and party-political records, election posters and handbills, pamphlets, and newspaper reports, it argues that the theoretical framework that generated labourist responses to the war was not new. As before the war, labourists articulated a conciliatory vision of society that, while undoubtedly based on an exclusivist conception of class, was not rooted in a recognition of the class struggle. And far from undergoing a significant ideological conversion, labourists felt that wartime developments proved the veracity of their assumptions about democracy, liberty, the state and other concepts that had formed the core of both pre-war labourism and, before it, working-class radicalism.

The eighth and final chapter considers the impact of Labour's decision to adopt a new constitution and publish its first comprehensive policy document, *Labour and the New Social Order*, in 1918. These changes were part of a deliberate effort to shift Labour's image from a trade union pressure group to a party of government. As intended, middle-class defectors from the Liberal Party and women of all classes joined the party in considerable numbers from 1918 onwards. This chapter, however, argues that we should not overstate the intellectual significance of these changes. Male labourists continued to hold restrictive assumptions about groups that had historically been marginalised within the party. Labourist conceptions of the social order remained influential at a local level and, like their political ancestors, labourists exhibited a strong sense of class while rejecting the theory of the class struggle. And while the constitutional changes of 1918 expanded the intellectual space in which non-labourist currents could exist and grow, labourism remained a major intellectual current in the party as it prepared to form its first government in January 1924.

Constructing a general picture of popular politics at a local level has involved examining a multitude of sources held in libraries, archives and record offices across Britain. As the period 1867–1924 was a time when 'out-of-doors' speech-making became a technique of mainstream public life, a special effort was made to consult sources that contain reports of speeches delivered on street corners, in market places and at political clubs.[52] As well as interrogating speeches published in pamphlet form, this meant mining national and provincial newspapers, most of which were accessed at the British Library site in Colindale, London, before their migration to the online British Newspaper Archive.

The pace at which digitisation has occurred demonstrates the speed of technological development and its potential for historical analysis. After all, as Luke Blaxill has argued, it is now possible to 'analyse the newly liberated textual sources of millions (sometimes billions) of words which are beyond feasible scholarly endeavour to read in entirety'.[53] Taking advantage of this development, this book is largely based on now-digitised political speeches, election addresses, letters, advertisements, poems, songs and meeting reports. For Blaxill, though, this analysis could be taken further by conducting an additional *quantitative* analysis of digital sources. Among other things, this could involve comparing language patterns across different regions, tracking the rise and fall of certain words and phrases, and, as Joseph Meisel has shown, identifying the 'overall patterns and underlying structures' of an individual's speech-making.[54]

This endeavour is not without its problems, especially for those wishing to study the language of local activists who operated on the fringes of mainstream politics. At the time of writing, the British Newspaper Archive is dominated by newspapers that aligned with the Liberal or Conservative parties. Though these papers reported on the activities of radical, labour and socialist activists, this was not consistent or comparable to the coverage given to the major political parties. Of course, this is likely to change as digitised versions of non-Liberal and non-Conservative newspapers are added to the British Newspaper Archive. But in the meantime, it is difficult to conduct a study of localised radical or labour oratory along the lines suggested by Meisel, who was able to compare the 'oratorical productivity' of William Gladstone and Winston Churchill because near-complete collections of their speeches have been published and digitised.

A more serious issue is the contestability of words, phrases and concepts. For example, the activists discussed in this book often used 'English' and 'British' interchangeably, which explains why the book's title refers to 'England' and not 'Britain'. Another reason is that the nations that make up the United Kingdom have separate national histories. As Naomi Lloyd-Jones and Margaret Scull have recently argued, while the histories of England, Ireland, Scotland and Wales shaped and informed one another's histories, 'developments in the one were not always present in the other(s)'.[55] This book, then, is a study of English politics rather than an Anglocentric study of British politics. Examining the interplay between 'British' and 'national' narratives is certainly a worthwhile scholarly endeavour, but it is something that falls outside the scope of this book.

The meaning of words like 'reform' and 'radical' also changed over time and could differ depending on the context in which they were used. In the 1880s, for instance, a 'radical' in Northampton, a 'labour' activist in Bristol and an 'independent liberal' in Lincoln were all part of same intellectual tradition. In both national and provincial newspapers, the terms 'labour party' and 'liberal party' did not always refer to actual political organisations. The difficulty in conducting a quantitative analysis of 'unofficial' political languages becomes even more obvious when we consider that liberal-leaning newspapers often referred to labour activists as 'liberals' and socialists as 'progressives', and conservative-aligned papers sometimes described the Liberal Party as 'separatists' or 'the radical party'. While the innovative methods proposed by Blaxill and others merit more careful investigation than this study can provide, it may be necessary to wait until more sophisticated tools are available before conducting a comprehensive quantitative analysis of radical and labour languages.

Notes

1 For examples of the stagist interpretation, see S. Webb and B. Webb, *The History of Trade Unionism, 1666–1920* (London, 1920); G. D. H. Cole, *British Working Class Politics, 1832–1914* (London, 1965); R. Harrison, *Before the Socialists: Studies in Labour and Politics, 1861–1881* (London, 1965); E. Hobsbawm, *Worlds of Labour: Further Studies in the History of Labour* (London, 1984); N. Kirk, *Change, Continuity and Class: Labour in British Society, 1850–1920* (Manchester, 1998).
2 For a comprehensive overview of the methodological differences between these historians, see J. Lawrence, *Speaking for the People: Party, Language and Popular Politics in England, 1867–1914* (Cambridge, 1998), pp. 41–61.
3 G. Stedman Jones, *Languages of Class: Studies in English Working Class History, 1832–1982* (Cambridge, 1983), p. 23; P. Joyce, *Visions of the People: Industrial England and the Question of Class, 1840–1914* (Cambridge, 1991); J. Vernon, *Politics and the People: A Study in the English Political Culture, c. 1815–1867* (Cambridge, 1993).
4 E. F. Biagini and A. J. Reid (eds), *Currents of Radicalism: Popular Radicalism, Organised Labour and Party Politics in Britain, 1850–1914* (Cambridge, 1991), p. 5; E. F. Biagini, *Liberty, Retrenchment and Reform: Popular Liberalism in the Age of Gladstone, 1860–1880* (Cambridge, 1992). For non-traditionalist work that argues for important discontinuities in radicalism, see M. Taylor, *The Decline of British Radicalism, 1847–1860* (Oxford, 1995), pp. 331–346.
5 Biagini and Reid, *Currents of Radicalism*, p. 4; Biagini, *Liberty, Retrenchment and Reform*, pp. 11, 51.
6 Joyce, *Visions of the People*, p. 11.
7 See J. Lawrence, 'Popular radicalism and the socialist revival in Britain', *Journal of British Studies*, 31:2 (1992), pp. 163–186; L. Barrow and I. Bullock, *Democratic Ideas and the British Labour Movement, 1880–1914*

(Cambridge, 1996); A. Taylor, '"The Old Chartist": Radical veterans on the late nineteenth- and early twentieth-century political platform', *History*, 95:4 (2010), pp. 458–476; M. Bevir, *The Making of British Socialism* (Princeton, NJ, 2011); J. Owen, *Labour and the Caucus: Working-Class Radicalism and Organised Liberalism in England, 1868–88* (Liverpool, 2014). See also Kirk, *Change, Continuity and Class*, p. 185.

8 See also S. Pierson, *Marxism and the Origins of British Socialism: The Struggle for a New Consciousness* (London, 1973); E. Royle, *Radicals, Secularists and Republicans: Popular Freethought in Britain, 1866–1915* (Manchester, 1980); L. Barrow, *Independent Spirits: Spiritualism and English Plebeians, 1850–1910* (London, 1986).

9 For similar criticisms, see J. Belchem, *Popular Radicalism in Nineteenth-Century Britain* (New York, 1996), pp. 2–3; Lawrence, *Speaking for the People*, p. 46; J. Thompson, 'After the fall: Class and political language in Britain, 1780–1900', *Historical Journal*, 39:2 (1996), pp. 793–794, 802; M. Worley, *Labour inside the Gate: A History of the British Labour Party between the Wars* (London, 2005), pp. 6–7; Owen, *Labour and the Caucus*, p. 14.

10 E. P. Thompson, *The Making of the English Working Class* (Aylesbury, 1968), pp. 9–10: emphases added.

11 They were more independent-minded than Patrick Joyce's deferential northern factory proletariat and more political than Gareth Stedman Jones's London-based working class. In some respects, this conception of class corresponds with what Peter Clarke described as 'the social democratic theory of the class struggle', whose proponents accepted the class dimension of democracy and worked within 'class parties' but denied the desirability of class conflict. Clarke, though, was describing the views of early Fabians and Edwardian new liberals. P. Clarke, 'The social democratic theory of the class struggle', in J. Winter (ed.), *The Working Class in Modern British History: Essays in Honour of Henry Pelling* (Cambridge, 1983), pp. 3–18; P. Joyce, *Work, Society and Politics: The Culture of the Factory in Later Victorian England* (Aldershot, 1991), pp. 291–292; Stedman Jones, *Languages of Class*, pp. 179–238; R. McKibbin, *The Ideologies of Class: Social Relations in Britain, 1880–1950* (Oxford, 1991), p. 36; R. McKibbin, *Classes and Cultures: England 1918–1951* (Oxford, 2000), p. 131; see also B. Jackson, *Equality and the British Left: A Study in Progressive Political Thought, 1900–64* (Manchester, 2007), p. 27.

12 For examples, see P. Thompson, *Socialists, Liberals and Labour: The Struggle for London, 1885–1914* (London, 1967); P. Clarke, *Lancashire and the New Liberalism* (Cambridge, 1971); D. Clark, *Colne Valley, Radicalism to Socialism: The Portrait of a Northern Constituency in the Formative Years of the Labour Party 1890–1910* (London, 1981); M. Savage, *The Dynamics of Working-Class Politics: The Labour Movement in Preston, 1880–1940* (Cambridge, 1987); J. Lawrence, 'Popular politics and the limitations of party: Wolverhampton, 1867–1900', in E. F. Biagini and A. J. Reid (eds),

Currents of Radicalism: Popular Radicalism, Organised Labour and Party Politics in Britain 1850–1914 (Cambridge, 1991), pp. 65–85.
13 D. Tanner, *Political Change and the Labour Party, 1900–1918* (Cambridge, 1990), p. 284.
14 Worley, *Labour inside the Gate*, p. 2; M. Worley (ed.), *The Foundations of the British Labour Party: Identities, Cultures and Perspectives, 1900–39* (Farnham, 2009), pp. 2–3; Tanner, *Political Change and the Labour Party*, pp. 13, 79.
15 D. Caramani, *The Nationalization of Politics: The Formation of National Electorates and Party Systems in Western Europe* (Cambridge, 2004), p. 1: emphasis added.
16 This is the belief that fundamental liberties were established under the Anglo-Saxons but suppressed or curtailed by the Norman Conquest of 1066. Historians have exaggerated the decline of this idea in the years after Chartism. C. Griffiths, *Labour and the Countryside: The Politics of Rural Britain, 1918–1939* (Oxford, 2007), pp. 25–50; M. Chase, 'George Howell, the Webbs and the political culture of early labour history', in K. Laybourn and J. Shepherd (eds), *Labour and Working-Class Lives: Essays to Celebrate the Life and Work of Chris Wrigley* (Manchester, 2017), p. 22.
17 P. Readman, *Land and Nation in England: Patriotism, National Identity, and the Politics of Land, 1880–1914* (Woodbridge, 2008), p. 12.
18 Norfolk Record Office, Norwich (hereafter NFRO), MS 4265/26/1, papers of J. F. Henderson, letter from Keir Hardie to J. F. Henderson, 5 December 1898.
19 M. Freeden, *The New Liberalism: An Ideology of Social Reform* (Oxford, 1978); M. Freeden, *Liberalism Divided: A Study in British Political Thought, 1914–1939* (Oxford, 1986); M. Freeden, *Ideologies and Political Theory: A Conceptual Approach* (Oxford, 1998).
20 Freeden, *Ideologies and Political Theory*, pp. 77–84, 438, 444–449, 459.
21 J. Harris, 'Labour's political and social thought', in D. Tanner, P. Thane and N. Tiratsoo (eds), *Labour's First Century* (Cambridge, 2000), p. 11.
22 Freeden, *The New Liberalism*, p. 246.
23 H. Emy, *Liberals, Radicals and Social Politics, 1892–1914* (Cambridge, 1973), p. 63.
24 M. Worley, 'Building the Party: Labour Party activism in five British counties between the wars', *Labour History Review*, 70:1 (2005), p. 75.
25 Harrison, *Before the Socialists*, p. 3.
26 Note its absence in M. Freeden, L. T. Sargent and M. Stears (eds), *The Oxford Handbook of Political Ideologies* (Oxford, 2013).
27 Freeden, *Ideologies and Political Theory*, pp. 78–79, 156, 165.
28 Freeden, *Ideologies and Political Theory*, p. 98.
29 *Leicester Pioneer*, 23 August 1902; 30 August 1902; 6 September 1902; 13 September 1902; 27 September 1902.
30 Freeden, *Ideologies and Political Theory*, pp. 69–79.
31 Vernon, *Politics and the People*, p. 7.

32 *Lincolnshire Chronicle*, 21 November 1868.
33 H. Cunningham, 'The language of patriotism, 1750–1914', *History Workshop*, 12:1 (1981), p. 11.
34 R. Saunders, 'Parliament and people: The British constitution in the long nineteenth century', *Journal of Modern European History*, 6:1 (2008), pp. 75–76.
35 J. Parry, *The Politics of Patriotism: English Liberalism, National Identity and Europe, 1830–1886* (Cambridge, 2006), p. 10; J. Parry, 'The impact of Napoleon III on British politics, 1851–1880', *Transactions of the Royal Historical Society*, 11 (2001), pp. 147–175; G. Pentland, 'Parliamentary reform', in D. Brown, R. Crowcroft and G. Pentland (eds), *The Oxford Handbook of Modern British Political History, 1880–2000* (Oxford, 2018), pp. 386–391.
36 Pentland, 'Parliamentary reform', p. 386.
37 Stedman Jones, *Languages of Class*, pp. 94–96.
38 For other discussions that focus on the way different groups contested the meaning of ideas, concepts and movements, see T. Tholfsen, *Working Class Radicalism in Mid-Victorian England* (London, 1976), pp. 16–17, 86; Vernon, *Politics and the People*, p. 296; M. Finn, *After Chartism: Class and Nation in English Radical Politics, 1848–1874* (Cambridge, 1993), pp. 221–222.
39 A view put forward in Webb and Webb, *The History of Trade Unionism*, pp. 362, 366, 369, 374.
40 Cole, *British Working Class Politics*, p. 81; W. Wolfe, *From Radicalism to Socialism: Men and Ideas in the Formation of Fabian Socialist Doctrines, 1881–1889* (London, 1975), p. 70.
41 Harris, 'Labour's political and social thought', pp. 14–15.
42 R. Miliband, 'Socialist advance in Britain', *The Socialist Register*, 20 (1983), p. 107.
43 P. Anderson, 'Origins of the present crisis', *New Left Review*, I:23 (1964), pp. 40–43. For an overview of the new left and labourism, see M. Davis, "Labourism" and the new left', in J. Callaghan, S. Fielding and S. Ludlam (eds), *Interpreting the Labour Party: Approaches to Labour politics and history* (Manchester, 2003), pp. 39–56.
44 G. Foote, *The Labour Party's Political Thought* (Beckenham, 1986), p. 5.
45 Stedman Jones, *Languages of Class*, p. 22.
46 D. Tanner, 'The development of British socialism, 1900–1918', *Parliamentary History*, 16:1 (1997), pp. 48–66; M. Pugh, *Speak For Britain! A New History of the Labour Party* (London, 2010), p. 9.
47 Harris, 'Labour's political and social thought', p. 47.
48 Tanner, *Political Change and the Labour Party*, p. 12.
49 H. Pelling, *Popular Politics and Society in Late Victorian Britain* (London, 1968), pp. 14–15, 118.
50 Harris, 'Labour's political and social thought', p. 9.

51 Modern Records Centre, Warwick (hereafter MRC), 547/P/1/9, National Union of Operative Boot and Shoe Rivetters and Finishers: monthly reports (hereafter NUBSO MR), March 1893; *Northampton Mercury*, 18 August 1899; *Leicester Pioneer*, 6 July 1901; MRC, 547/P/1/18, NUBSO MR, April 1902; MRC, 547/P/1/18, National Union of Operative Boot and Shoe Rivetters and Finishers: conference reports (hereafter NUBSO CR), 1902; *Manchester Evening News*, 8 September 1903. Note: the National Union of Operative Boot and Shoe Rivetters and Finishers (NUBSRF) changed its name to the National Union of Boot and Shoe Operatives (NUBSO) in 1890. In references to primary sources I have used the latter acronym only for the organisation, even when referring to pre-1890 materials.
52 J. Meisel, *Public Speech and the Culture of Public Life in the Age of Gladstone* (New York, 2001), p. 277.
53 L. Blaxill, 'Elections', in D. Brown, R. Crowcroft and G. Pentland (eds), *The Oxford Handbook of Modern British Political History, 1880–2000* (Oxford, 2018), p. 410.
54 J. Meisel, 'Words by the numbers: A quantitative analysis and comparison of the oratorical careers of William Ewart Gladstone and Winston Spencer Churchill', *Historical Research*, 73:182 (2000), p. 263.
55 N. Lloyd-Jones and M. M. Scull, 'A new plea for an old subject? Four nations' history for the modern period', in N. Lloyd-Jones and M. M. Scull, *Four Nations' Approaches to Modern "British" History: A (Dis)United Kingdom?* (London, 2018), pp. 4–6; Cunningham, 'The language of patriotism', p. 28.

1

Radicalism, class and populism

> [John Stuart Mill] said that politicians of Liberalism constituted a Broad Church. It is so, and what he meant to convey was that we strove to combine with a firm devotion to the general principles in which we are united [while making] a reasonable allowance for those variances of opinion which will prevail among men, intelligent and conscientious.
>
> *William Gladstone speaking in Birmingham, 1877.*[1]

If one of Gladstone's contemporaries had wished to test the thesis that liberalism constituted a broad church, they would have found it useful to take a journey across the East Midlands, East Anglia and the South West of England. On arriving in Bristol, Leicester, Lincoln, Northampton or Norwich, they would have been struck by just how sharp the variations of opinion had become in strongholds of the Liberal Party. They would also have discovered that the broad church of liberalism was not always broad enough to include those who described themselves as 'ultra liberals', 'extreme liberals', 'true liberals', 'advanced liberals' or, more commonly, 'radicals'. Standing firmly on the left of the mid- to late Victorian political spectrum, radicals spent as much time challenging the perceived elitism and moderation of local Liberal organisations as they did in attacking the Conservatives. On attending a public meeting of radical activists, our traveller would likely have found participants in a determined spirit, obstinate and sometimes aggressive in their desire to see liberal politics transformed into an inclusive and democratic movement. If the traveller had stayed in these towns for a little longer, they would also have been able to identify more subtle differences in the way radicals and liberals talked about the social and political order and the way they articulated certain terms, phrases and concepts. With these differences in mind, our traveller may well have concluded, quite understandably, that radicalism and liberalism were two distinct political traditions.

But until recently, it was Gladstone's inclusive vision of liberal politics that found favour among historians of mid- to late Victorian England. In both 'stagist' and 'continuity' accounts of this period, radicals have often been portrayed as compliant partners in a broad cross-class coalition whose members worked in relative harmony under the guiding influence of 'the People's William'. For proponents of a class-based model of political development, radicals and liberals grew close in the years following the defeat of the 'class-conscious' Chartist movement, when the working classes, driven above all by economic concerns, abandoned their commitment to independent class politics and accepted the political and intellectual leadership of middle-class reformers.[2] This once-dominant narrative has been challenged by scholars who have questioned the idea that the formation of a radical–liberal coalition represented a turning-point in popular politics. If radicalism in its Chartist form was already a cross-class movement in which populist modes of thought and language were prevalent, as Gareth Stedman Jones and others have argued, then there is little need to use a model of discontinuity to explain the populist nature and appeal of radicalism in the post-Chartist era.[3] As Eugenio Biagini and Alastair Reid have argued, popular radicalism after 1850 remained a broad movement of artisans, small tradesmen and organised workers who considered themselves to be part of 'the people' rather than a class.[4] When considered collectively, this work has done much to demonstrate the coherence of a 'popular radical' worldview and the ease with which former Chartists and those inspired by the same lofty ideals could find a place in Gladstone's broad church.

More recent studies have cast doubt on the idea that radicalism was a well-integrated member of the liberal family. Since the early 1990s, several scholars have made attempts to untangle these two traditions by pointing to the enduring vitality of a semi-independent radical subculture whose members sustained a lively and widely read national press and played a leading role in popular campaigns, including the agitation over the Tichborne claimant, which operated outside the confines of official liberal politics.[5] Shedding light on these activities has been a worthwhile endeavour, not least because it has helped to revive the idea, common among both radicals and liberals at the time, that despite their sharing common ground on a whole range of political issues, there existed important social and intellectual differences that divided the two traditions.

Such differences existed in the towns and cities discussed in this book. In Bristol, Lincoln, Leicester, Norwich and Northampton, radical activists frequently heckled and withheld their votes from undeserving Liberal candidates, publicly denounced unpopular Liberal personalities, criticised the candidate selection process used by local Liberal organisations, and conducted heated debates with more moderate activists in public meetings and through the correspondence pages of the provincial press. But identifying differences between radicals and liberals only partially explains the configuration of popular politics in these towns. In the same towns, there also existed a decidedly *working-class* radical tradition that was in many ways distinct from both mainstream liberalism and populist forms of radicalism. Differences between these different traditions reveal themselves in the way their proponents spoke about themselves and the socio-political order, and the way they understood and used certain terms, phrases and concepts.

In short, working-class radicals viewed the world through the lens of class. When delivering speeches or writing letters, they described themselves as bona fide working men whose experiences gave them a unique insight into the needs and concerns of their class. They were mostly male manual workers and active trade unionists who considered trade unionism to be a defensive movement that protected the legitimate interests of the workers against tyrannical practices and despotic employers. While they often criticised 'the lords of the land, *and* lords of the mill', they did not see the trade union movement as antagonistic to employers as a class and always refuted accusations that they recognised or hoped to instigate a class war.[6] And though they tended to vote for Liberal candidates at election time, they were vehement critics of the 'wire pullers' in local Liberal organisations who, in their view, had long ignored the wishes of the working classes. Radicalism, they believed, was the natural political expression of the working classes, and it was through trade unionism and the enactment of the radical programme that the working class would obtain a fair day's wage for a fair day's work and their 'just' share of political representation.

Radicalism, like other ideologies, had its local dialects and accents.[7] But as varieties of a broader linguistic family, these dialects and accents are mutually intelligible to their respective speakers. To put it another way, despite their geographical separation, radicals in different parts of the country articulated a remarkably similar vision of the socio-political order. Radicalism was also a parent ideology with a coherent conceptual framework that was capable of both variation and mutation. Though this may seem like an uncontroversial claim, it is not one that has featured prominently in previous studies on the topic. In stagist accounts, radicals are often depicted as either passive consumers of middle-class ideas or lacking 'any clear ideological basis' at all.[8] While advocates of the continuity thesis have done a great deal to challenge this view, their work has still tended to blur the ideological boundaries between radicalism and liberalism. And though more recent studies have drawn attention to differences between radical and liberal political programmes, comparisons of policy proposals only go so far in revealing what was truly distinctive about the ideologies of radicalism and liberalism.

One way of determining what was unique about radical ideology is to uncover the conceptual framework on which radical proposals were based. It would be futile to try and list all the concepts that constituted radical ideology, but an examination of radical speeches, letters, poetry, songs, literature and election campaign material suggests that radicals were above all guided by the core concepts of democracy, liberty, individuality, progress and rationality. Adjacent concepts such as equality, the general interest and rights, and a set of marginal concepts such as the state, helped to constrain the potentially 'indefinite variety' of radicalism's core concepts. Radicalism also contained a set of perimeter concepts such as manhood suffrage, triennial Parliaments, vote by ballot, equal electoral districts, Irish Home Rule, and reform or abolition of the House of Lords which helped to link its core and adjacent concepts to the 'real world'.[9]

Liberals were also fond of stressing the importance of liberty, individuality, progress and equality. But while radicals and liberals drew upon a shared pool of concepts when expressing their views on the key issues of the day, the divergent configuration of their conceptual morphologies led them to assign different meanings to these concepts. For example, recognising democracy as an adjacent concept in liberalism makes it easier to account for the 'tempered democratic inclinations' of many of its proponents.[10] Conversely, the presence of democracy as a core concept in radicalism helps to explain why radicals tried so hard to convert local and national governing bodies into truly representative institutions. Democracy's central position in radical morphology and its relationship with other concepts yielded a version of democracy that led radicals to demand, among the other things, the right of all male members of the community to participate in the selection of their representatives.[11]

Contests over the meaning of democracy, liberty and other concepts had important implications for radical–liberal relations. They also helped to bring to light the existence of working-class and populist variants of radical ideology. The subtle differences between these two variants can be explained by seeing class and trade unionism as adjacent concepts in the former while recognising their absence from the latter. These concepts led to the notion that the struggle of the working class to obtain (or regain) their political rights was a struggle against both the upper classes and the 'middleocracy'.[12] They also sharpened working-class radical understandings of the general interest. While radicals and liberals of all classes spoke of 'the people' or 'the nation', *working-class* radicals believed that special remedial action on behalf of the working classes would inevitably contribute to the common good of society. By privileging the demands of one section of the community over all others, working-class radicals distinguished themselves from both populist radicals and liberals, both of whom were far more likely to frame their arguments in an inclusive and non-class language of populism.

Radical–liberal relations

During the Victorian era, commentators often referred to the East Midlands, East Anglia and the South West as strongholds of political and religious radicalism. Weaving together stories of local protests, rebellions and martyrdoms, local radicals embraced this reputation and promoted the idea that a consistent radical thread ran through the historical fabric of their towns and cities. Leicester's reputation as a bastion of Chartism, religious dissent and secularism convinced one member of the Leicester Labour Party that his home city had an atmosphere 'that tended towards liberty'.[13] Religious and political radicalism was strong in Bristol, a 'notorious centre' for Lollardism in the fourteenth century, a site of 'intense agitation around the question of religious reform' in the sixteenth century, and the scene of fierce rioting in 1831 after the House of Lords rejected a Reform Bill.[14] Nonconformity was firmly established in Lincoln, particularly among the city's working-class communities, who were also not averse to rioting if their demands were not met.[15] Northampton's radical thread can be traced back to the fourteenth century, when Lollardism gained an influence among the town's residents, while the town's support for Puritanism and Parliament during the Civil War and the political radicalism of the town's large body of shoemakers bolstered its reputation as a 'Mecca of Radicalism'.[16] Norwich and the surrounding county of Norfolk also acquired a reputation as a 'perfect hotbed of Radicalism' for its historical association with Lollardism, Quakerism, Chartism and Primitive Methodism, as well as for being the home of Boudicca's Iceni tribe and the site of the anti-enclosure Kett's Rebellion of 1549.[17]

These narratives inspired the activities of those who sustained local radical subcultures in the years following the defeat of Chartism. Throughout the 1860s and 1870s, radicals formed a vocal presence in political life and led campaigns that offended conservatives and embarrassed liberals. Their involvement in the campaigns for republicanism, trade unionism, secularism and various other causes convinced many, including one Lincoln-based Conservative, that radicals formed a 'schismatic sect' whose 'violent democratic principles' brought the good name of liberalism into disrepute.[18] Radicals were undoubtedly driven by a firm belief in democracy. They were also openly critical of Liberal organisations and certain Liberal personalities. But they did not seek to tarnish the legacy of liberalism as a political philosophy. This was the duality at the heart of radical politics, and it shaped radical–liberal relations throughout this period. Radicals often worked outside Liberal organisations to achieve their objectives, but often with the intention of democratising and improving the machinery of liberal politics. They condemned the actions of Liberals who refused to accede to radical demands, but regularly campaigned and voted for Liberal candidates. And while they regularly bemoaned the state of contemporary liberal politics, it was also common for them to express pride in the historical achievements of the Liberal Party.

To contemporary eyes, this attitude may appear inconsistent. But when radicals spoke of 'the Liberal Party', they were often referring to a symbolic entity rather than a political party in the modern sense. In fact, radicals were frustrated with the Liberal Party precisely because it was not a party in the modern sense, with structures in place to accommodate membership involvement in the candidate selection process. One of their key objectives during this period was to turn their vision of an ideal Liberal Party into reality. To do this, they attempted to convince local Liberal personalities to establish inclusive organisations whose leaders would be accountable to the mass of Liberal voters. While there would be a place for Whigs and moderate elements in these organisations, they would no longer be allowed to control the candidate selection process. The Liberal Party of the future was to be a broad-based democratic coalition that embraced all sections of anti-Conservative opinion and which would only put forward candidates deemed acceptable by the party's working-class base.

How radicals attempted to achieve this objective differed from town to town. In some places, radicals formed their own organisations in the hope that a declaration of independence would spur Whigs and moderate Liberals into action. In double-member constituencies, radicals formed independent organisations to provide the necessary organisational and financial clout to support an independent parliamentary candidate if and when the opportunity arose. This was the situation in Bristol, where tensions between radicals and liberals principally revolved around working-class participation in the political process. By the 1870s, radicals in Bristol had grown frustrated with the unrepresentative nature of the Bristol Liberal Association and the refusal of its leaders to adopt working-class candidates. To remedy this, they established political organisations such as the Radical Association (1870), the Direct Representation of Labour League (1873) and the Working Men's

Reform Association (1877). As their names suggest, these organisations were largely composed of working men and trade unionists, a fact that added a social dimension to radical–liberal relations.[19] Indeed, many radicals were happy to admit that they had lost faith in the Bristol Liberal Association precisely because of its middle-class character and composition. As in the 1830s and 1840s, class served as a major fault line that separated the radical and liberal movements in Bristol.[20]

After the passage of the 1867 Reform Act, radicals in Bristol reasserted their independence from mainstream liberal politics by prioritising the issue of labour representation. This demand, which appeared in all Bristol radical programmes during this period, emanated from a belief that the Bristol Liberal Association and its candidates did not represent the working-class majority of the broadly conceived Liberal Party. This sense of frustration was not unique to Bristol, and it did not go unchallenged.[21] At a by-election in 1870, radicals made an ambitious attempt to send a working man to Parliament by supporting the candidature of George Odger, a nationally renowned trade unionist and a key figure in the First International and the Reform League. Although Odger's campaign was unsuccessful, it left a lasting impression on the Bristol radical movement. The refusal of the middle-class Liberal Association to adopt a labour candidate convinced radicals of the need to establish exclusivist, class-based organisations composed of and led by trade unionists. This explains the formation and names of the Direct Representation of Labour League and the Working Men's Reform Association, both of which were led by manual workers associated with the Bristol Trades' Council, a self-described parliament of trade union societies founded in 1873. It also explains why trade unionists stood as 'representatives of the working classes' in school board elections throughout the 1870s despite being advised not to by leading members of the Liberal Association. Again, while most of these campaigns ended in failure, local radicals remained determined to achieve an objective that, as one activist declared in 1877, was the 'first item' in their programme.[22]

Bristol radicalism was an unashamedly working-class movement whose members, despite professing broad sympathy with the historical achievements of the Liberal Party, felt obliged to work outside the local Liberal Association to achieve their goals. The same spirit of independence shaped the character of radicalism in Leicester, a city that had become an important centre of the hosiery and footwear trades.[23] Working men from these industries became the backbone of the city's burgeoning secularist movement and helped to establish the Leicester Democratic (later, Republican) Association in 1871. This organisation became an important centre of gravity for those described by the

Leicester Chronicle as the 'very Advanced Liberals of Leicester', a group that campaigned for universal (not just manhood) suffrage, secular education, direct labour representation, and the formation of trade unions for men and women. Like its counterparts in Bristol, the Democratic Association had an identifiable working-class image and was intended as an 'extensive scheme of organization on the part of the working-classes of Leicester … to secure the objects of … advanced Liberalism'.[24]

Radicals in Leicester were far more successful at achieving their objectives than those in Bristol. Even before the Reform Act of 1867, they had managed to secure the election to Parliament of Peter A. Taylor, a member of the Courtauld textile family whose views on secularism, republicanism and Italian unification made him a popular figure in radical circles.[25] They were also more successful in convincing leaders of the Leicester Liberal Association to support their demand for labour representation. Still, while radicals and liberals often worked together during election contests, theirs was not an entirely harmonious relationship. At radical meetings, it was not uncommon for speakers to express their dissatisfaction with Liberal MPs and Liberal governments. Not even Gladstone was immune from criticism. At the first meeting of the Democratic Association in 1871, held in the aptly named Gladstone Hall, a founding member denounced Gladstone's 'policy of economy' and hoped for a time when England would have a prime minister 'who would not only look after the interests of the middle and upper class, but of those of the working class.'[26] This insistence on using a language of class when discussing political matters and a tendency to prioritise the needs of the working classes over those of other sections of community distinguished radicals from their allies and rivals. The radical–liberal alliance in Leicester, though successful at containing the electoral challenge of the Conservative Party, was always a strategic partnership of two distinct groupings whose members had different priorities and often-contrasting interests.

Radicals in Lincoln showed little desire to establish a similar alliance in their city. At the 1868 general election, they used their new-found political influence not only to impose their candidate on the Lincoln Liberal Party, but also to secure his unopposed return to Parliament. This show of defiance surprised local Liberal leaders, who were forced to ask one of the sitting MPs to retire. It also surprised John Hinde Palmer, the radical candidate, whose narrow defeat in a previous election contest had caused riots in the city. After his victory in 1868, Palmer, who only became aware of his nomination after the declaration of poll, was greeted with a joyous spectacle of fireworks, tar barrels, music, processions and a large meeting of supporters. In opening the meeting, the chair of

Palmer's election committee showed little indication that he wanted to the heal the divide between radicals and liberals. Instead, he praised 'the working-men' for forcing the retirement of the junior Liberal MP and for showing 'the gentlemen who profess to steer the helm of Liberalism in this city' that the working men '[had] the power'. 'The working men,' Palmer confessed in a letter to his father, '[had] done it all'.[27]

Working-class radicals remained a thorn in the side of the Lincoln Liberal party throughout the 1870s. Palmer's victory proved that a determined show of strength could force Liberal leaders to bow to the will of the new voters. Buoyed by this new-found sense of confidence, this 'little coterie of amateur legislators', as the *Lincolnshire Chronicle* called them, formed a Working Men's Liberal Association with the aim of uniting 'all true liberals in the city'.[28] Conciliatory statements of this kind failed to convince leaders of the local Liberal Party, who remained wary of Palmer's radicalism and the involvement of his supporters in the trade union agitation of the early 1870s. Consequently, a good number of Liberals refused to cast their votes for the radical–Liberal ticket at the 1874 general election, which not only ensured Palmer's defeat but also allowed a Conservative to top the poll. The loss of a seat convinced several prominent Liberals to reorganise the Liberal Party on the 'Birmingham model', but, for many, this was too late. The 'amateur legislators' remained steadfast in their support for Palmer and continued to promote what the local media referred to as 'Independent Liberalism'. And as this description suggests, radicals in Lincoln resisted attempts to downplay differences between 'independent' and mainstream forms of liberal politics. When informed during the run-up to the 1880 general election that these differences had disappeared and that 'those who had any crotchets [should] bury them' for the sake of electoral success, radicals raised such a storm of protest that the speaker had to qualify his remarks. 'Well, then, if not … bury them, at least … lay them on one side for the present.' Radicals agreed to this request on the condition that they could reopen discussions about the 'subordinate questions of the day' once the election was over.[29]

Palmer's return to Parliament in 1880 restored a semblance of radical–liberal unity in Lincoln. Palmer was joined in the House of Commons by a number of other radicals, including Henry Labouchère (Northampton), Sir Charles Dilke (Chelsea), Thomas Burt (Morpeth), Alexander Macdonald (Stafford), Robert Reid (Hereford) and Sir Wilfrid Lawson (Carlisle), who also benefited from the anti-Conservative tide. He was also joined by Jacob Henry Tillett, a nonconformist solicitor and newspaper proprietor who had spent twelve years attempting to become MP for Norwich. During his first attempt in 1868, Tillett and his supporters attracted considerable hostility from the Whig section of the Norwich Liberal Party that had long controlled the candidate selection process.[30] To co-ordinate his campaign and demonstrate their numerical superiority over rival sections, radicals formed the Electoral Organization of the Working Classes with a claimed initial membership of 1,800 working men. After nominating Tillett, the Organization's leaders promised to support 'any other Liberal candidate' who stood alongside him, but also declared their intention to fight the election with or without Whig support.[31] This attitude, not uncommon among radicals at the time, rested on a dual understanding of liberal politics. Even as they expressed their commitment to 'Liberal principles' and acknowledged the 'genius and patriotism of Mr. Gladstone', radicals in Norwich believed that they could best further their objectives by 'work[ing] independently of both parties'.[32] At the same time and without apparent contradiction, they promoted the eventual unification of all anti-Conservative forces into a single organisation while clinging firmly to their political and cultural independence in the meantime.

Unperturbed by criticism that their strategy would lead to certain electoral defeat, radicals in Norwich went to the poll in 1868 believing that they could 'beat the Whigs and the Tories'. When they found out that they could not, moderates and Whigs felt vindicated. The *Norwich Mercury* was adamant that the loss of a seat to the Conservatives was 'the result ENTIRELY of Mr. Tillett's course of proceeding' and argued that the episode served as a 'good lesson to the whole Liberal party'.[33] In fact, the defeat was largely the result of corrupt practices carried out by a Conservative organiser who used the promise of free beer to entice voters to the polls. Despite this flagrant example of electoral corruption that saw the 1868 contest declared void on petition, Whigs still refused to back Tillett. During the resulting by-election in 1870, Whigs demanded a 'more agreeable candidate' while radicals directed their anger at the 'political clique' and 'wire-pullers' who treated working men as 'mere electoral puppets'.[34] Tillett was successful in the by-election contest, but, again, his election was declared void as a result of electoral abuses, this time carried out by his own supporters. Though radicals succeeded in convincing moderate Liberals to support another candidate from the 'extreme section', they remained determined to clear Tillett's name. This task became harder when Tillett was again unseated on petition after another by-election 'victory' in 1875.

Radicals in Northampton encountered similar difficulties when attempting to send their political hero to Parliament. Though political and religious radicalism had long been prevalent among Northampton's traders, shopkeepers, merchants and shoemakers, Charles Bradlaugh's arrival on the political scene added a new dimension to local politics. Bradlaugh was not only a keen radical but also an avowed republican, democrat, atheist and advocate of birth control who had founded the National Secular Society in 1866. In short, he was on the 'extreme wing of the extreme wing of the Liberal party', a position that endeared him to Northampton's large community of politically engaged shoemakers, one of whom claimed that they were 'the most radicallest set of fellows … in the kingdom.'[35]

Bradlaugh's political and theological views alarmed those of a moderate liberal disposition, and his decision to contest the general elections of 1868 and 1874 angered the leaders of the Northampton Liberal Party. Despite claiming that he wanted to unseat the Whig MP, Lord Henley, Bradlaugh encountered hostility from the Whig and moderate sections of the local party, whose leaders refused to endorse his candidature on both occasions. Attacks on Bradlaugh's character and the social basis of his support deepened the rift between radicals and other non-Conservative forces in the town, which culminated in a violent riot after Bradlaugh's narrow defeat in a by-election in 1874. Significantly, the rioters aimed their anger (and stones) not at the successful Conservative candidate, but at the committee rooms of Bradlaugh's Liberal opponent, the offices of the town's leading Liberal newspaper and the headquarters of the Liberal Party.[36] Eventually, the electoral damage caused by ongoing divisions led to a compromise, and Bradlaugh was elected alongside Henry Labouchère, with the support of the Liberal Party, at the 1880 general election.

Radicals and the problem of class

By examining the language of local radical activists, it is possible to identify more than one radical tradition in England. While populist radicals and working-class radicals agreed on the need for far-reaching measures of political reform, they differed in their interpretation of what 'radicalism' actually meant. In general, populist radicals held that the fundamental division in society was not between labour and capital but between 'the idle' and 'the industrious' classes.[37] When putting forward their demands, they emphasised the benefits that their enactment would bring to the community as a whole, which often went hand in hand with a stress on the need to organise around political principles rather than class interests. Working-class radicals, on the other hand, preferred to frame their demands in a language of class. They used inclusive terms such as 'the people' side by side with and sometimes as an alternative description for 'the working classes'. They claimed that, as workers themselves, they were best placed to speak on behalf of working men. And very often, they justified their political activities by explaining how the return of a certain candidate to Parliament or the amendment of an existing law would further the interests not only of the community as a whole but of working men in particular.

Working-class radicals used a language of class when discussing a variety of topics. Among allies and opponents and in large meetings and more intimate settings, they proudly proclaimed their working-class credentials, the narrow social composition of their organisations and their willingness to prioritise the needs of their class. Expressions of exclusivist sentiments were most common when they discussed the lack of direct labour representation on local and national governing bodies. For working-class radicals, this state of affairs was unjust, not only because it meant that governing bodies were not representative of society but also because only bona fide working men could truly articulate the wishes of their class. Consequently, while working-class radicals in Bristol praised certain middle-class 'friends of the people', they believed that that those 'not born in the ranks of the working classes', as one activist explained in 1878, were 'not fit to represent that class'.[38] Members of the Leicester Democratic Association expressed similar sentiments when running 'working men candidates' in municipal elections throughout the 1870s. As in Bristol, working-class radicals were comfortable with the idea of introducing the politics of class into election contests. For Daniel Merrick, the leader of the Sock and Top Union who became the first working-class member of the Leicester City Council in 1873, working men were best placed to convey the views of their fellows on questions that 'vitally affected working-men' but which only affected 'the middle class ... indirectly.' Education was one such question, which is why Merrick and others spent so much time trying to place on the School Board those who were 'well acquainted with the life of [the] working man, his difficulties and wants, and fully alive to the true value of education to that class'.[39]

Radicals in Bristol and Leicester were in the advance guard of the campaign for labour representation. The classist assumptions that underpinned their demands, however, were just as prevalent in towns where labour representation was not the primary objective of working-class radical activists. In Norwich, for example, working-class radicals celebrated the fact that their organisations were composed of and led by working men and trade unionists, particularly during meetings of the Electoral Organization of the Working Classes. Journalists both sympathetic and hostile to this organisation often reported that its meetings were attended almost exclusively by working men, who, on one occasion, gave cheers for the 'Liberty of the Working Classes' and sang songs that honoured the struggles of 'the sons of labor [sic]'.[40] Journalists also noted how audience members offered their own views on the key issues of the day. 'As a working man ...' was a popular opener to such statements, as it conferred on the speaker a certain authenticity and served to demonstrate their pride in their social position. At a campaign meeting during the 1868 parliamentary election, for instance, one of Jacob Tillett's supporters expressed his delight that the Reform Act had given men like him, who spent their lives toiling 'from Monday morning to Saturday night for the bread that perisheth', the opportunity to exercise their 'constitutional rights' in nominating and voting for a candidate of their own choosing.[41]

Populist radicals and liberals were not averse to emphasising (and exaggerating) their humble origins.[42] But statements of this kind were exceptions rather than the rule, and it was far more common for middle-class radicals to portray themselves as spokespersons for an inclusive, heterogeneous movement of 'the people' that had historically fought to improve the lives and conditions not only of the working classes but of all sections of the community. For populist radicals, the people was composed of a vast brotherhood of shopkeepers, tradesmen, manual labourers, industrialists and, in some conceptions, everyone except the idle or privileged orders. In their view, the great political struggles in English history over free trade, parliamentary sovereignty and the extension of the franchise were fought in the interests of 'the masses of the people' against the entrenched political power of 'the uppermost circles'. This reading of history shaped populist radical understandings of contemporary issues, not least the question of labour representation. As the people rather than the working class were at the centre of their political analysis, it followed that populist radicals did not always agree with the logic behind this demand. While they were not opposed to the idea of sending more working men to Parliament, they ultimately believed that the working classes could be fairly and fully represented by any man, irrespective of his class background, who supposedly understood the needs of working men.[43]

Foreshadowing a common criticism directed at the Labour party in the twentieth century, populist radicals felt that political representatives should first and foremost represent the interests of the nation rather than those of a single class. Working-class radicals approached this question from the opposite standpoint. If representatives paid special attention to the demands of the working classes and worked to satisfy their wants as an immediate priority, then it followed that they would be doing a service to the nation as a whole. This was a slight but important difference that explains some of the idiosyncrasies that can be found in working-class radical and, later, labourist discourse.

A sharp class-centred analysis of political representation has rarely been attributed to the mid- to late Victorian radical movement. But as we have seen, workerist and class-based sentiments were a constant feature of working-class radical discourse during this period. Such sentiments serve to highlight the differences that existed not only between radicals and liberals, but also between those supposedly united in a broad-based radical movement. Some of these tensions revolved around questions that, for some scholars, only became politically divisive in later decades. For example, working-class radicals played a key role in the trade union agitation of the 1870s by forming trade union societies and, in some towns, trades' councils. Though they obtained support from middle-class radicals like Charles Bradlaugh and Samuel Morley, they encountered hostility or ambivalence from some employers who, while earnestly radical in politics, resented the perceived ingratitude of their employees.

The rise of trade unionism threatened to rupture the Northampton radical movement, which ostensibly had all the elements of a genuinely populist coalition. The Northampton Radical Association was under the control of an eclectic band of bakers, merchants, tailors, drapers, shoe manufacturers, printers and booksellers.[44] But the voice of a decidedly working-class radical tradition became more audible in Northampton after 1873 when the newly formed National Union of Operative Boot and Shoe Rivetters and Finishers (NUBSRF) began to organise the town's shoemakers.[45] From that time on, local trade union societies began to put forward candidates at school board elections, often without the sanction or support of Liberal and Radical organisations, and campaigned against Conservative, Liberal *and* Radical candidates who they deemed unworthy of support.[46] For trade unionist radicals, the wages question was intimately tied up with questions of a political nature, and the actions of employers in the workplace were often more important than their professed political convictions.

Leading members of the Northampton Radical Association rejected this view and informed trade unionists that industrial questions could not be discussed at political meetings. This drew the ire of trade unionists such as William France, the secretary of the Northampton NUBSRF and a member of Bradlaugh's election committee, who criticised middle-class radicals for 'howl[ing] at you as if you were some inferior animal' for attempting to organise shoemakers.[47] France and his supporters eventually resigned from the Radical Association, but not before condemning its leaders in strong class terms. France told readers of the *Northampton Mercury* that he had left the Radical Association 'not because [he was] any less a Radical, but because [he had] noticed, for a long time, that the association [was] fast growing into a middle-class association'. Continuing, France bemoaned the fact that working-class radicals had lost their sense of independence and urged them to form a 'working men's society of their own', separate from those who, he believed, were not radicals in the true sense of the term.[48]

That this feud erupted just months prior to Bradlaugh's election victory in 1880 challenges the notion that radicalism in Northampton was a populist movement free of internal divisions. It is possible to identify these differences, as well as the existence of a working-class section within the movement, by examining the way in which political leaders addressed their audiences. For instance, a speaker's use of flattery may help to reveal the social composition of an audience. The frequency with which speakers urged audience members to be patient with their leaders, to show respect when listening to their representatives and to refrain from doing anything that could divide the anti-Conservative vote tells us much about the political unreliability of the radical rank and file. Similarly, the abuse that radical activists and voters received from their opponents sheds light on the classist assumptions of Liberal and Conservative leaders and the social backgrounds, educational qualifications and behavioural practices of the ordinary radical voter. Writers for the Liberal *Norwich Mercury* revelled in this form of abuse in the aftermath of the Second Reform Act, an Act that one writer believed had given encouragement to the 'extreme section' of 'roughs' who delighted in 'intimidation', 'violence' and 'mob law'.[49]

By the time of the 1868 general election, working men formed a majority of the electorate in the towns and cities studied in this book. This may explain why candidates and activists of all parties directed their appeals to working-class voters and why their literature often included a sharp analysis of class distinctions. This was especially true in Northampton, where Liberals and Conservatives published numerous handbills, posters and songs that tried to convince Charles Bradlaugh's working-class supporters that their idol was little more than a dishonest, middle-class agitator. In 1868, Liberals released a poster featuring a fictional dialogue between two working men, one who intended to vote for two sitting Liberal MPs and another who intended to vote for Bradlaugh and Frederick Lees because they were working men. After informing his colleague that Lees was 'not a working man' but a 'middle-class tradesman', the Liberal voter criticised Bradlaugh in similar terms:

> He says he is a working man, and a good many of his supporters really think so, whereas the account of his life which I see in their own windows,

shows that he was first a soldier, and after that, as far as I can make out, a lawyer's clerk, and has never been a working man at all.[50]

This poster, as well as election literature from other towns, suggests that the politics of class had a certain level of electoral purchase at this time.[51] After all, its creator did not seek to loosen Bradlaugh's and Lees' hold over working-class voters by evoking universalist themes or criticising their views on political questions. Rather, they sought to draw attention to the boundaries that separated social groups that, for many contemporaries, were constituent parts of the people. Liberal activists, perhaps feeling that their strategy had contributed to Bradlaugh's defeat in 1868, continued this line of attack at the 1874 general election. In a poster revealingly titled 'A Contrast!' (see Figure 1) its creator sought to drive a wedge between Bradlaugh and his working-class supporters by implying that he lived a life of luxury off the back of the 'dirty fellows' that supported him.[52] That the Liberal candidates were not working men themselves did not seem to matter. What mattered was that Bradlaugh was shown to be a hypocrite, and that working-class voters, who presumably cared a great deal about a candidate's honesty, were made to question their faith in a man who claimed to be the true working-man's candidate.

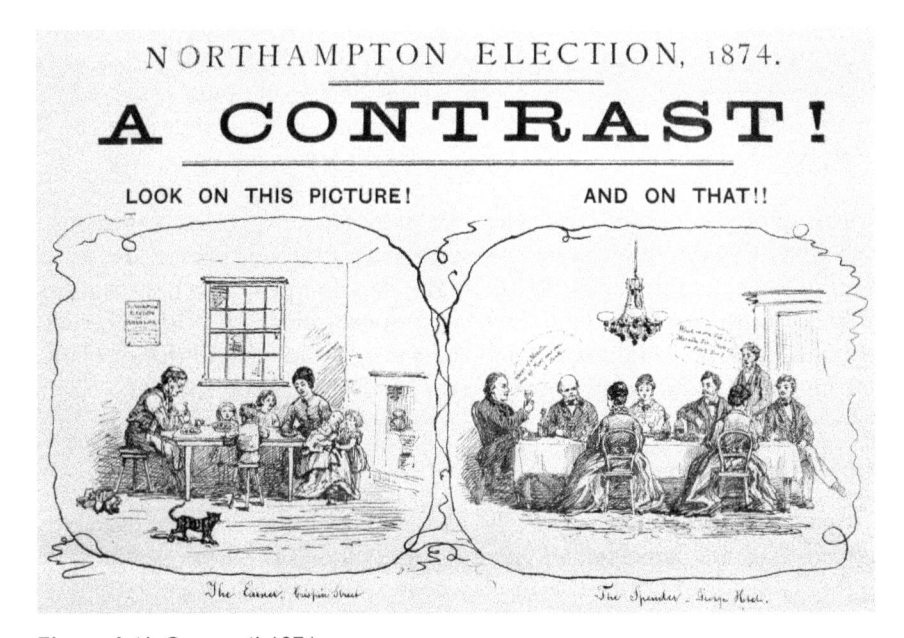

Figure 1 'A Contrast!', 1874

Liberals and Conservatives were keen to exploit any divisions in the radical movement. We must be wary, therefore, of reading too much into the way opponents attacked radical candidates and should try as much as possible to examine the way radicals spoke about themselves and their movement. Thankfully, these were topics that radicals were more than happy to discuss. Through interrogating discussions of this kind, it becomes clear that radicals differed in their view of the radical movement and the social basis of its support. In general, populist radicals portrayed radicalism as a populist movement of the people rather than the movement of a single class. Thomas Purser, a house agent and leading activist in the Northampton Radical Association, provided a succinct summary of this view at a meeting in 1875:

> When he spoke of people, he did not allude to one class only, although there were many who thought the Radical portion of the community were meant. It was true that the Radicals of the present day and of former days had been more especially the advocates of the working classes, but in speaking of the people he meant all classes.[53]

One of Purser's political colleagues, a grocer by trade, had offered a similarly inclusive definition of the radical movement at a meeting two years earlier:

> Radicalism, then, what does this mean? Legislation for the working classes, demolition of the rights of property, destruction of social order, the tyranny of a majority, the subjection of masters to men, of capital to labour, the reign of demagogism or of the professed agitator. None of these; none of these.[54]

This interpretation of radicalism was most often expressed by populist radicals, or as one Northampton-based activist called them, those who had 'raised themselves a little above the position at which they started in life'.[55] But it was not the only version of radicalism on offer. Whereas populist radicals sought to detach radicalism from the politics of class, working-class radicals attempted to do precisely the opposite.

Purifying the constitution

At a meeting organised in 1878, liberals and radicals from Leicester agreed that 'the principles of Liberalism' included the struggle for civil and religious liberty, the disestablishment of the Church of England and the maintenance of free trade. But for Daniel Merrick, this list was incomplete. A prominent radical and one of the best known trade unionists in

Leicester, Merrick told those present that there were 'great differences of opinion among Liberals as to the chief questions that were soon to be settled by the legislature'. He felt that 'special thought should be directed to the extension of the franchise to the counties', something that previous speakers had neglected to mention. He believed that the Liberal Party should support the principle of direct labour representation so that the House of Commons would represent 'the different classes of society'. And he demanded that MPs be paid for their services to ensure that all classes had a 'fair and equal chance of being represented'. It was this last question in particular that Merrick hoped would claim the attention of the Liberal Party in the years to follow.[56]

Seeing democracy as an adjacent rather than a core concept in liberalism makes it easier to understand why Merrick's fellow speakers failed to mention these demands. Because of democracy's adjacent position in liberalism, liberals could logically remain liberals while expressing concern about 'mob rule' or 'the tyranny of the majority'.[57] Conversely, seeing democracy as a core rather than an adjacent concept in radicalism explains why Merrick placed such a strong emphasis on these demands. Because of its close connection to liberty and individuality, radicals viewed democracy as a system of self-government in which power would be exercised by the people through their elected representatives. The radical notion of democracy was augmented by a belief in the rationality of human beings and an assumption that men had the ability to determine their own lives. These concepts were bound to a particular notion of progress that radicals took to mean gradual socio-political advance along democratic lines.

Adjacent concepts encircled the core concepts of democracy, liberty, individuality, rationality and progress and, in doing so, helped to limit the number of meanings that individuals could assign to them. Equality, 'decontested' as the equality of all citizens before the law and the right of all adult males to participate in the government of their country, was an integral component of radical ideology.[58] The idea of a general or common interest was important for radicals of all persuasions, but especially for populist radicals. It is here that we begin to see divisions in the radical ideological family. The contrasting tone of populist and working-class forms of radicalism makes sense when we see class as an adjacent concept in the latter but absent from the former. Though the impulse behind their activities stemmed from their exclusion from the *political* process, working-class radicals often presented their demands in a language of class. Class and trade unionism influenced working-class radical understandings of the general interest, which is why they placed special emphasis on the unique concerns of the working class. And by giving priority to the demands of a single class, working-class radicals revealed how they differed from intellectual currents whose advocates preferred to articulate their demands in the language of populism.

Rights was another influential concept in radical ideology. In fact, without recognising the salience of rights in shaping the radical worldview, it would be extremely difficult to understand the focus of radical politics during this period. As a prioritising concept 'definitionally attached to any political value or concept it is designed to protect and prioritize', rights was located in radicalism's adjacent band.[59] Its proximity to the concepts of liberty, democracy, individuality, equality and other core and adjacent concepts yielded an array of radical policy proposals such as the right to vote, the right to secrecy when voting and the right to participate in the selection of a candidate. As one working-class radical from Norwich explained, most men had a right to:

> A voice in the representation of the country, a right to consent to the making of the laws that they were compelled to obey, and a right to say what amount of the taxes which they were called upon to pay should be levied upon them.[60]

But working-class radicals articulated a class-based notion of rights. For example, trade union radicals often singled out employers for trampling on the 'rights of labour', which, for them, included the right to form and join a trade union. By drawing on the concepts of class, equality, the general interest and individuality, they also campaigned for legal changes that would place workers 'on the same footing as the rest of the community' and end industrial practices which had 'sprung up in the dark ages'.[61] As this quote indicates, working-class radicals believed that each section of the community, including employers, had a right to guard their interests and protect their rights. If representatives of the workers and employers were given the freedom to negotiate on fair and equal terms, then disagreements would be resolved to the satisfaction of all parties. In this view, trade unions were not necessarily 'opposed to an employer's interest'. They had been formed to 'protect, but not to injure', and responsible trade unionists such as Daniel Merrick advocated a 'moderate and temperate policy' for settling differences in a 'kindly and impartial way'.[62] By using their collective strength to persuade employers of the justice of their demands, trade unionists, for one activist from Norwich, would be able to obtain the 'full enjoyment of those rights and privileges which [they] long ago ought to have possessed'.[63]

Working-class radicals attempted to translate these principles into action in several ways. Their efforts to democratise local liberal politics stemmed from a belief that male members of the community, as rational beings capable of making informed political decisions, should be allowed to participate in the selection of those who legislated on their behalf. Again, while this demand was political in nature, its articulation took on a marked class inflection. As a leading member of the Bristol Working Men's Reform Association remarked in 1877, working men 'had a right to be heard in the selection of their representatives' because the Liberal Party was a party of 'working men' rather a 'coterie of employers'.[64] What mattered most for radicals was the manner in which Liberal candidates were chosen, or, more precisely, whether or not 'the masses of the people' had been consulted in the process.[65]

Radicals sought to make nominally representative bodies more accountable. To do this, they advocated a comprehensive programme of political reforms that included universal manhood suffrage, triennial Parliaments, vote by ballot and equal electoral districts. Some favoured the abolition of the monarchy and the House of Lords, while others, including members of the Lincoln Working Men's Liberal Association, were content to bring the Lords 'more into harmony with the intelligent wishes of the country and the House of Commons'.[66] *Working-class* radicals agreed with these demands but, again, justified them in class terms. When 'Citizen' Payne of the Leicester Democratic Association complained of the 'needless grants and dowries to Royalty', he made it clear that his opposition to 'this kind of oppression' stemmed from his direct experiences as a working man and his belief that the diversion of resources to the monarchy 'press[ed] heavily on the hard earnings of [his] class'.[67] Working-class radicals in Bristol were more forthright in their criticisms of the royal family. At a meeting of republicans in 1871, one activist described the royal family as a 'herde [sic] of locusts' who had 'flock[ed] over … from Germany and Prussia [to marry] the Queen's daughters' so they could '[run] away with the bread of the children of the working classes'. Those in attendance at the meeting adopted a strongly worded resolution that, in characteristic fashion, was littered with references to 'the working community', the 'working classes' and the 'toiling millions'.[68]

Working-class radicals hoped that the election of more labour representatives would make local and national governing bodies more representative of the population as a whole. This demand flowed from the close conceptual relationship between democracy, class, trade unionism and equality, and the connection between these concepts and the general interest produced a proportionate understanding of political representation. Far from seeking to deny the right of the 'upper and middle classes' to choose their own representatives, working-class radicals simply believed that the 'numerous industrial class' were also entitled to a fair share of representation.[69] But despite the expansion of the franchise in 1867, which made working men the majority of the electorate, working-class radicals still felt that the middle and upper classes enjoyed a disproportionate share of political power. This being the case, the working classes, for one Bristol-based trade unionist, had a 'greater right, or at least an equal right', to send men of 'their own order' to legislate on their behalf.[70]

A raft of cultural constraints, including the notion that men and women inhabited separate spheres, shaped the articulation of radical ideology. These constraints also influenced radical interpretations of the constitution. While contemporary critics accused them of seeking the 'total subversion of the monarchy, and all other existing institutions', radicals thought of themselves as ardent constitutionalists who endeavoured 'to maintain intact the institutions of this country' while seeking to bring them into line with the core principles of the constitution.[71] Far from wishing to subvert the constitution, radicals claimed that they were its staunchest defenders. The conceptual connections between democracy, liberty, progress, rights and equality, and the meanings that the idea environment of mid- to late Victorian England bestowed upon them, invited radicals to see themselves as part of a centuries-old tradition whose members had resisted arbitrary power and tyrannical government. At times, they even harked back to the myth of the 'Norman Yoke' and praised the 'old Saxon assemblies' for recognising the right of 'every free man to exercise his judgement on the affairs and conduct of the Government'.[72]

Radicals campaigned against 'the evils of the present system of Government', which, in their view, included unjust and oppressive laws that imposed restrictions on the franchise and which concentrated political power in the hands of an unaccountable elite.[73] As Jonathan Parry has shown, such inclusive, Anglocentric readings of the constitution were not the preserve of radicals alone. Victorian liberals also developed a constitutional conception of Englishness that placed parliamentary reform at the centre of progressive accounts of England's past. By presenting themselves as 'the more reliable interpreters of the historic English constitution' and 'the sounder defenders of popular liberties', Liberals showed that a constitutionalist language of patriotism, based on political rights and liberties rather than respect for traditional institutions, could rival that of the conservatives.[74]

Radicals largely accepted this view of the constitution and its history. By insisting that reform was a crucial part of the English political tradition, radicals, following the example of their eighteenth- and early-nineteenth-century predecessors, were able to present their defence of popular liberties and their critique of institutional exclusiveness as patriotic acts.[75] Like liberals, they also used comparisons of England and the continent to prove that they could achieve their objectives through legal channels.[76] While radicals wished to 'alter great questions ... at once', these changes would come about through peaceful agitation and moral persuasion rather than revolutionary action, though this strategy might be necessary in autocratic countries.[77] And while it was likely that radicals sometimes overstated their commitment to the constitutionalist order in the years following the Reform Act, the frequency with which they used the language of constitutionalism suggests that their commitment was genuine. The 'great ends' for which radicals were working, as the first report of the Norwich Electoral Organization made clear, would come about 'gradually and peacefully and by Constitutional methods only.'[78]

Still, there were subtle differences between radical and liberal forms of constitutionalism. To some extent, it was the speed at which radicals attempted to accomplish their objectives, rather than the fact that they wished to uproot the foundations of the constitutional order, that made them truly 'radical'. But another point of disagreement between radicals and liberals was the question of which laws and practices contravened the constitution. While it was increasingly difficult for them to claim that the post-1867 state (let alone the monarch) was tyrannical, radicals still drew upon the themes of freedom, tyranny and arbitrary power when engaging in discussions with conservatives and liberals on issues such as parliamentary reform, institutional exclusivity, and the influence of sectional and vested interests in political life. And for *working-class* radicals, the absence of working men from Parliament contravened the constitution by preventing the representative system from operating on a 'complete and national' basis. As George Odger explained during his unsuccessful campaign in Bristol in 1870, this would only be rectified when working men were sent to Parliament to 'purify the constitution' and dismantle 'bad laws which ... had been created by the higher and middle classes'.[79]

Conclusion

For William Gladstone, as for later historians, radicals were integral members of a broad church of liberalism. Based on the case studies discussed in this chapter, however, it would be more accurate to see radicals as members of an independent church, similar in many ways to the grander church of liberalism but with distinct features of its own.

To be sure, radicals in Bristol, Leicester, Lincoln, Northampton and Norwich tended to vote Liberal when a radical candidate was absent from the field. They also claimed to stand for 'liberal principles' and revered figures who also held a special place in the hearts of moderate liberals. But there was much more to the radicalism of the post-1867 era, and it is to the idiosyncrasies of the movement that we must turn if we are to more fully understand its distinctiveness and its complex relationship with other political and intellectual forces.

Radicals were not obedient partners in a broad-based Gladstonian coalition. In some towns, they formed independent organisations and stood their own election candidates. In others, they worked in fragile alliances with moderate liberals and gave qualified support to official Liberal candidates. In both scenarios, though, their behaviour, attitudes, language and focus all served to reinforce the view that they were different, in several important respects, from those who inhabited the world of mainstream liberal politics. Whether in spite of or because of this, radicals developed and sustained a national network of local subcultures whose interests and activities often ran counter to those of official liberalism.

Radicals articulated a distinct ideology that rested on a unique blend of concepts. Democracy, liberty, individuality, progress and rationality were located at the heart of radicalism's internal morphology, while equality, the general interest and rights were situated in its adjacent band. The state, which radicals deemed to be of comparatively little use, was to be found on the margins of radical ideology, although in time it would come to gravitate to a more central position. A range of institutions, practices, policies and attitudes, from the constitution and assumptions about separate spheres to manhood suffrage and the House of Lords, helped to link these concepts to their 'real-world' contexts, thus ensuring that they did not exist only at the level of abstraction. While many of these concepts could be found in liberalism and some forms of conservatism, conceptual overlap does not rule out a distinction between two or more ideologies.[80]

Like other ideologies, radicalism played host to a number of variations. This chapter has identified two such variations – working-class radicalism and populist radicalism – whose respective proponents offered different interpretations of radicalism's core messages. The concepts of class and trade unionism shaped working-class radical interpretations of democracy, liberty, rights, the general interest and other concepts in radical morphology and led its advocates to prioritise the demands of the working class over other sections of the community. They also led working-class radicals to participate in activities that angered liberals, conservatives and, at times, populist radicals. By forming socially exclusive organisations, framing political struggles in social terms, emphasising the protection and extension of the rights of labour, accepting a class-based reading of the constitution and showing a keen interest in the thorny question of labour representation, working-class radicals distinguished themselves not only from their traditional Conservative foes but also from those who considered themselves devoted members of Gladstone's broad church.

Notes

1 *London Evening Standard*, 2 June 1877.
2 For examples, see Hobsbawm, *Worlds of Labour*, pp. 182, 219, 221; Kirk, *Change, Continuity and Class*, pp. 26–27; N. Kirk, 'Class and the "linguistic turn" in Chartist and post-Chartist historiography', in N. Kirk (ed.), *Social Class and Marxism: Defences and Challenges* (Aldershot, 1996), p. 116.
3 For Stedman Jones, 'in radical discourse the dividing line between classes was not that between employer and employed, but that between represented and unrepresented'. Stedman Jones, *Languages of Class*, pp. 106–107.
4 Biagini and Reid, *Currents of Radicalism*, p. 4; Biagini, *Liberty, Retrenchment and Reform*, pp. 11, 51.
5 For the Tichborne case, during which an Australian butcher claimed to be the long-lost aristocrat Sir Roger Tichborne, see R. McWilliam, *The Tichborne Claimant: A Victorian Sensation* (London, 2007).
6 Record Office for Leicestershire, Leicester and Rutland, Wigston (hereafter LRO), M766/1, poems by Joseph Green, shoemaker of Lower Sandacre Street, Leicester, 1876 (hereafter Joseph Green poems).
7 Belchem, *Popular Radicalism in Nineteenth-Century Britain*, p. 5.
8 Harrison, *Before the Socialists*, p. 3.
9 Freeden, *Ideologies and Political Theory*, pp. 68–69, 78–79, 165.
10 Freeden, *Ideologies and Political Theory*, pp. 154–155.
11 Freeden, *Ideologies and Political Theory*, p. 98.
12 A radical activist used this term at a meeting of the Bristol Industrial, Social, and Political Association of Working Men in 1870. *Western Daily Press*, 9 March 1870.
13 British Library of Political and Economic Science, London (hereafter LSE), JN1129.L3, Labour Party conference reports (hereafter LP CR), 1911; S. Roberts, 'Thomas Cooper in Leicester, 1840–1843', *Transactions of Leicestershire Archaeological and Historical Society*, 61 (1987), pp. 62–76; B. Lancaster, *Radicalism, Cooperation and Socialism: Leicester Working-Class Politics 1860–1906* (Leicester, 1987), p. 63; H. Pelling, *Social Geography of British Elections 1885–1910* (London, 1967), pp. 210–211.
14 P. Fleming, 'The emergence of modern Bristol', in M. Dresser and P. Ollerenshaw (eds), *The Making of Modern Bristol* (Tiverton, 1996), p. 6, 13; Pelling, *Social Geography of British Elections*, pp. 145, 157.

15 F. Hill, *Victorian Lincoln* (Cambridge, 1974), pp. 180, 253–254.
16 Pelling, *Social Geography of British Elections*, p. 110; W. Adkins, *The Position of Northampton in English History* (Northampton, 1897), pp. 14–19; J. Howarth, 'The Liberal revival in Northamptonshire, 1880–1895: A case study in late nineteenth century elections', *The Historical Journal*, 12:1 (1969), p. 83.
17 S. Cherry, *Doing Different? Politics and the Labour Movement in Norwich, 1880–1914* (Hunstanton, 1989), p. 11; *Norfolk Chronicle*, 25 August 1888; LSE, ILP/5/1915/76, Independent Labour Party (hereafter ILP) pamphlets and leaflets, report of the Norwich Conference, April 1915.
18 *Lincolnshire Chronicle*, 17 February 1865.
19 S. Bryher, *An Account of the Labour and Socialist Movement in Bristol: Part 1* (Bristol, 1929), p. 16; *Reynolds's Newspaper*, 13 March 1870; *Bristol Mercury*, 20 September 1873; *Western Daily Press*, 16 July 1877.
20 J. Cannon, *The Chartists in Bristol* (Bristol, 1964), p. 16.
21 Owen, *Labour and the Caucus*, p. 24.
22 *Western Daily Press*, 15 September 1877.
23 By 1891, workers in these trades constituted 62.5 per cent of Leicester's industrial workforce. Lancaster, *Radicalism, Cooperation and Socialism*, p. xx.
24 *Leicester Chronicle*, 4 March 1871; 28 March 1874; *Leicester Daily Mercury*, 7 February 1879.
25 Lancaster, *Radicalism, Cooperation and Socialism*, p. 77.
26 *Leicester Chronicle*, 4 March 1871.
27 *Lincolnshire Chronicle*, 21 November 1868; J. Hinde Palmer had contested Lincoln on three previous occasions, including in 1862 when his narrow defeat led to riots. Hill, *Victorian Lincoln*, pp. 34–36.
28 *Lincolnshire Chronicle*, 2 January 1869; 29 April 1870.
29 *Lincoln, Rutland and Stamford Mercury* (hereafter *Stamford Mercury*), 5 March 1880.
30 In 1868, Liberal magistrates, councillors, Guardians and members of the 'Registration Society' invited candidates to stand. *Norwich Mercury*, 11 July 1868.
31 *Norfolk News*, 18 April 1868; 11 July 1868.
32 *Norfolk News*, 18 April 1868.
33 *Norwich Mercury*, 7 November 1868; 21 November 1868; *Norfolk News*, 2 January 1869.
34 *Norfolk News*, 1 June 1870; 18 June 1870.
35 Harrison, *Before the Socialists*, pp. 181–182; F. A. D'Arcy, 'Charles Bradlaugh and the world of popular radicalism, 1833–1891' (unpublished doctoral thesis, University of Hull, 1978), p. 307.
36 *Northampton Mercury*, 10 October 1874.
37 Lawrence, 'Popular radicalism and the socialist revival in Britain', pp. 170, 182.
38 *Bristol Mercury*, 30 October 1878.
39 *Leicester Chronicle*, 31 December 1870; 27 December 1873.

Radicalism, class and populism

40 *Norfolk News*, 16 May 1868; *Norwich Mercury*, 13 June 1868.
41 *Norfolk News*, 4 July 1868.
42 In 1868, Bradlaugh told working-class voters that he had lived in their midst and felt 'the biting grip of their wants'. *Northampton Mercury*, 18 July 1868.
43 Tillett, for example, 'didn't believe it was necessary that working men should be represented by working men, in order to have their views expressed and their wrongs righted'. *Norfolk News*, 18 July 1868.
44 *Northampton Mercury*, 29 October 1881; 23 December 1882; 30 October 1886; 25 October 1895.
45 A. Fox, *A History of the National Union of Boot and Shoe Operatives 1874–1957* (Oxford, 1958), p. 78. In 1831, a third of men living in Northampton were shoemakers; this had risen to two-fifths by 1871. V. Hatley, *Shoemakers in Northamptonshire 1762–1911: A Statistical Survey* (Northampton, 1971), pp. 5, 10.
46 Northamptonshire Central Library, Northampton (hereafter NCL), 198–781/9/1880, Northampton election ephemera including printed addresses, handbills and posters (hereafter NEE), 'To Trade Unionists and Non-Unionists', 1880. Conservative Party literature also criticised radical candidates for 'grinding the wages down'. See NCL, 198–781/9/1880, NEE, 'A Conversation overheard between two Working Men, Friday, October 22nd, 1880'.
47 Quoted in Fox, *A History of the NUBSO*, p. 78.
48 Letter 'Robert McMillan' to NM, 22 March 1879; letter 'William Cory France' to *NM*, 23 August 1879.
49 *Norwich Mercury*, 11 July 1868; 18 July 1868. See also *Stamford Mercury*, 30 October 1874.
50 NCL, 198–781/9/1868, NEE, 'What The Little Bird Heard: A Dialogue', 1868.
51 Working-class-orientated songs such as 'Non-Electors' Hymn', 'Rally Round the Glorious Standard' and 'Cheer, Boys, Cheer!' featured in the Leicester Liberal songsheet for the 1880 general election. LRO, 10D64/1, Leicester Liberal Songsheet, 1880.
52 NCL, 198–781/9/1874, NEE, 'A Contrast!', 1874.
53 *Northampton Mercury*, 24 April 1875; 10 February 1877.
54 *Northampton Mercury*, 11 January 1873.
55 *Northampton Mercury*, 20 September 1879.
56 *Leicester Chronicle*, 25 May 1878.
57 Freeden, *Ideologies and Political Theory*, pp. 154–155.
58 For Freeden, 'decontesting' is the process through which concepts within an ideology acquire their specific meanings. See Freeden, *Ideologies and Political Theory*, pp. 75–91.
59 Freeden, *Ideologies and Political Theory*, p. 162.
60 *Norfolk News*, 4 July 1868.
61 Merrick, addressing the Trades Union Congress in 1877. *Leicester Chronicle*, 22 September 1877.

62 *Leicester Journal*, 24 January 1879; *Leicester Chronicle*, 22 June 1872; 22 September 1877. For similar sentiments, see *Norfolk News*, 18 April 1868; *Northampton Mercury*, 3 February 1872; *Bristol Mercury*, 15 May 1880.
63 Letter 'A. F.' to *Norfolk News*, 21 January 1871.
64 *Western Daily Press*, 16 July 1877.
65 *Norfolk News*, 16 May 1868.
66 *Stamford Mercury*, 28 July 1871.
67 *Leicester Chronicle*, 1 July 1871.
68 *Reynolds's Newspaper*, 3 December 1871.
69 Letter 'A Working Man' to *Western Daily Press*, 25 February 1870.
70 *Western Daily Press*, 18 December 1873.
71 *Leicester Journal*, 12 January 1872; *Lincolnshire Chronicle*, 21 November 1868.
72 Jacob Tillett, addressing a meeting in Norwich. *Eastern Daily Press*, 10 March 1880.
73 *Leicester Chronicle*, 4 March 1871.
74 Parry, The Politics of Patriotism, p. 10; Parry, 'The impact of Napoleon III on British politics'; Pentland, 'Parliamentary reform', pp. 386–391.
75 Cunningham, 'The language of patriotism', pp. 8–33.
76 Parry, 'The impact of Napoleon III on British politics', p. 150; Pentland, 'Parliamentary reform', p. 386.
77 *Lincolnshire Chronicle*, 21 November 1868.
78 *Norfolk News*, 18 April 1868.
79 Letter 'A Voter' to *Western Daily Press*, 25 February 1870; *Reynolds's Newspaper*, 27 March 1870.
80 E. Harding, 'Conceptualising horizontal politics' (unpublished doctoral thesis, University of Nottingham, 2012), p. 208.

2

Charles Bradlaugh and the constitution

Charles Bradlaugh's struggle to enter Parliament was one of the most controversial political and legal campaigns of the Victorian era. Trained initially as a solicitor's clerk, Bradlaugh became a well-known figure for his controversial lectures on secularism, birth control and republicanism and for founding the National Secular Society in 1866. After being elected as the radical member for Northampton in 1880, Bradlaugh, like all Members of Parliament, was expected to declare allegiance to the Crown before taking his seat. As an atheist, though, Bradlaugh considered the religious Oath of Allegiance to contain words of an 'idle and meaningless' character, and so asked for permission to affirm instead. A specially convened Select Committee of the House of Commons rejected this request, whereupon Bradlaugh announced that he would take the oath after all. But this request was also denied and the House of Commons resolved that Bradlaugh should not be allowed to make an affirmation or take the oath. After effectively being barred from entering the House of Commons, Bradlaugh's seat fell vacant and a by-election was called.

'The Bradlaugh case', as the debacle became known, attracted a great deal of public attention and discussion. Those who supported Bradlaugh's right to take his seat began a nationwide political movement and organised legal challenges, petitions and protest meetings to fight against this violation of civil and religious liberty. Bradlaugh's supporters in Northampton also refused to accept the decision of the House of Commons and re-elected Bradlaugh five times in five years in the face of hostility from a holy alliance of conservatives, liberals, Anglicans, nonconformists and Catholics. Finally, after a tumultuous six-year campaign during which he received death threats and spent time imprisoned in the Palace of Westminster's Clock Tower, Bradlaugh was allowed to take the oath and his seat in 1886.[1]

The pro-Bradlaugh movement has long been seen as one of several popular radical campaigns that enlivened British political life in the mid- to late nineteenth century. Strangely, though, the case has received little attention in accounts that have emphasised the resilience of liberalism throughout this period, perhaps because the semi-autonomous and rebellious nature of the movement complicates the notion that radicals and liberals were united under the inclusive flag of Gladstonian liberalism. When Bradlaugh has been discussed, he has often been portrayed as an exemplar of militant radicalism (or 'unofficial' liberalism) whose activities placed him on the extreme outer edges of mainstream liberal politics. While Bradlaugh and his supporters exhibited broad sympathies with what they saw as the 'true' liberal tradition, they were also part of a plebeian subculture that tended to embarrass the sensibilities of Liberal Party leaders.[2]

These studies have gone some way towards reaffirming the historical significance of the case and its importance for understanding the dynamics of late Victorian popular politics. Still, the case can tell us a great deal more about the social, political and intellectual landscape of the time. The quick succession of election and by-election contests in Northampton between 1880 and 1886, all of which were widely reported on in the national and provincial press, offers historians a unique window into the political culture of 1880s England. Bradlaugh's actions provoked heated discussions among a broad cross-section of society and encouraged political actors at a 'high' and 'low' level to debate questions of a constitutional, theological, social, political and ideological nature. In the House of Commons and on street corners, Bradlaugh's supporters and opponents engaged in fierce debates about a range of delicate topics, from the true meaning of the constitution and the rights and duties of elected representatives to the boundaries of civil and religious liberty and the relationship between religious institutions and the state. As Bradlaugh's profanation of a religious oath deeply offended many Christians, it should come as no surprise that participants often conducted these debates in a vitriolic manner. They also introduced personal elements into their verbal and written attacks which served to reveal the deeply rooted assumptions about class, gender, nationality, education and other issues that would likely have remained hidden in debates of a less controversial nature.

It is strange that the internal dynamics of the pro- and anti-Bradlaugh campaigns have featured so little in scholarly discussions. This chapter aims to fill this gap in the historiography by untangling the complex web of alliances and rivalries that formed in response to the case in Northampton, Bristol, Leicester, Lincoln and Norwich. Untangling these webs is not an easy task, mainly because attitudes did not divide neatly along party lines. Radicals, who were Bradlaugh's strongest supporters, viewed the case as a straightforward battle for religious, civil and constitutional liberty. Conservatives thought that Bradlaugh represented all that was wrong with Victorian England and feared that his 'monstrous hybrid' of 'communistic radicalism' and 'atheism' would tear up by the roots 'all that is dear to Christian lovers of the British Constitution'.[3] Liberal responses were more diverse, ranging from highly favourable to openly hostile. Notwithstanding their commitment to the principle of civil and religious liberty and the close historical affinity between liberalism and dissenting religious traditions, some liberals opposed Bradlaugh's right to take his seat in Parliament on theological and ideological grounds. This apparent disregard for liberal principles drew the ire of Bradlaugh's radical supporters and disappointed a large number of liberals who felt that the House of Commons should not be able to exclude an elected representative from taking their seat, however distasteful or immoral their political or theological opinions might be.

Exploring the dynamics of the radical–liberal relationship at a local level makes it easier to explain the diversity of liberal attitudes to the case. In towns where liberals and independent-minded radicals had recent experience of mutual acrimony and electoral conflict, liberals were more likely to view Bradlaugh's campaign with indifference, irritation or hostility. In towns where radicals and liberals had recent experience of working together or where radicals had managed to gain a certain foothold in Liberal organisations, liberals were more likely to be supportive of Bradlaugh's campaign. And yet even in these towns, radicals and liberals still assigned varying degrees of importance to the case, with the former viewing it as a national political and constitutional crisis and the latter seeing it as a nuisance that prevented liberals from focusing on issues of greater importance. While the formation of temporary alliances served to obscure the reality of these tensions, radicals and liberals offered contrasting interpretations of Bradlaugh and his campaign.

Untangling the debates surrounding the Bradlaugh case strengthens our understanding of ideological differences between radicalism and liberalism. In particular, it sheds light on the differences between radical and liberal forms of constitutionalism. Contests over the meaning of the constitution were at the centre of the Bradlaugh debate. Songs, poems, posters, articles, handbills and other materials produced during the case contained a great deal of constitutional doctrine, as did speeches delivered by orators representing the pro- and anti-Bradlaugh campaigns. These texts provide historians with key insights into contemporary perspectives on the constitution, as its uncodified nature enabled 'low-level' activists and 'high-level' politicians to offer their own views on the rights and duties of electors, the powers and responsibilities of elected representatives, and, of course, the right of atheists to sit in Parliament.

Radicals and liberals shared a broadly similar view of English history and the English constitution. However, this did not necessarily mean that they viewed the Bradlaugh case in the same light. In general, those who opposed Bradlaugh's campaign considered the admission of atheists to Parliament to be contrary to the constitution. In this view, an elected representative should be morally as well as legally qualified to serve as an MP. Radicals and liberals who supported Bradlaugh, while not denying the obvious theological implications of the case, believed that the central issue at stake was whether constituencies had a right to choose their own representatives. This, they argued, was a constitutional right and one that had been passed down to them by their forefathers. By refusing to accept the 'unconstitutional' actions of the House of Commons, Northampton's electors were involving themselves in a long historical struggle to defend the political, civil and religious rights of the English people.[4]

Discussions surrounding the case also touched on democracy, rights, equality, liberty and other concepts that comprised the frameworks of radical and liberal ideologies. These discussions reveal that even when they stood on the same side of the Bradlaugh debate, radicals and liberals tended to endow these concepts with different meanings. That Bradlaugh received the support of both radicals and some liberals can be accounted for by acknowledging the conceptual overlaps between radicalism and liberalism. The centrality of democracy and the arrangement of concepts in radical morphology helps to explain the strength of radical support for Bradlaugh. To paraphrase Michael Freeden, the radical belief in the right of electors to choose their own representatives can be decoded as encompassing a core belief in the value of democracy, understood as rule by the people, attached to other core and adjacent concepts such as rights, equality and the general interest (jointly decontested as the right of all members of the community to participate in the selection of representatives to a democratically elected body), and rounded off by peripheral concepts such as Parliament and manhood suffrage.[5]

Liberals could also find a logical route through their conceptual framework to support Bradlaugh's campaign. But, crucially, they arrived at this conclusion via a different route. This reflected differences between radical and liberal morphologies and emanated from the presence of democracy as a core concept in the former and an adjacent concept in the latter. The second-ranking importance of democracy in liberalism meant that liberals could logically support the notion of 'popular rule ... tempered by quality control' as a way of preventing sectional rule by the uneducated masses, which, for some, threatened to do immeasurable harm to the pursuit of the general interest.[6] This went hand in hand with a belief that democracy should serve an educational and ethical function and that voters should elect those who would not only represent their interests in Parliament, but would also exert a benevolent and moral influence on society. Seen in this way, it becomes easier to see why some liberals considered Bradlaugh to be unqualified to serve as an elected representative and why they deemed Northampton's electors to be irresponsible for refusing to choose a 'fit and proper' person to represent them in Parliament.

The final section of the chapter seeks to add an additional layer of complexity to our understanding of radical–liberal relations in the late nineteenth century by uncovering the social identities of those who comprised the pro-Bradlaugh movement at a local level. With a focus on campaign songs, poems, handbills, writings and speeches, it considers the way 'Bradlaughites' were depicted by their allies and rivals, as well as the way in which they spoke and wrote about themselves. The question of social class is one of the major and consistent themes at work in these sources, as the 'typical' Bradlaugh supporter was portrayed as a male manual worker. Depending on the political proclivities of the author or speaker, Bradlaugh's supporters were also portrayed as either politically engaged or ignorant, respectful or insubordinate, sober or drunk, morally responsible or prone to immorality. Though they rejected many of the labels given to them, these working-class radicals embraced their reputation as working men. Subscribing to what Ross McKibbin called 'a kind of folk-Marxism', they saw their labour as 'the source of all value [and] the only work that mattered' and believed that without their work, 'society would not exist'.[7]

But this was not an inclusive conception of class. Through their writings and speeches, working-class radicals constructed an invisible but well-understood set of boundaries that served to limit membership of 'the working classes' to a certain kind of worker, namely the male, regularly employed, English urban worker. This conception of class was heavily informed by assumptions about gender, work, nationality and race, though local socio-economic contexts often influenced the articulation of these assumptions. For instance, while sailors from the port city of Bristol often articulated a highly racialised notion of the working classes, workers from Norwich, an isolated urban centre in a largely agricultural region, spoke more frequently about the threats posed by agricultural rather than foreign labourers. Still, the working-class radical conception of class was broadly consistent across different regions, and its proponents articulated it in two ways: first, by implying that the traits and struggles of the English working man were fundamentally different to those of 'other' workers, and then by using terms and expressions that served to draw attention to the presumed otherness of the long-term unemployed, the 'undeserving poor', and female, non-British and agricultural workers. It was in this sense that class had an influence on the tone of popular politics at a time when the working classes, according to 'stagist' and 'continuity' accounts, were either docile consumers of middle-class values or favourable to non-class, populist visions of the social order.

'The choice of the people's voice'[8]

Charles Bradlaugh contested the seat of Northampton on six occasions between March 1880 and July 1886. He was opposed each time by a Conservative candidate, and it was members and supporters of the Conservative Party, both in Northampton and throughout the country, who proved to be Bradlaugh's fiercest and most vocal opponents. It is difficult to do justice to the sheer level of anger and invective that Conservatives directed towards Bradlaugh during these campaigns. For the *Norfolk Chronicle*, Bradlaugh's profanation of the oath had single-handedly caused the 'greatest scandal' to disgrace the parliamentary records of Britain 'for the last hundred years'.[9] Conservative statements often blended political and religious themes, a strategy that some, including Bradlaugh himself, suspected of being part of a deliberate ploy to use the 'cloak of religion for party purposes'.[10] An election handbill distributed in Northampton during the 1880 contest, for example, advised voters that a vote for Bradlaugh would mean 'deny[ing] Him who laid Himself down for us. It [was] to despise Him who gave Himself for us.'[11] A reporter for the Conservative-aligned *Leicester Journal* described Bradlaugh as a modern-day Jonah who, like the biblical prophet of the same name, deserved to be drowned in the ocean for disobeying God's command.[12] On another occasion, the paper even blamed Bradlaugh for causing the agricultural depression that swept through Britain during the late nineteenth century, presumably because his election to Parliament had displeased a wrathful God.[13]

Bradlaugh was undoubtedly an unpopular figure among Conservative voters, but some within the Conservative Party hierarchy welcomed his refusal to accept the decision of the House of Commons. As the Liberal *Norwich Mercury* explained, Bradlaugh was 'the best weapon in the Tory armoury' because his campaign revealed the fragile nature of the radical–liberal 'coalition'.[14] As we saw in the previous chapter, there is much truth to this claim. Despite the best efforts of Liberal leaders to downplay tensions within the coalition, there were important differences between its radical and liberal sections. For those in the former camp,

Bradlaugh was a hero. His republicanism and hostility to the landed elite, his support for trade unionism and manhood suffrage, his sympathy with foreign nationalist movements and strenuous opposition to the game laws, all served to endear him to radical activists in Northampton and further afield.

Consequently, radicals from across Britain, including those active in Bristol, Lincoln, Leicester, Sheffield, Plymouth, London, Wolverhampton, Glasgow, Leeds, Newcastle upon Tyne, Macclesfield, Norwich and Bradford, gave generous moral and financial support to Bradlaugh's campaign.[15] Bradlaugh received support from avowed secularists, including those from the secularist stronghold of Leicester, but also from radicals who were not atheists. In fact, some of his strongest supporters in Northampton were devout churchgoers and devoted Christians who joined the cause to defend the principle of religious liberty rather than the theological views of Bradlaugh. For them, Bradlaugh represented a principle. Some even claimed that Bradlaugh's supporters were 'acting according to the principles of Christianity', which created an unusual situation in which Christian language was used to justify the election of an atheist to Parliament.[16]

Between Bradlaugh's conservative opponents and radical supporters stood a large mass of liberals who proved to be the pivot on which the election contests in Northampton turned. Both radicals and conservatives directed their election literature to this influential group of voters and presumed that they could be won over by appealing either to their Christian faith or to their sense of loyalty to the principle of religious liberty. Liberal responses to these appeals, however, were far from uniform. There certainly does not appear to be a correlation between religious affiliation and liberal attitudes to the case. While the towns that form the basis of this book were all strongholds of nonconformism where the working classes were generally apathetic towards organised religion – both key ingredients in producing what Henry Pelling called a 'strong bias towards Liberalism' – this did not produce consistent responses to the Bradlaugh case.[17]

If anything, the relationship between radicals and liberals seems to have been a more decisive factor in determining liberal responses to the case. In general, where radicals and liberals had recent experience of working together on specific campaigns, liberals seemed more likely to defend Bradlaugh's right to sit in Parliament, however much his political and theological views differed from their own. In these towns, the case served to direct attention away from questions that divided the two movements, and clarified some of the issues on which they agreed. On the other hand, in towns where liberals and radicals stood apart from one another, liberals were more likely to express hostility to Bradlaugh, his cause and those who supported him. Traditional hostilities were sometimes just as difficult to discard as traditional loyalties.

The delicate nature of the radical–liberal alliance in Northampton certainly seemed to influence local liberal responses to Bradlaugh's campaign. A semblance of radical–liberal unity had been established in the town just prior to Bradlaugh's election win in 1880, when leaders of the two sides agreed to set aside their differences to prevent another Conservative victory. Unity was the dominant theme of the 1880 radical–liberal campaign, and handbills, posters and songs all emphasised the uncontroversial aspects of Bradlaugh's programme that moderate liberal voters would have found easy to accept. This strategy succeeded in convincing a sufficient number of liberals to back Bradlaugh and his running mate, Henry Labouchère, but it was not universally successful. When Bradlaugh had to contest by-election contests in 1881, 1882 and 1884, several local Liberal and nonconformist figures actively campaigned for Bradlaugh's Conservative opponent, including some who had voted *for* him in 1880 as a way of bringing down the Conservative government.[18] While Bradlaugh was able to ward off these challenges, a certain number of liberals still voted against him, which one of his opponents saw as proof that some liberals preferred 'the principles of Christianity to those of politics'.[19]

The divisions that separated pro- and anti-Bradlaugh campaigners were sharper in Bristol, where radicals and liberals had long been organised into two warring camps. If anything, the Bradlaugh case simply gave Bristol radicals another opportunity to attack the leaders of the 'conservative' Bristol Liberal Association. Radical interest in the case was piqued when Samuel Morley, the senior Liberal MP for the city, announced that he opposed Bradlaugh's right to sit in Parliament. In 1882, Morley even urged Northampton's electors to vote for Bradlaugh's Conservative opponent 'as an act of allegiance to God and to public morality', a quote that local Conservatives quickly put on a handbill.[20] Unsurprisingly, Morley's intervention in the debate angered Bristol's radical community, who had long held Bradlaugh in high regard.[21] Radicals accused Morley of forsaking the principle of civil and religious liberty and urged him to see Bradlaugh's campaign as part of the long struggle for religious toleration that had brought emancipation for Catholics, Jews and nonconformists. Morley's utterances on the topic placed members of the Bristol Liberal Association in an awkward position, though they eventually reaffirmed their faith in Morley and his commitment to liberal principles. Nevertheless, Morley decided to retire his seat in 1885, a move that delighted local radicals.

Bradlaugh's brand of radical politics found fertile ground in Leicester, a city where he had built up a dedicated following among local secularists and trade unionists. After his exclusion from the House of Commons, working-class radicals turned out in great numbers to attend protest meetings alongside Liberal councillors and aldermen, key members of the Leicester Liberal Association, and Peter A. Taylor, the city's radical MP, who had once described Bradlaugh as a 'good democrat and a sound Republican'.[22] Even the *Leicester Chronicle*, the mouthpiece of moderate liberalism, lent its support to Bradlaugh's cause. In an editorial from early 1882, one writer bemoaned the fact that Bradlaugh 'enjoyed a notoriety which … [was] not proportional to his abilities' but admitted that there was a broader issue at stake. In short, it was 'a simple question of political principle and political freedom – nothing more and nothing less'. While they may not have shared Bradlaugh's theological or political views, liberals and radicals in Leicester could see that the 'illegal and unconstitutional' actions of the House of Commons violated the principle of 'free election'.[23]

In Norwich, the Bradlaugh case served to reopen old political wounds that had only begun to heal after the 1880 general election. After spending twelve years trying to convince the Norwich Liberals to back their choice of parliamentary candidate, radicals were once again engaged in a campaign that offended the sensibilities of the town's key Liberal personalities. As in the 1860s and 1870s, they also encountered hostility from the Liberal *Norwich Mercury*, whose editor regarded the prolongation of the case as a 'national disaster' that drew too much attention to the Bradlaugh's 'obnoxious' and 'objectionable' opinions.[24] Working-class radicals disagreed and put pressure on the two local MPs, Jeremiah James Colman and Jacob Tillett, to keep their promises and support Bradlaugh's cause at Westminster. In the run-up to the 1885 general election, activists withheld their support from the newly adopted Liberal candidate until he had clarified his position on the case, and, like their counterparts in other towns, they organised and delivered petitions to Parliament and held protest meetings that local dignitaries considered 'immoral, illegal, or likely to lead to a breach of the peace'.[25]

'The true rights of an Englishman'[26]

One way of teasing out the ideological differences between those who participated in the 'Bradlaugh debate' is to examine the divergent and often conflicting ways in which they spoke about the constitution. Conservative interest in the case largely emanated from a belief that an MP's theological views *did* matter to voters and that the admission of atheists to Parliament was contrary to the constitution. 'God', as the *Lincolnshire Chronicle* put it, was 'inevitably involved in this question'.[27] Though many conservatives used biblical language to pour scorn on Bradlaugh and his supporters, others phrased their arguments in legalistic terms by insisting that representatives needed to be legally *and* morally qualified to sit in Parliament. Bradlaugh, in their view, did not meet this criterion, as his atheism prevented him from either taking the Oath of Allegiance or making an affirmation, both of which had been framed for religious believers and which included an undeniable recognition of God. The House of Commons, therefore, had acted within its rights in excluding Bradlaugh and, in doing so, had served to sustain the 'honour and dignity' of that ancient assembly.[28] The House had also taken a stand for the principle of religious liberty, which, among other things, meant the right of anyone *with religious feeling* to serve as a Member of Parliament.[29]

Radicals and many liberals rejected these arguments and offered their own readings of the constitution to defend Bradlaugh's campaign. To some extent, the Bradlaugh case, like the cause of Italian unification in the 1850s, had the potential to strengthen the bond between radicals and liberals.[30] After all, despite being divided on many issues, radicals and liberals would surely resist any infringement on the civil and political rights of electors. Accordingly, liberals who took up the cause used uncontroversial slogans, such as the right of constituencies to choose their own representatives, which were consistent with both radical and liberal views on the constitution. This phrase, and others like it, rested on a set of culturally and historically contingent assumptions. For those who used it, the 'right of constituencies' derived from the historic English constitution. Consequently, the actions of the House of Commons were deemed 'unlawful', 'unconstitutional' and 'subversive of the constitutional rights of the whole body of electors of this kingdom'. The refusal of Northampton's electors to accept the decision of the House of Commons was also viewed as a noble stand for constitutional principles:[31]

> They say, 'For Northampton we don't care a bit,
> Turn him out and issue a writ;'
> But we are determined that he shall sit
> Up at St. Stephen's Hall.[32]

In keeping with the idea that popular rights and liberties were deeply rooted rather than contingent on the whim of the monarch or the government, Bradlaugh's supporters also insisted that they had been 'inherited from their forefathers', who, like themselves, had had to fight valiantly to resist 'encroachments' on their 'political freedoms'.[33]

References to the 'whole body of electors' imply a complex understanding of the concepts of equality, rights and democracy. Throughout the controversy, it was common for both radicals and liberals to speak of an 'equality of rights' to which all men (but not women) were entitled regardless of their political or theological opinions. This egalitarian notion of rights had a long history in English radical and liberal thought, stretching back to the Peasants' Revolt via the Levellers and Diggers of the seventeenth century, the Corresponding Societies of the eighteenth century and the Chartists of the early to mid-nineteenth century. As we have seen, Bradlaugh's supporters often drew parallels between their struggle and those of their ancestors. One activist from Bristol likened the 'unconstitutional' actions of the Conservative Party to the actions of Civil War-era royalists who 'bowed [their necks] under the foot of the king, and aided King Charles in trampling on the liberties of Englishmen'.[34] The experiences of John Wilkes, a radical journalist whose election victories in February, March and April 1769 were overturned by Parliament, also served as an important reminder that Bradlaugh was not the first duly elected person to be excluded from the House of Commons.[35] 'Bradlaugh & Liberty', a song written and popularised in Northampton during the controversy, noted the similarity between the two cases:

> In times of old, by fraud and gold,
> For long they kept Wilkes out,
> But England's voice proclaimed her choice
> And put wrong to the rout!
> And though they try now to deny
> The Champion of the Poor,
> Vox POPULI! shall be the cry
> That will unbar the door.[36]

On one occasion, Bradlaugh's opponents in Northampton even distributed a handbill that referred to Bradlaugh as the Tom Paine of his age, an epithet that Bradlaugh would likely have embraced.[37]

Bradlaugh's supporters often invoked the sovereignty of the people and, like the radicals and reformers of old, contended that the authority of Parliament derived from and rested on the consent of the governed. As elected representatives only acquired their powers 'from us as voters, and from us alone', the *Leicester Chronicle* believed that MPs could not possibly override the rights of constituencies.[38] Similar language can be found in other radical and liberal campaigns, including the campaign to extend the franchise to agricultural labourers. As the general secretary of the NUBSRF told the crowd at a 'Great Reform Demonstration' in Leicester in 1884:

> These two million men shall have the franchise, not as a boon from the House of Commons but as a right. We do not want nor do we ask for privileges, but we do insist upon each man having what is his birthright.[39]

As Jonathan Parry has argued, by reaching into the past and appealing to the ancient constitution and the notion of 'birthrights', radicals and liberals could insist that their freedoms needed to be restored rather dispensed to them by elites.[40]

But despite the overlaps between radical and liberal forms of constitutionalism, radicals and liberals still found much to disagree on. Radicals often bemoaned liberal indifference to the case and criticised the weakness of the Liberal government in dealing with the question. And in perhaps the clearest sign that radicalism and liberalism could generate diverse responses to a political issue, some liberals even opposed Bradlaugh's right to take his seat. This created a peculiar situation in which ideological liberals, many of whom had long defended the political rights of nonconformists, Jews and Catholics, now found themselves sharing platforms with those who had been on the opposite side in previous political struggles. This did not necessarily mean that they had ceased to be liberals. Rather, it simply demonstrates how members of the same ideological family could, at different times and in certain contexts, accord different proportional weight to the concepts at the heart of their ideology.

Seeing democracy as an adjacent rather than a core concept in liberal ideology helps to account for the variety of liberal responses to the case. If we accept Michael Freeden's definition of mid-Victorian classical liberalism, then its core structure consisted of liberty, individuality, progress, rationality, the general interest, sociability, and limited and responsible power, while concepts in the adjacent band included democracy, rights, property and education. Each of these concepts obtained a particular meaning through their interrelationship with one another, which resulted in a form of liberalism that 'place[d] the protection of individual capacities at the core of its programmatic concerns' and that was 'geared to ensuring that free individuals will be able to develop their rational and sociable attributes'.[41] For many liberals in the late nineteenth century, the form of government that would best nurture this kind of environment was one based on the responsible, accountable and educated exercise of power. This could lead liberals to favour reforms that enhanced the participation of the people in the political process, but it could just as easily steer them away from movements that took this notion too far.

The diversity of liberalism was evident in Bristol, where two Liberal MPs found themselves on opposite sides of the Bradlaugh debate. A 'Great Liberal Meeting' at Colston Hall in November 1882 provided radicals and liberals with a perfect opportunity to share their views on the subject. Lewis Fry, the junior MP for the city, reiterated his view that the House of Commons had no right to disqualify a duly elected representative from taking his seat. Samuel Morley, the senior MP for Bristol, took the opposite view, opposing Bradlaugh's campaign because he had profaned the parliamentary oath. How, Morley asked, could an oath imbued with religious connotations mean anything to a man who had been 'a persistent, a violent, and a coarse opponent of Christianity'? This put Morley at odds with radicals and many liberals in Bristol, but, again, this did not mean that he had ceased to be a liberal. During the same speech, he maintained that the liberal principles 'which he had advocated from his earliest recollection' continued to guide his political practice. He also admitted that, ideally, inquiries into the religious opinions of elected representatives 'ought not to be made by anyone in the House of Commons'. Disagreements on the Bradlaugh case in Bristol, then, had arisen not 'because [Morley] failed to hold the great principles' of liberalism, but, in the words of Fry, because opinions differed 'as to the mode and extent to which the principles should be applied in that particular case'.[42]

Morley could logically oppose Bradlaugh's admission to the House of Commons while remaining a liberal because of the essential contestability of ideological concepts, a non-specificity that allows diverse interpretations to be attached to them through their relationship with other core, adjacent and peripheral concepts. In contrast, radicals would have found it extremely difficult to oppose Bradlaugh's right to take his seat without also abandoning their commitment to radicalism. This is because democracy was located at conceptual core of radical ideology, which placed stricter limits on the possible number of meanings that radicals could assign to it. Radicals' insistence that 'the whole body of electors' had a right to choose their own representatives flowed from the conceptual connections between democracy (rule by the people), other core and adjacent concepts such as rights, equality and the general interest, and a range of peripheral concepts such as Parliament.[43] These connections generated a distinct perspective on the case and convinced its proponents, including the secretary of the Bristol Radical Reform Association, to argue that the rights of the 'faithful and determined people of Northampton [to] their full share of representation in the

House of Commons' overrode the rights of lawmakers to prevent an elected representative, 'against whom no taint of bribery or undue influence have ever been truthfully breathed', from taking his seat.[44]

These subtle conceptual differences account for the varying degrees of importance assigned to the case. To again use the example of Bristol, it is clear that liberals wanted to downplay Samuel Morley's transgression and avoid discussion of the issue. While some liberals acknowledged that it was a battle that needed to be fought, they also considered it an irritant that drew attention away from more important issues. Morley, in their view, was either not guilty of violating the principles of civil and religious liberty or guilty only of making an uncharacteristic mistake. At public meetings and in the provincial press, leading members of the Bristol Liberal Association declared that they disagreed with Morley on this issue but denied that his actions damaged his reputation as a sound liberal. The liberal press took a similar line, with the *Bristol Mercury* expressing regret that the 'agitation and excitement' generated by the controversy had 'block[ed] the course of needed legislation'.[45] The *Western Daily Press* also reaffirmed its trust in Morley and denied that the difference of opinion that had arisen in Bristol on the question was a 'matter of great importance'.[46] Liberal papers in other localities also expressed reservations about the nature of the movement that backed Bradlaugh and its pernicious influence in popularising the idea that constituents could control the actions of their elected representatives once they had been chosen to serve in Parliament.[47]

These examples highlight the risk of overstating the similarities between radical and liberal forms of constitutionalism. Though they both developed an inclusive, patriotic conception of the constitution and presented a broadly similar narrative of English history, there was no guarantee that radicals and liberals would agree on the case's significance in the historic struggle for English liberties. And if a not insubstantial number of liberals could downplay the importance of the case, view the whole matter as a nuisance or, in some cases, oppose Bradlaugh's right to sit in Parliament altogether, then we must question the similarity between radical and liberal understandings of the constitution. For radicals in Northampton and elsewhere, Bradlaugh and his political and theological opinions were not of supreme importance; what mattered was that the House of Commons refused to allow a body of electors to choose their own MP. For the 'Hundreds of Liberals' who endorsed and distributed a pamphlet in Northampton during the 1881 by-election campaign, however, Bradlaugh's 'conduct in Parliament', the embarrassment he caused the Liberal government, his ambition to 'swell his own importance and advance Secularism', his 'mockery ... of a solemn ceremony' and the 'obstruction to legislation' that the whole debacle had caused were seemingly more important than the constitutional principles which Bradlaugh claimed to be defending.[48]

But radicals were adamant that this was a case of utmost importance. The sheer number of meetings they organised to discuss the issue between 1880 and 1886 testifies to the importance they attached to the case, as does the emotional tone of their speeches and writings on the subject. For example, at the meeting in Bristol described above, radicals in the audience responded passionately and angrily to suggestions that Morley deserved the continued support of those who had voted for him in 1880. For his radical critics, Morley had violated the trust reposed in him by going back on pledges that he had previously made, including his promise to further 'the cause of civil and religious liberty … and the equality of all men before the law'.[49] He had disregarded a principle that all radicals and all liberals should hold dear, namely each individual's 'liberty to think and judge for himself, and to allow those who differed from him the same indulgence as he enjoyed'.[50] Radicals considered the Bradlaugh case not as a matter of minor importance or a nuisance that should be relegated to the very bottom of the political agenda, but as a 'CRISIS so important for the constitutional liberties of the country', a war against 'the tyranny of a lawless majority in the House of Commons' and a battle over a principle that radicals were willing to 'wage … perpetual warfare' to defend.[51]

'The friend of the working classes'[52]

The 'war' in which Bradlaugh and his supporters were engaged was more than a political and theological conflict. There was also an important social dimension to the controversy – a fact that both sides of the debate drew attention to. As pro-Bradlaugh songs and poems indicate, radicals interpreted the struggle in both social and political terms. Though it would be misleading to suggest that there was a direct relationship between one's social position and one's attitude to the case, it was certainly true that the national debate engendered by the controversy helped to cultivate socially inflected images of Bradlaugh's supporters. These images rested on a broad set of assumptions about gender, class, education, race, religion and nationality, as well as on generalisations about the cultural habits of Bradlaugh's supporters.

Conservatives were particularly keen to define the traits and habits of the typical Bradlaughite. In the words of the Conservative *Lincolnshire Chronicle*, they were nothing more than 'infidels', an 'unthinking people' and a 'common' and 'insubordinate mob'.[53] By 1880, radicals in

Northampton had become used to this kind of abuse. During Bradlaugh's first attempt to capture the Northampton seat in 1868, an opposition handbill had made an explicit reference to Bradlaughites' supposed criminality, drunkenness and ignorance (note the misspelling of Bradlaugh):

> The shades of night were falling fast,
> As down a dirty entry passed
> A chap (so drunk, he scarce could stand),
> Clutching a poster in his hand–
>   For Bradlor![54]

One of the assumptions implicit in these attacks was the idea that radical voters could not think rationally about the political choices that they were expected to make. Accusations of this kind, particularly those directed towards working-class voters, were a common feature of election debates. For example, Liberals often claimed that working men only voted for Conservative candidates because they had a penchant for beer, betting and the bible.[55] While similar tropes featured in anti-Bradlaugh literature, Bradlaugh's atheism added an additional flavour to the contests. Bradlaughites were accused of being not only ill-educated and easily swayed but also immoral. At the 1880 general election, handbills warned voters that if they elected Bradlaugh as one of their representatives, then Northampton was 'in danger of inflicting upon itself the greatest Dishonour, if not Infamy that can fall upon any Community'. Several commentators did, indeed, cast aspersions on the town's reputation in the wake of the controversy surrounding Bradlaugh's exclusion from Parliament.[56]

Radicals embraced the idea that Bradlaugh was especially popular among the working classes.[57] One of his supporters in Leicester went so far as to describe him as 'a representative of the working-classes of the kingdom, elected by a working-class constituency, supported by the working-classes of the country'.[58] While this was an exaggeration, its emphasis on the class composition of Bradlaugh's core support was not exceptional. Statements of this kind also contained a kernel of truth, especially in Northampton, where Bradlaugh found favour among the town's politically engaged shoemakers. His cause was also taken up by working-class radicals in towns and cities across Britain, including by shoemakers in Norwich, who, like their counterparts in Northampton, had garnered a reputation for 'Atheistical Radicalism and Republicanism'.[59]

Bradlaugh's working-class supporters often articulated a narrow conception of class that valorised the experiences of the male, regularly employed, English urban worker at the expense of women, agricultural labourers, foreign workers, the long-term unemployed and the 'undeserving poor'. They regarded their work as the 'great source of wealth', viewed working men as the 'wealth producers of the country' and insisted that society would be 'nothing without labour'.[60] Workers in trades that required a comparatively high degree of skill also exhibited great pride in their work. As Joan Scott and Eric Hobsbawm have noted, shoemakers in particular had long held a 'remarkable reputation ... as political radicals'.[61] According to an 1879 article in the NUBSRF's monthly report, 'cobblers have always had the character of being notorious politicions [sic] and radicals' because they sat 'day after day on their stools' discussing 'the affairs of state until they have deemed themselves capable of ruling nations even better than the trained statesmen'.[62] The political consciousness and independence of shoemakers regularly featured in the poems of John Gregory, the Bristol-based shoemaker poet:

> Oh, when this iron bell I ring,
> I laugh at care and feel
> More independent than a king
> That never earned a meal,
> The idle may, they ought to pray
> Their prayers for daily bread;
> I ask for health instead of wealth,
> And work for mine instead, my boys,
> I work for mine instead.[63]

Gregory's poems provide a rich source for examining the social and political identities of working-class radicals during this period. In his poems, Gregory often drew a sharp distinction between the male manual worker and the 'worthless drone' who 'subsists on the toil and sweat of the Laboring [sic] Man'.[64] The 'drone' in this case was a 'perfumed aristocrat', but it could have been just as easily applied to the idle or undeserving poor. Discussions that touched on the various gradations within 'the poor' and the distinctions that separated the working classes from the poor were commonplace during the early to mid-1880s, when the proportion of trade union members unemployed ranged between 5 and 7 per cent.[65] But while radical trade unionists participated in relief efforts and, in some places, encouraged town and city councils to provide work for the unemployed, they were keen to emphasise that they only wished to assist the hard-working, deserving and industrious elements among the unemployed, and, in particular, those who were 'unemployed through no fault of their own'.[66] Consequently, they often drew attention to the distinction between 'loafers' and honest working men who cared for their families and refused to take parochial relief because they feared the stigma of pauperism.

Working-class radical conceptions of class were also highly gendered. This was despite the fact that women made up a substantial proportion of the workforce, including in the Leicester hosiery trade and the Northampton boot and shoe trade.[67] In some places, male trade unionists took active steps to organise their female co-workers, while, in others, women took it upon themselves to form their own societies.[68] In general, though, trade unionism was weak among women workers at this time, often because of the actions, or inaction, of male trade unionists. In Bristol, where large numbers of women were employed in the chocolate, tobacco, cotton, stationery and packaging industries, the local trades' council refused to organise women at a cotton factory in 1874 because they had acted as blacklegs during a strike.[69] Similarly, although women formed the majority of members of the Leicester Amalgamated Hosiery Union (LAHU), the all-male executive accused women of being poor trade unionists and worked tirelessly to retain male exclusiveness over certain operations in a trade that was in the process of mechanising.[70]

Radical working men drew attention to the 'otherness' of women workers by using gendered terms and phrases. During political and trade union meetings, they used seemingly inclusive terms ('the working classes') alongside exclusivist descriptors ('working men'), even in the presence of women workers. They stressed the experiences and traits of the typical working man, emphasising, among other things, his determination, loyalty and manliness. Gendered assumptions informed their analysis of constitutional principles, and they tended to use words such as 'people', 'person', 'citizen' and 'England' in ways that excluded women without explicitly saying so.[71] They also propagated the notion that men and women inhabited separate spheres of activity.[72] For instance, at a well-attended meeting of 'working men and their wives and daughters' held in Norwich in May 1868, a leading radical activist explained that organisers had invited women to the meeting because they, more than most, '[felt] where the shoe pinches when the loaf is small and the price is high'. After all, it was 'the woman who has to prepare her husband's meals, and who has to see that the little ones who hang about her skirts are fed'. Continuing, the speaker reminded listeners that:

> We as working men expect our wives to keep our houses comfortable, to have our meals prepared when we come home from daily labor [sic], and to work hard indoors while we are working hard out of doors.[73]

Some of the hostility that male trade unionists expressed towards women could be attributed to the assumption that women workers depressed wages. This fear also accounts for urban workers' attitudes to agricultural labourers. Agrarian issues were of considerable importance in late Victorian England and remained so well into the Edwardian period. During the 1870s and 1880s, urban-based radicals expressed sympathy with the plight of the 'sons of toil' and offered moral support to those who wished to unionise and enfranchise them. But they also 'othered' the experiences and concerns of the rural poor, which served to reinforce the distinctions between the urban and the rural. They viewed the concerns of the labourer through the prism of the urban worker, considering, for example, how potential solutions to 'the land question' would impact those residing in towns and cities. At meetings organised to discuss this topic, they often spoke of the diminution of labour and the dependency of Britain on foreign imports while, revealingly, neglecting or relegating the discussion of labourers' wages, conditions and concerns.

This is surprising considering that so many urban radicals felt a connection to rural life.[74] Such attitudes were particularly common in towns where the urban–rural boundary remained fluid. The boot and shoe industry in Northamptonshire, for example, was scattered across the county in a network of small towns and rural villages, and some shoemakers even worked at their trade for one part of the year while working in the fields at harvest time.[75] Still, this attachment to rural life did not seem to stop urban workers from seeing low-paid rural migrants as a threat to their position. Trade unionists in the footwear and hosiery trades in Leicester, Norwich and Northampton complained about the tendency of manufacturers to send 'outwork' to non-unionised villages, where costs were lower and where trade unionism was weak.[76]

As Paul Readman has shown, debates about the land question often involved patriotic issues and values.[77] And while radical and liberal understandings of Englishness were tied up with a progressive view of history and a particular reading of the constitution, the *working-class* radical understanding of Englishness was also tied up with the notion of class. In this view, English workers had certain traits, including a strong sense of 'fair play', a tendency towards moderation, a high quality of craftsmanship and an enthusiasm for hard work, as well as traits common to all Englishmen such as self-reliance and a respect for the law, which distinguished them from their counterparts in other countries.[78] Working-class radicals invoked the language of patriotism to criticise their political opponents (including liberals) who acted in an 'unpatriotic' manner, claiming, for example, that it was 'un-English to claim representation for a minority'.[79] They also questioned the patriotism of unscrupulous employers who showed a preference for hiring foreign workers for jobs that 'naturally belonged to the English artisan'.[80] By drawing on a class-based language of patriotism, working-class radicals were able to criticise employers and politicians, whether conservative, liberal or radical, while also defending themselves from accusations that they favoured the revolutionary doctrines of foreign radicals. This was a form of patriotism that was to become an important tool in the armoury of socialists, labourists and others who continued the working-class radical cause in the final decades of the nineteenth century.

Conclusion

Charles Bradlaugh served as MP for Northampton until his death in January 1891. Just three years later, a public statue of Bradlaugh was erected on Abington Square, Northampton, in the presence of what the *Northampton Chronicle and Echo* described as 'one of the greatest concourses of people ever seen' in the town. The unveiling ceremony was a truly cross-class affair. Work was suspended in many of the town's shoe factories to enable shoemakers and manufacturers to join the pre-ceremony procession, while various 'Liberal and Radical Associations and Clubs of the county and district' congregated at the foot of the statue and, later, in the Corn Exchange to listen to a variety of radical and liberal speakers. At these meetings, speakers focused on Bradlaugh's courage, heroism and 'nobleness' and praised him for his work on India and for the battles he fought for 'the rights of humanity and freedom of thought and action'. In the words of the inscription on his statue, Bradlaugh was 'a sincere friend of the people' who devoted his life to 'progress, liberty, and justice'.[81]

Perhaps mindful that this was an occasion of solemn remembrance, speakers avoided issues of a controversial nature. Still, there was general unanimity that Bradlaugh's struggle to enter Parliament in the 1880s had been a noble and necessary fight for constitutional principles. As we have seen, though, this view exaggerates the extent to which radicals and liberals were united during the campaign. While a battle for civil and religious liberty seemed the perfect opportunity for anti-conservatives to set aside their differences and work towards a common objective, an examination of the pro- and anti-Bradlaugh campaigns at a local level suggests that radicals and liberals still found much to disagree on. Radicals and liberals who defended Bradlaugh believed that the case was a national and constitutional crisis that required the urgent attention of all true reformers. Other liberals, while acknowledging that the case had to be fought, felt that it was a distraction from more important concerns, or an unfortunate diversion that gave too much attention to someone whose political and theological views could damage the wider liberal cause. A smaller group of liberals opposed Bradlaugh's campaign outright and favoured the return of his Conservative opponents, mainly on moral or religious grounds.

One of the aims of this chapter was to suggest that this divergence of opinion between radicals and liberals and between liberals of different persuasions rested on more than just electoral, tactical or theological grounds. Ideological differences also played an important part, and the case serves as a useful case study for highlighting how radicals and liberals could approach questions from a different perspective. It is also useful for comparing radical and liberal readings of the constitution. Both radicals and liberals offered broadly similar accounts of English history, viewing it as an arena of struggle in which the people forced elites (and would continue to force elites) to restore their ancient rights and liberties. Radicals characterised Bradlaugh's struggle in precisely these terms and portrayed his exclusion from the House of Commons as a clear violation of constitutional principles. Many liberals agreed with this view, particularly in towns and cities where liberalism was of a 'progressive' nature. But others did not consider Bradlaugh's struggle to be as important as historical struggles for civil and religious liberties and questioned its similarity to older campaigns involving religious minorities.

This chapter has suggested that contrasting perspectives emanated at least partly from the precise location of democracy in the radical and liberal morphologies. Due to its central location in radicalism, radicals believed that democracy meant 'rule by the people' and felt that the political system allowed constituencies to choose their own representatives. Due to its adjacent position in liberalism, liberals *could* adopt this attitude to democracy as long as it did not threaten liberty and individuality. But this adjacent position could also encourage them to view democracy in a more sceptical light and to keep their distance from campaigns that threatened to take the idea too far. As Michael Freeden has argued, liberals of the classical school who feared the tyranny of the majority also sought competence in government, which required an 'educated, developed, and critically aware' electorate. And if liberals preferred 'the educated and talented ... to the untrained', then this explains why so many pointed to Bradlaugh's uncouth behaviour in the House of Commons and the supposedly ignorant and immoral state of his supporters to justify their indifference or opposition to Bradlaugh's campaign.[82]

As these accusations suggest, class was an important element in the pro- and anti-Bradlaugh campaigns. Liberals and conservatives had been guilty of using elitist arguments against Bradlaugh and his supporters since his first election campaign in the town in 1868. Bradlaugh's working-class supporters embraced their reputation for political radicalism and exhibited a strong but narrow sense of class that privileged the concerns of the male, employed, English urban worker. As we saw in the previous chapter, this could cause issues not only between working-class radicals and liberals, but also between working-class radicals and those who offered a more populist version of radicalism. And as the nineteenth century began to draw to a close, the social and ideological tensions that existed between and within radicalism and liberalism were about to come into sharper focus with the emergence of new political forces that aimed to detach workers from their traditional allegiances. Indeed, on the very day that the *Northampton Mercury* urged readers to attend the unveiling of the Bradlaugh statue in June 1894, it was reported that 'dissension' had arisen in the 'camp of Northampton Radicalism' after a prominent trade unionist announced his intention to stand in the next general election to advance 'the principle of direct Labour representation'.[83]

Notes

1 For a summary of the case, see W. Arnstein, *The Bradlaugh Case: A Study in Late Victorian Opinion and Politics* (Oxford, 1965).
2 See Biagini, *Liberty, Retrenchment and Reform*, pp. 220–222. Rohan McWilliam interprets the 'populist agitations of the mid-Victorian era', which could be extended to include the Bradlaugh agitation, as 'a variant form of liberalism' or 'liberalism lite'. R. McWilliam, 'Liberalism lite?', *Victorian Studies*, 48:1 (2005), pp. 104–105.
3 *Lincolnshire Chronicle*, 16 March 1883.
4 See, for example, *Reynolds's Newspaper*, 17 April 1881.
5 Freeden, *Ideologies and Political Theory*, p. 81.
6 Freeden, *Ideologies and Political Theory*, pp. 154–155.
7 McKibbin, *Classes and Cultures*, p. 139.
8 The heading is a line from a pro-Bradlaugh song. See NCL, 198–781/9/1882, NEE, 'Up At St. Stephen's Hall. A Parody', 1882.
9 *Norfolk Chronicle*, 3 July 1880.
10 *Lincolnshire Chronicle*, 21 March 1884.
11 NCL, 198–781/9/1880, NEE, 'To The Electors of Northampton', 1880.
12 *Leicester Journal*, 4 March 1881.
13 *Leicester Journal*, 26 November 1880.
14 *Norwich Mercury*, 11 March 1882.
15 For examples, see *Western Daily Press*, 21 July 1880; *Lincolnshire Chronicle*, 21 March 1884; *Leicester Chronicle*, 3 July 1880; *Western Morning News*,

19 July 1881; *Sheffield Independent*, 19 July 1881; *Beverley and East Riding Recorder*, 17 February 1883; *Leeds Times*, 13 August 1881; Lawrence, *Speaking for the People*, p. 114.
16 *Leicester Chronicle*, 3 July 1880.
17 Pelling, *Social Geography of British Elections*, pp. 110, 90–92, 144–146, 210–213.
18 NCL, 198–781/9, NEE, 'Liberals! Shall we Vote for Mr. Bradlaugh?', 1881.
19 NCL, 198–781/9/1881, NEE, 'Borough Election, 1881. To My Friends & Supporters', 1881.
20 NCL, 198–781/9/1882, NEE, 'Reply of Samuel Morley, Esq., M. P. to a LIBERAL NON-CONFORMIST ELECTOR when asked "How he would act in the Present Contest"', 1882.
21 Bryher, *Labour and Socialist Movement in Bristol: Part 1*, p. 16.
22 *Leicester Chronicle*, 1 October 1881.
23 *Leicester Chronicle*, 3 July 1880; 4 March 1882; 1 March 1884.
24 *Norwich Mercury*, 11 March 1882.
25 *Norfolk Chronicle*, 21 May 1881.
26 NCL, 198–781/9/1882, NEE, 'Up At St. Stephen's Hall. A Parody', 1882.
27 *Lincolnshire Chronicle*, 16 March 1883.
28 *Norfolk Chronicle*, 25 February 1882.
29 *Lincolnshire Chronicle*, 3 June 1881.
30 Parry, *The Politics of Patriotism*, p. 233.
31 *Bristol Mercury*, 8 March 1882; *Norwich Mercury*, 8 April 1882. *Leicester Chronicle*, 3 July 1880.
32 "Up at St. Stephen's Hall. A Parody." NCL, 1882.
33 *Leicester Chronicle*, 3 July 1880; 14 May 1881; 4 March 1882.
34 *Western Daily Press*, 21 June 1883.
35 See A. C. Cash, John Wilkes: The Scandalous Father of Civil Liberty (London, 2006).
36 NCL, 198–781/9, NEE, 'Bradlaugh & Liberty! Constitutional Song', undated.
37 NCL, 198–781/9/1880, NEE, 'To the Electors of the Borough of Northampton', 1880.
38 *Leicester Chronicle*, 3 July 1880; 4 March 1882.
39 *Leicester Chronicle*, 26 July 1884.
40 Parry, *The Politics of Patriotism*, p. 55.
41 Freeden, *Ideologies and Political Theory*, p. 153.
42 *Western Daily Press*, 23 November 1882.
43 Freeden, *Ideologies and Political Theory*, p. 81.
44 *Bristol Mercury*, 8 January 1883.
45 *Bristol Mercury*, 19 February 1883.
46 *Western Daily Press*, 3 April 1882.
47 See, for example, *Leicester Chronicle*, 14 May 1881.
48 NCL, 198–781/9, NEE, 'Liberals! Shall we Vote for Mr. Bradlaugh?', 1881.
49 *Bristol Mercury*, 8 March 1882.

50 *Western Daily Press*, 23 November 1882.
51 NCL, 198–781/9, NEE, 'Fellow-Workmen and Electors of Northampton', undated; *Leicester Chronicle*, 3 July 1880.
52 NCL, 198–781/9/1882, NEE, 'Up At St. Stephen's Hall. A Parody', 1882.
53 *Lincolnshire Chronicle*, 16 March 1883.
54 NCL, 198–781/9/1868, NEE, 'Bradlor's Friend', 1868.
55 NCL, 198–781/9/1874, NEE, 'A Conservative Appeal' handbill, 1874.
56 NCL, 198–781/9/1880, NEE, 'To the Electors of the Borough of Northampton', 1880; the *Norfolk Chronicle* described Northampton as a 'degraded constituency' for electing Bradlaugh. *Norfolk Chronicle*, 16 April 1881.
57 NCL, 198–781/9, NEE, 'Bradlaugh & Liberty! Constitutional Song', undated.
58 Letter 'An Anti-Tory' to *Leicester Chronicle*, 27 January 1883.
59 *Norfolk Chronicle*, 21 May 1881.
60 McKibbin, *Classes and Cultures*, p. 139; *Leicester Chronicle*, 4 March 1871; 26 July 1884; *Bristol Mercury*, 22 January 1880.
61 E. Hobsbawm and J. W. Scott, 'Political shoemakers', in E. Hobsbawm, Worlds of Labour: Further Studies in the History of Labour (London, 1984), p. 104.
62 MRC, 547/P/1/2, NUBSO MR, September 1879.
63 MRC, 547/P/1/2, NUBSO MR, 'Saint Crispin's Bell', June 1879.
64 MRC, 547/P/1/2, NUBSO MR, 'He's only a Laboring Man', November 1879.
65 H. Clegg, A. Fox and A. Thompson, *A History of British Trade Unions since 1889: Volume 1, 1889–1910* (Oxford, 1977), p. 53.
66 LRO, DE1655, minutes of the Leicester Amalgamated Hosiery Union (hereafter LAHU M), Special Trade Meeting, 15 June 1887.
67 Lancaster, *Radicalism, Cooperation and Socialism*, p. 189; Fox, *A History of the NUBSO*, p. 75.
68 By the mid-1880s, women were eligible to join certain trade unions, including the Leicester Amalgamated Hosiery Union and the NUBSO. B. Drake, *Women in Trade Unions* (London, 1984), p. 143; S. Boston, *Women Workers and the Trade Union Movement* (London, 1980), p. 45.
69 Bristol Records Office, Bristol (hereafter BRO), 32080/TC1/2A, Bristol Trades' Council minutes 1873–1899 (hereafter BTC M), 2 April 1874; K. Kelly and M. Richardson, 'The shaping of the Bristol labour movement, 1885–1985', in M. Dresser and P. Ollerenshaw (eds), *The Making of Modern Bristol* (Tiverton, 1996), p. 212.
70 Lancaster, *Radicalism, Cooperation and Socialism*, p. 17.
71 J. Barnes, 'The British women's suffrage movement and the ancient constitution, 1867–1909', *Historical Research*, 91:253 (2018), p. 512.
72 See J. Hannam and M. Martin, 'Women in Bristol 1835–1914', in M. Dresser (ed.), *Women and the City: Bristol 1373–2000* (Bristol, 2016).
73 *Norfolk News*, 16 May 1868.
74 For example, see LRO, M766/1, Joseph Green poems, 1876.

75 Fox, *A History of the NUBSO*, p. 18; J. H. Saxton, *Recollections of William Arnold* (Northampton, 1915), p. 3; J. Hawker, *A Victorian Poacher: James Hawker's Journal* (Oxford, 1978), p. 2.
76 LRO, DE1655, LAHU M, 21 September 1887; Lancaster, *Radicalism, Cooperation and Socialism*, pp. 17–19; Howarth, 'The Liberal revival in Northamptonshire', p. 81; MRC, 547/P/1/3, NUBSO MR, December 1882; Cherry, *Doing Different?*, pp. 8–11.
77 See Readman, *Land and Nation in England*.
78 Parry, *The Politics of Patriotism*, p. 62.
79 *Norfolk News*, 4 July 1868.
80 *Western Daily Press*, 20 December 1877; BRO, 32080/TC1/2A, BTC M, 8 May 1879.
81 *Northampton Chronicle and Echo*, 26 June 1894.
82 Freeden, *Ideologies and Political Theory*, pp. 155–158.
83 *Northampton Mercury*, 22 June 1894.

3

Radicalism, socialism and labourism

A series of developments in the final years of the nineteenth century forced working-class radicals to reflect on the relevance of their political and ideological doctrines. For some, the revival of socialist politics in the 1880s convinced them to renegotiate or end their historic relationship with the Liberal Party. The experiences of the 'new unionist' strike wave that swept across Britain in the late 1880s and early 1890s had a similar psychological impact, persuading many of them to see political trade unionism as the instrument through which to effect change. The period also witnessed the emergence of collectivism as a hotly debated topic in political circles. Often used synonymously with 'socialism', collectivism became a topic of interest for individuals from across the political spectrum, many of whom engaged in fierce discussions, at both local and national level, about the merits and feasibility of using the state to alleviate unemployment, low pay, long working hours, poverty in old age and other social ills. Working-class radicals actively participated in these debates and often took the lead in organising lectures and public discussions on these topics.

This chapter examines the various ways in which working-class radicals responded to these developments. With a particular focus on Bristol, Leicester, Lincoln, Northampton and Norwich, it traces the political and intellectual paths taken by those who came to identify as labour and socialist activists during the 1880s and 1890s. By interrogating the way in which they spoke about these developments during election campaigns, in public debates and through the correspondence pages of the provincial press, it sheds light on the emergence and evolution of these political movements. It allows us to establish a coherent conceptual framework for the ideology of 'labourism', which became the dominant ideology among labour activists and which differed in several respects from the ideologies of liberalism and socialism. It deepens our understanding of the organisational configuration of late Victorian popular politics and casts fresh light on the close relationship between political identities, including the 'labourist' identity, and the politics of class. And it offers a fresh perspective on the evolution of 'progressive' identities and ideologies in response to the new unionist strike wave, which, initially at least, threatened to rupture long-established political alliances and strategies.

The central aim of this chapter is to demonstrate that there were significant continuities between working-class radicalism and labourist forms of politics, identity and ideology. Establishing these connections strengthens the case against the stagist narrative of British political and social history, whose proponents suggest that deep structural changes beginning in the 1870s led to the emergence of class politics in Britain.[1] What this narrative of discontinuity fail to account for, and what several studies have since drawn attention to, was the survival of older ways of thinking about the socio-political order. For proponents of the continuity thesis, the late nineteenth century was a period of continuity rather than change. More precisely, it was a period of *populist* continuity in which liberals, labourists and socialists remained attached to the non-class identities and inclusive practices that had been a feature of popular politics throughout the 'long' nineteenth century.[2]

But in the towns and cities that form the basis of this book, labourist politics and ideology emerged from a *working-class* radical tradition. Locating the roots of labourism in a class-conscious political tradition offers a novel challenge to the interpretations described above. In particular, it allows us to explain the emergence of labour politics without having to account for major discontinuities in local politics, and without having to minimise the importance of class as a tool of historical analysis. More generally, it makes it far easier to explain the narrow social composition and 'workerist' tone of labour politics as it developed in these towns in the 1880s, 1890s and beyond. Labourists followed their working-class radical predecessors in articulating a class-based conception of society while rejecting the theory of the class struggle. Like their predecessors, they also thought of themselves as spokespersons for the working class, whose interests they claimed to champion and on whose behalf they claimed to speak. At the same time, they continued to acknowledge the right of all classes to political representation and the right of all, including employers, to peacefully defend their interests. Their commitment to a non-adversarial view of class and class relations was deeply entrenched, and in most cases was able to survive the tumultuous industrial warfare of the early 1890s intact.

Labourists' understanding of class relations gave them a unique political identity that set their movement apart from mainstream liberalism and various forms of socialism. In some places, such as in Bristol and

Leicester, the emergence of labour politics coincided with the establishment of local labour parties. In other towns, such as Norwich, Northampton and Lincoln, labour activists followed the example set by their predecessors and advocated a strategic alliance with local Liberal Associations, many of which were led by prominent employers. But even those who worked within or alongside Liberal Associations still retained a strong sense of cultural and ideological independence and refused to be subsumed within cross-class coalitions. They too described themselves as spokespersons for the 'labour party' even though a labour party in an organisational sense did not exist. They claimed that they would prioritise the needs of the workers if elected to public office and bemoaned the lack of representation afforded to trade unionists on local and national governing bodies. They also accused local Liberal Associations of failing to represent the true feelings of the workers, even as they stood as electoral candidates on Liberal platforms. Labour activists, whether or not they worked within the confines of organised liberalism, helped to sustain a strong and distinctive identity that would go on to make a strong contribution to English political life.

Many of the elements that made up this identity, including a veneration of male manual labour and a privileging of the needs of the working class, had been associated with the tradition from which it had emerged. In this sense, continuity was more prevalent than change. But this was not a narrative of continuity in which labourists embraced the non-class values of the *popular* radical movement. In fact, using the term 'populism' to describe labourist values and identities would only obscure the complexities inherent within them. The same is true of ideology. As shown in the previous two chapters, radicalism was a conceptually coherent ideology that differed from mainstream liberalism and that accommodated both populist and working-class variations of its core concepts. Like all ideologies, radicalism was also capable of mutation in response to real-world events and developments.

This is what occurred in the 1880s and 1890s, when radicals began to promote what G. D. H. Cole called an 'advanced Radicalism with certain marked collectivist tendencies'.[3] Inspired by the formation of socialist organisations, the demands of the new unions, research into the conditions of the poor and a broader acceptance of the doctrine of scientific evolution, radicals began to display an increasing interest in using the power of the state to remedy social ills.[4] Their willingness to consider new approaches to social problems can be seen in their active participation in localised public debates about collectivism and socialism. Often reported verbatim in the provincial press or published in pamphlet form, these debates commenced with a lecture by a prominent speaker and ended with an open-forum discussion about the topic in question. These forums functioned as local sites of intellectual conflict where individuals from across the political spectrum could discuss, challenge and reinterpret ideas about politics, the state and society.[5] In many cases, these contests helped individuals to determine how they could incorporate new ideas into their existing patterns of thinking, a development that served to alter their interpretation of the concepts at the core of their ideology. Consequently, these local-level discussions can be treated as historical texts that reveal how local political actors reconstructed the national-level meaning of the terms and phrases that made up the language of late Victorian English politics.

Working-class radicals who came to describe themselves as labour activists embraced the idea that the state could be used to improve the conditions of the working class. As a result, they began to include a wide range of collectivist demands in their programmes, including the municipal employment of the unemployed and the establishment of a state system of pensions. Although this book uses the term 'labourism' to describe this ideology, it was conceptually almost identical to working-class radicalism. The labourist core was composed of the concepts of democracy, liberty, individuality, progress and rationality, while the concepts of equality, the general interest, rights, class and trade unionism, which had surrounded the working-class radical core and provided its concepts with distinctive meanings, comprised labourism's adjacent band. This conceptual similarity explains why the central demands of labourists in the 1880s and 1890s bore a resemblance to those put forward by working-class radicals in the 1860s and 1870s. It also helps to account for similarities in the way working-class radicals and labourists presented their demands. Like their predecessors, labourists claimed to be staunch defenders of the English constitution who sought the reform of political institutions and practices that had corrupted the constitution. They associated the principle of democracy with the struggle of the working classes for a fair share of political representation and believed that an increase in the number of direct labour representatives on local and national governing bodies would help to achieve this goal. And in contrast to popular radicals, they interpreted the concepts of rights, liberty and equality through a lens of class, which led them to lay stress on the rights of labour and the liberties of trade unions.[6]

This is not to suggest that working-class radicals and labourists put forward an identical set of demands. Labourists were undoubtedly more persistent in their efforts to achieve direct labour representation. But the inclusion of new demands in their programmes does not necessarily confirm that a deep shift in thinking had taken place. Instead, it may have signified a change in the way they interpreted concepts that had long informed their political agenda. In this instance, the gravitation of the state from a marginal position in working-class radicalism to an adjacent position in labourism served to add a collectivist gloss to labourist programmes.[7] Labourist understandings of democracy came to be associated not only with the extension of the franchise but also with the need for the democratic (i.e. state) ownership and control of certain industries. Labourists also expanded the notion of rights to include not only the right of trade unionists to resist the tyrannical actions of employers but also the 'right to work', which they believed the state should guarantee by providing employment to those temporarily out of work. Labourists remained firmly attached to, while broadened the meaning of, the concepts at the heart of working-class radical ideology.

Half a loaf or the whole loaf?

From the early 1880s, working-class radicals who had grown disillusioned with organised liberalism established new organisations, including the SDF (1881) and the Socialist League (1885), which promoted the revived doctrine of socialism.[8] For some, socialism represented an existential threat that, if left unchallenged, could irrevocably destabilise the established order. But many others chose to engage with this seemingly new political phenomenon. In market places and on street corners, they congregated, often in large numbers, to hear speeches delivered by the leading socialist orators of the day, including William Morris, Annie Besant, Henry Hyndman, George Bernard Shaw, John Burns and, on rare occasions, Prince Peter Kropotkin.[9] They organised and attended public debates that pitted leading socialists against their critics, and they conducted good-natured discussions with socialists through the correspondence pages of the provincial press. They also arranged informative lectures on topics such as collectivism and individualism with the intention of summarising or, as was more often the case, condemning socialist doctrines.

These public discussions were often reported verbatim in the provincial press, which provides us with an invaluable window into the essence of political life in late Victorian England. Crucially, the reports also describe how and when audience members heckled, cheered, posed questions and provided detailed counter-arguments to the speakers, which helps to reveal the way socialist ideas were both promoted and received. It is through such reports that we can identify the emergence of labourist ideology. In Bristol, Leicester, Lincoln, Northampton and Norwich, labourism was chiefly associated with working-class radicals who rejected what they perceived to be the impracticality of the socialist worldview. Their eagerness to differentiate themselves from the socialist movement was sometimes born out of a sense of frustration at the way socialists spoke about certain individuals, such as Charles Bradlaugh, who they felt had done a great deal of good for the working classes.[10] But the differences between socialists and labourists ran much deeper than this. In short, there were subtle yet important conceptual differences between the ideologies of socialism and labourism – differences that would have long-lasting implications for popular politics in Britain.

It is possible to tease out some of these differences by examining newspaper reports of the public discussions described above. Northampton was a common site of such discussions during this period. The town's standing as a centre of political and religious radicalism convinced the SDF, at that time the largest socialist organisation in the country, to conduct an aggressive local propaganda campaign from early 1886 onwards.[11] In the following August, Henry Hyndman delivered a speech on the town's Market Square, where he attempted to convince the radicals of Northampton, whom he described as 'half-a-loafers', to embrace the doctrines of the SDF, who went in 'for the whole loaf'. According to the *Northampton Mercury*, a 'working man' interrupted Hyndman midway through his speech to ask whether force would be needed to bring about this new society. 'It might be so', Hyndman replied. Another listener continued this line of questioning and asked whether 'all property, no matter how acquired, would have to be surrendered' to the socialist state, to which Hyndman replied 'certainly'.[12] Unsurprisingly, Hyndman's views on political violence and the pervasiveness of the future state found little favour among Northampton's leading radicals, such as Charles Bradlaugh, who offered a detailed critique of socialism at a well-attended lecture in the Town Hall in September 1886.[13] The SDF's position on these issues also formed the basis of numerous challenges by local-level radicals who expressed discomfort with the seemingly unconstitutional and authoritarian principles inherent in the socialist worldview.

Northampton was not the only site of such discussions. In Leicester, Lincoln, Norwich and elsewhere, socialists regularly attended and explained their theories at meetings organised by an assortment of political and social organisations.[14] Discussions about the relationship between liberalism, radicalism, socialism and labour politics also featured in the correspondence pages of provincial newspapers. A discussion of this nature commenced in the *Bristol Mercury* after the formation of a local Labour League in mid-1885, a development that had prompted one liberal critic to accuse the League's leaders of advocating a 'war against capital and capitalists'.[15] The League's organising secretary denied this accusation and claimed that socialism was 'never advocated and scarcely ever spoken of at ... League meetings'. He also denied that the League promoted the view that there was an 'irreconcilable antagonism' between capital and labour. On the contrary, its members were guided by a belief in the possibility that these two social groups could be reconciled by 'the one being represented as fairly as the other in our Parliament'.[16] By engaging in discussions of this kind, labourists began to portray their organisations as distinct, both politically and ideologically, from liberalism and socialism.

The forcefulness with which labourists tried to distinguish themselves from socialists obscures the fact that they agreed on several important issues. During this period, many labourists came to agree that the local or national state had a right and a duty to provide work for the unemployed. They also came to favour the municipalisation of local monopolies such as tramways, waterworks, gasworks and electricity providers. But unlike socialists, they did not support state-based solutions because they were intrinsically socialistic or because they were stepping-stones to a future socialist society. Labourists gave only qualified and partial support to the idea of using the state to remedy social ills, which set them apart from the main currents of socialism. They tended to downplay the millenarian undertones of their demands and preferred to point to real-world examples of state intervention in the economy. In Northampton, for example, labourists had come to believe that the state should provide the unemployed, in the words of a local trade unionist, with the 'means whereby they may ... labour to support themselves'. While this demand was certainly statist in tone, its author was no socialist. He did not wish to see the state become the sole employer of labour, and he only advocated the demand after the government had 'admitted its duty' to 'the people' by providing them with education. He also thought that the state should play a limited role in the workings of the market by intervening only when 'the Capitalists [could not] profitably employ the labourer'.[17]

The state was not the institutional manifestation of a future socialist community but an instrument that workers could use to achieve some of their long-standing goals.[18] Labourist attitudes to state intervention were also evident in discussions about the establishment of a universal eight-hour day. Socialists had few qualms about letting Parliament legislate on this question. In some places, such as in Bristol, labourists agreed with them.[19] But elsewhere, attitudes were more diverse. In Leicester, trade unionists were initially divided between those who favoured a parliamentary solution to the problem and those who opposed all legislative interference with the hours of labour.[20] Views were just as diverse in Northampton. In the summer of 1889, the secretary of the Northampton Trades' Council publicly denounced Charles Bradlaugh's opposition to a universal eight-hour day because, in his view, it would be beneficial 'to the community at large, and the workers in particular'. Still, he believed only that Parliament had a right to limit working hours in government establishments, on railways, in gasworks and in municipal undertakings. Again, he advocated state intervention on this issue not because it would be an early step on the road to a socialist society but because it would benefit both employers and employees by allowing 'both parties more leisure for study and recreation'.[21]

The differences between socialist and labourist attitudes to the state may appear trivial in hindsight, but political actors at the time considered them to be vitally important. Disagreements of this kind led to heated arguments and political splits, and continued to do so into the twentieth century. To a certain extent, this was because they were not trivial differences at all. They were rooted at a deep theoretical level and indicated that socialists and labourists thought differently about the social order. While 'whole loafers' had come to embrace a new conceptual framework for understanding the socio-political order, this was not the case for labourists. Their willingness to see the state as an effective instrument of reform did not fundamentally alter the conceptual framework that had guided the activities of their working-class radical predecessors. Rather, it represented the emergence of the state as an adjacent concept in their ideological morphology, a shift that modified the meaning of democracy, liberty, individuality and other concepts that had formed the core of working-class radical ideology.

Seeing labourism as the ideological successor to working-class radicalism explains why labourists continued to advocate demands that had featured in older radical programmes. During the 1880s they continued to call for the democratisation of the political system, which they hoped to achieve by extending the franchise, paying MPs and abolishing property qualifications in local government. Their understanding of democracy remained intimately tied up with broader assumptions about class and class interests, a conceptual interlinkage that generated the demand for an increase in direct labour representation, which labourists thought would make nominally democratic bodies more representative of society as whole. This was because they clung to a proportionate understanding of political representation and viewed each social class as entitled to its fair share of representation on school boards and town councils and in the House of Commons. As one Bristol-based trade unionist wrote in late 1888, while labourists felt that working men had 'no better right than any class' to political representation, the relative absence of 'bona fide' workers and trade unionists from these bodies meant that they had a 'prior claim', all things being equal.[22]

Conceptual continuities between working-class radicalism and labourism were also evident in the way labourists embraced the constitutionalist ethos of the English radical tradition. Like their predecessors, labourists articulated a democratic understanding of the constitution and a progressive view of English history that privileged the struggles of the English people to assert their rights and increase the power of the House of Commons in the constitution. Because of the flexible nature of the constitution and the political system, labourists did not feel a need to use the extra-parliamentary tactics favoured by their continental counterparts. Consequently, they drew attention to the 'legal and justifiable' nature of their activities, the honesty and integrity of their demands and the 'determined and peaceful' temperament of their strategy, particularly at times when socialist activists engaged in what many considered to be subversive and violent activities.[23]

In his seminal 1981 article on the languages of patriotism, Hugh Cunningham argued that 'a patriotism of the left' became impossible to demarcate from the 1870s onwards when the Liberal and Conservative parties laid claim, with varying degrees of success, to the language of constitutionalism.[24] But this exaggerates the decline of patriotism as a creed of opposition. As Paul Ward and Paul Readman have shown, socialists articulated a 'radical patriotism' that drew upon 'oppositional notion[s] of Englishness' well into the twentieth century.[25] Privileging Parliament within the national history, emphasising the role of modern capitalism in destroying rural communitarianism, attacking non-parliamentary socialisms as 'foreign', and presenting the English past as a 'site of struggle to gain political liberties', socialists challenged the dominant paradigms of patriotism that emerged in the late nineteenth century.[26]

Labourists did not have to go to such lengths to refute allegations of 'foreignness'. As a tendency deemed to be pragmatic rather than ideological, labourism was shielded from one of the most common criticisms levelled at socialists, namely that their fondness for collectivist and revolutionary theories ran counter to the pragmatism and cautiousness of the English character. By rejecting the millenarian tone of much socialist rhetoric as well as the populist tone of liberal and conservative forms of patriotism, labourists expressed a class-based form of patriotism rooted in the pragmatism, resilience and 'common-sense' values of the English working class. Thus, they evoked the themes of tyranny and unchecked power when discussing industrial relations, portraying trade unions as defensive institutions formed to 'battle for the right of … workmen' to defend themselves against the 'despotism' and 'great oppression' of 'unjust' employers.[27] And by working to send more working men to Parliament, labourists believed that they were continuing the patriotic struggle of their forefathers to restore the corrupted constitution to its former purity and to realise the principles that underpinned it, namely the 'representation of the people for the people by the people'.[28]

The emergence of 'labour parties'

Labourism was the dominant ideology among those who helped to form 'labour parties' during the 1880s and 1890s. In some towns and cities, labour parties took on tangible organisational forms. In Bristol, working-class radicals involved in the city's trade union movement formed a Labour League in 1885 to co-ordinate efforts to achieve direct labour representation on local and national governing bodies.[29] Founded on a broader institutional basis than its predecessors, the Labour League was firmly rooted in the class-conscious tradition of Bristol radicalism. Trade unionists took leading positions on the League's executive body and restricted membership to those who worked for weekly wages. Those deemed 'superior in social position to working men' were prohibited from standing as Labour League electoral candidates and were largely ignored in the League's election literature.[30] Its activists also embraced the independent political strategy of the Bristol radical tradition because the acceptance of the 'social and political patronage of the upper and middle classes' was nothing less than a 'venal prostitution of their liberties'.[31] Consequently, the League ran electoral candidates 'to fight the battle in the interest of [their] own class' against both major parties at the municipal and, in 1886, parliamentary level.[32]

As these statements suggest, labour politics in Bristol was anything but populist in tone. In other towns, such as Northampton, Lincoln and Norwich, labour parties either failed to materialise or existed ephemerally. But even in these towns, politicians, journalists and political activists all used 'labour party' to describe those who took a prominent role in trade union matters and who sought to promote the trade union interest in the political arena. And like their predecessors, these labour parties, despite maintaining strong connections to the forces of organised liberalism, were never subsumed within broad, populist coalitions. Rather, they were assertive political forces whose members fought doggedly to achieve their self-defined goals by forming pragmatic political alliances. To ignore or downplay the instrumentalist basis of this strategy would only serve to conceal the fragility of liberal–labour relations in these towns.

Tensions in the liberal–labour alliance manifested themselves during election campaigns and at candidate selection meetings, where labourists often reminded Liberal leaders that the support of the labour party was conditional and could be withdrawn. On occasion, frustration at the unwillingness of Liberal Associations to accommodate the needs of the labour party even led to controversial electoral challenges. In Lincoln, working men helped to defeat official Liberal candidates in two wards during the 1883 municipal elections.[33] In Norwich, 'advanced radicals' managed to secure the election of an independent working-class candidate and the defeat of the Liberal leader of the city council in the municipal elections of 1886.[34] Even in Northampton, which could be considered a bastion of lib–labism during this period, it was not uncommon for trade unionists to stand their own electoral candidates, as they did in the aftermath of a bitter lockout in the boot and shoe trade in 1887. The resistance that the two labour candidates encountered from sections of the local Liberal and Radical Union, not to mention the fact that one candidate was opposed and defeated by a 'radical' shoe manufacturer, gives some indication of the instability of the liberal–labour alliance in this historically Liberal borough.[35]

Early labour politics in Leicester represented a middle ground between the independent strategy of labourists in Bristol and the critical-but-loyal approach to liberalism adopted by activists elsewhere. In 1887, trade union leaders in Leicester formed a Labour Association with the primary intention of electing working men to the city council.[36] The Labour Association's early leaders sought to work in harmony with the Leicester Liberal Association and often praised the city's Liberal MPs for voting 'with the labour party' in the House of Commons.[37] But even in Leicester, there were clear signs that the liberal–labour alliance was essentially a strategic one. When the Liberal Association refused to run a leading member of the NUBSRF as a candidate in the 1888 municipal elections, members of the Labour Association reacted angrily and expressed their disappointment often in strong class terms. One member argued that the Liberal Association's actions proved that the 'classes' did not admire the 'masses' and suggested that the latter 'would have to fight' the former 'before [their] strength was recognised'. William Inskip, another leading member of the NUBSRF, took a less combative approach to the situation but still warned Liberal leaders that the Labour Association would 'have to work independent' if their requests were not acceded to. Labour's 'true line of action', Inskip explained, 'should be to work in harmony with the [Liberal] association *if possible*', a crucial caveat that appeared frequently in labour discourse at this time.[38]

Labour activists, whether they worked on independent lines or in conjunction with local Liberal Associations, became an important presence in local political life during the 1880s. As well as promoting a unique set of ideological perspectives, they also offered a distinctive vision of class, class relations and the social order. Much like working-class radicals before them, labourists exhibited a strong sense of class identity while rejecting the politics of class conflict. Through their speeches and their writings, they rejected universalist conceptions of political representation in favour of more exclusivist understandings, which led them to advocate the direct representation of 'the labour interest' by 'bona fide' workers (or, as was more often the case, trade unionists). This, as they were keen to point out, was because only working men could truly understand the experiences and wants of their class. Only those who had experienced life as a working man could deal adequately and sensitively with questions such as unemployment, low pay, tyrannical employment practices and other issues that concerned their fellow workers. Working men, as one Leicester-based activist argued, could always represent workers 'better than the middle or upper classes could possibly do'.[39]

But labourists also continued to deny that they sought to stir up class hatred. As a leading member of the Bristol Labour League explained in 1886, labour politics was born not out of a 'spirit of revenge against the upper classes' but out of a desire to obtain the 'moral and material recognition of the dignity of labour'.[40] This strong but non-adversarial sense of class was fundamental to the identity of labourists in other towns, including Northampton. Charles Bradlaugh appealed to this sense of class when speaking to a well-attended meeting of trade unionists in the town in 1886. During his lecture, Bradlaugh declared his support for the principle of trade unionism, recognised that workers and employers had equal rights and expressed his hope for an eventual reconciliation between labour and capital. Interestingly, and despite Bradlaugh's claim to speak as a neutral observer on the topic, the secretary of the local NUBSRF branch felt that Bradlaugh's view of class relations perfectly encapsulated the 'labour point of view', and subsequently arranged for the lecture to be published in pamphlet form.[41]

New unionism

For socialists, Bradlaugh's views on the relationship between labour and capital were outdated and harmful to the cause of the workers. Some agitators, including members of the anarchistic Socialist League, often went further and actively encouraged open warfare between workers and their employers. For example, in Lincoln, a member of the Socialist

League admitted that he would 'preach a class war until there was no class to fight against'.[42] At a debate held in Leicester in 1892, a local anarchist admitted that he would use force and 'means quite outside any constitutional action' to achieve his objectives.[43] Similarly, a leaflet produced by anarchist groups in Birmingham and Walsall argued that capitalists and labourers formed 'two great hostile armies' engaged in a 'perpetual conflict', and urged English workers to follow the example of 'the brave and noble Wat Tyler and John Ball' and 'take up arms against their enemies'.[44]

Not surprisingly, many socialists and anarchists welcomed the wave of militant strike activity that gripped industrial centres from the summer of 1889.[45] In Bristol, unskilled workers in the newly formed Gasworkers', Dockers' and Sailors' Unions, as well as 'old' trade unionists employed in shoemaking, confectionery, tobacco and other industries, engaged in sometimes violent battles with their employers.[46] Growing discontent with the arbitration system and the introduction of machinery in the boot and shoe trade led to the eruption of unofficial strikes in Leicester and, consequently, the expansion of the local branch of the NUBSO to over 12,000 workers.[47] Similar developments were reported in Norwich, Lincoln, Ipswich, Northampton, Kettering, and several other towns and cities across England.[48]

The 'new unionist' strike wave was an important episode in British industrial history. For this reason, it has attracted a considerable amount of attention from historians. Those who adhere to a 'stagist' model of political development have suggested that because the strike wave served to broaden the composition and ideological character of the trade union movement, it represented a significant turning-point in working-class history that paved the way for the rise of 'class politics' in Britain. In particular, scholars in this tradition have attached a great deal of importance to the formation certain political organisations, including the ILP, and the apparent shift in workers' attitudes towards a more independent-minded and anti-Liberal political position.[49] Socialists played a crucial role in both of these developments. By gaining a foothold on local trades' councils, as they did in London, Manchester and Birmingham, or by helping to form or re-form trades' councils in areas where they did not exist, as in Halifax, Huddersfield, Keighley and Brighouse, socialists contributed to the detachment of local 'labour parties' from their old political strategies. Socialist influence in Britain's major trade unions also helped give support to the idea of independent labour representation, which would culminate in the formation of the LRC in 1900.[50]

These developments occurred in some of the places that form the basis of this book, including Bristol and Leicester, where there was a marked increase in the number of trade unionists seeking to achieve political office by running on independent lines. But it is important not to overstate the transformative impact of new unionism. Radical and labour politics in Bristol had always been tinged with a spirit of political independence. It is also be misleading to suggest that labourists in Leicester fully embraced the principle of independent labour politics during this period. The Leicester Trades' Council remained divided on this question throughout the early 1890s, and its leading members regularly cast doubt on the viability of working against the Liberal Party.[51] In fact, local support for the idea of a lib–lab alliance was confirmed at a double parliamentary by-election in 1894, when Henry Broadhurst, initially recommended by the Trades' Council but also adopted by the Liberal Association, headed the poll with 33 per cent of the vote. The ILP candidate, who also received the support of the Trades' Council, achieved an impressive 16 per cent vote share despite only campaigning for four days.[52] Support for some type of lib–lab alliance remained strong in Leicester until the First World War.

The strike wave also had little political impact in Lincoln, where the 'labour party', in the words of one local socialist critic, continued to make a 'fetish of Liberalism'. Although it put forward municipal election candidates on 'Labour and non-political lines', the candidates were in effect 'brought out by the Liberal Association'.[53] Trade unionists in Northampton also achieved representation on the town council by working through rather than against the Liberal and Radical Union. It is also likely that, if not for internal wrangling over the question of political independence, the general secretary of the NUBSO would have succeeded Charles Bradlaugh as the junior MP for the town.[54] The liberal–labour alliance also remained intact in Norwich, where the Liberal Association, with the support of the Norwich Trades' Council, selected the president of the General Railway Workers' Union as its second candidate in the 1892 general election.[55] While their efforts in the parliamentary arena were unsuccessful, trade unionists in Norwich did manage to establish a small but vocal presence on the town council by forming an effective though fragile electoral alliance with the Liberals.[56]

It is also possible to identify continuities in the way labourists spoke about class and the social order. Much like their working-class radical predecessors, labourists articulated a class-based but non-adversarial approach to political and industrial relations. What is significant and perhaps surprising is the fact that they remained committed to such an approach even as they engaged in fierce confrontations with their employers. For example, it was rare for them to speak of an interminable 'class war' between capital and labour, and 'defence not defiance' remained a popular slogan in trade union circles throughout the period.[57] It was also common for them to express disapproval of the antagonistic sentiments that featured in socialist discourse. Trade unionists, as many of them were keen to point out, were not 'hostile to Capital' and did not wish to set 'class against class'.[58] Such a conciliatory attitude explains why labourists (both 'old' and 'new') placed such a strong emphasis on the moderation of their demands and hoped to achieve their aims without resorting to strike action.[59] Indeed, for many, strike action was a damaging method of resolving industrial disagreements and part of a 'disastrous system' that would become a thing of the past when employers worked with trade unionists to establish Boards of Arbitration and Conciliation.[60] 'This is the way in which we should be only too glad to settle our differences', admitted one leading activist in Norwich, 'providing we could only get the employers in the same mind'.[61]

But this approach also rested on exclusivist assumptions about class and class politics. As Michael Freeden has noted:

> Labourism moved the concept of class to a salient adjacent position in such a way as to elevate the interests of the workers, and their protection, at the expense of a more embracing concept of community. Community was demoted to denote class solidarity.[62]

Both during and after the strike wave, labour election candidates sought to convince voters of their 'bona fide' working-class credentials by describing the hardships that they too had faced as working men. They continued to direct their appeals to the working-class section of the electorate and often admitted that, above all, they intended to serve 'the class to which [they] belonged', as a leading member of the Bristol Labour Electoral Association stated in 1893.[63] And on occasion, they even confessed that they had no interest in winning over 'the cultured, the refined, and the educated classes'. Rather, they wished to convince 'their own classes and ... fellow workers' that 'each class' should 'vote for its own candidates'.[64]

Labourism: A weaker version of socialism?

A strong sense of class and a commitment to constitutional methods of reform remained integral parts of the labourist worldview. But labourists also had to come to terms with new developments in the intellectual domain. The socialist demands put forward by leaders of the new unions and their relative success in achieving their short-term aims helped to bring formerly impracticable ideas into the realm of practicable politics.[65] The same can be said about the efforts of Charles Booth, an important social reformer and investigator whose research helped to popularise the idea of old-age pensions during the 1890s. Consequently, labourist solutions to a range of social and economic problems became increasingly collectivist in tone, and by the end of the decade most labourists had come to favour a parliamentary-enforced eight-hour day, a state-based system of old-age pensions, public works schemes for the unemployed, free education, the municipalisation of local monopolies, and the state ownership and control of 'natural monopolies' including railways, docks, mines and other means of transit.[66]

For many contemporaries, this was proof that socialism had infected the labour movement. There were certainly conceptual overlaps between socialism and labourism. Both socialists and labourists emphasised the concepts of equality, liberty, the state, democracy and the general interest, and laid great stress on the importance of peripheral concepts such as unemployment, old-age pensions and an eight-hour day. A strong case could also be made for seeing class and trade unionism as influential concepts in 'workerist' forms of socialism. But as Michael Freeden has argued, 'overlap, or reputed influence, are insufficient to establish membership of an ideological family', and rather than embracing a new conceptual framework, most labourists continued to give expression to an ideology that differed in several important respects from both liberalism and various forms of socialism.[67]

For Freeden, the socialist core is composed of five concepts: the constitutive nature of the human relationship (individuals constitute fraternities); human welfare as a desirable object; human nature as active (humans are productive); equality (all humans are equal); and history as the arena of change (a reading of history as movement and social advancement). This core is surrounded by the concepts of democracy, liberty, property, the state, nationalisation, power and rationality, though, like all ideologies, socialism is capable of accommodating different variations on this conceptual arrangement.[68] In the context of the late nineteenth century, the interplay between these concepts produced versions of socialism that emphasised the importance of *social* as well as *political* democracy and prioritised communitarian impulses over individual liberty. With this in mind, it is not surprising that liberals felt that socialism threatened to undermine the centrality of their core beliefs.

Socialism also threatened to undermine some of the solutions put forward by populist radicals. Differences between socialism and radicalism were laid bare at a public debate held in Northampton in February 1894, when Henry Hyndman, the leader of the SDF, and Henry Labouchère, the radical MP for Northampton, shared their views on the pervasiveness of the socialist state, the use of violence as a political strategy and the importance of social as well as political democracy. Both men acknowledged that there were significant areas of agreement between the two sides. But for Labouchère, Hyndman's 'millennial' version of socialism was not 'practicable' and, if carried out, would not 'effect the ends which he anticipates'. Labouchère also objected to the socialist idea of 'making us all children in the hands of the State', which, in his view, posed 'the greatest danger to our liberties'. While the 'modern Radical Party' would accept 'every reasonable idea of Socialism', it would always be in favour of 'both Collectivism *and* Individualism'.[69]

Labourists shared many of Labouchère's views on socialism and the role of the state. But just as there were differences between populist and working-class variants of radicalism, so there were differences between 'social' radicalism and labourism. In particular, the concepts of class and trade unionism, which were adjacent concepts in labourism but generally absent from social radicalism, served to influence the workerist direction and tone of labourist demands. This can be seen clearly in labourist speeches, letters and pamphlets, including in an 1889 pamphlet issued by the National Labour Electoral Association titled *The Policy of Labour*. Like Labouchère, the author of the pamphlet articulated a communitarian notion of liberty, arguing that individuals 'may not be interfered with beyond what is necessary to secure to others [the] same advantages'. And because 'unchecked competition in buying and selling labour, together with the private ownership of some of the necessaries of production' had led to unemployment, low pay and long working hours, labourists wished to 'check the free course of competition'. This, the author admitted, was a 'violation of liberty', as it interfered with the employer's liberty of action. But the absence of restraints on the activities of employers also interfered with freedom of the worker to refuse to work longer than eight hours a day. If society had to choose between these two 'losses of liberty', then the author believed that the inconveniences caused by state regulation 'would be less than the hardships which exist now as a consequence of the absence of restraint'.[70]

But whereas social radicals confessed a 'distaste for class politics', labourists tended to present their demands in a language of class.[71] In *The Policy of Labour*, the author makes frequent references to 'the workers' who 'cannot get employment' and who 'work for starvation wages', despite claiming that the Labour Electoral Association's proposals would assist in the 'advancement of the community'. At one point, the author even claims that England was divided between those who wanted 'more power and more wealth to Labour' and those who wanted 'more power and more wealth to Capital'. The weight that labourists accorded to class shaped their understanding of the other ingredients in labourist ideology. Their understanding of rationality and individuality rested on the assumption that 'industrious and sober' individuals of all classes had the capacity and desire to determine their own futures. These concepts were closely linked to the idea of progress and a belief that society, spurred on by the efforts of productive individuals and 'little knot[s] of honest men', would 'move gradually towards' a better (and more collectivist) future 'by progressive steps' without 'breaking any law of the country'. This future would also be more democratic. Because of the interplay between democracy and the concepts of class, equality, rationality and the general interest, labourist notions of democracy were rooted in a belief that 'every citizen, however poor, [was] concerned in the question of how he shall be governed'. This was an expansive and egalitarian view of democracy that encouraged labourists to campaign for increased labour representation and a range of political reforms that would help to bring representatives 'more immediately under the control of the electors' and ensure that the vote belonged 'to a person, not property'.[72]

Labourism retained the core concepts of working-class radicalism while elevating the state to a more prominent position in its conceptual framework. While this added a collectivist tone to their programmes, labourists were keen to downplay the socialistic connotations of their demands. They also placed an emphasis on the practicality and moderation of their demands. The state was envisaged not as the future owner and controller of the entire means of production and exchange but as an effective instrument that could be used to improve the lives and conditions of the workers in the framework of existing society. Labourists sometimes felt it necessary to make this important distinction. At the 1894 conference of the NUBSO, Edward Poulton, a delegate from Northampton, accused the SDF and the ILP of attaching a meaning to collectivism that misled and confused potential converts to their cause. Although Poulton described himself as an avowed collectivist, he told the 'advanced men' in the room that they had not 'thought the matter out properly' and that he and his fellow labourists offered the 'proper interpretation' of the principle.[73]

There may have been strategic reasons why Poulton downplayed the socialist connotations of his demands. Labour activists, in their capacities as trade union officials or election candidates, were principally concerned with winning over individuals who were either apathetic or hostile to the values of trade unionism, collectivism and socialism. But while it is important to appreciate the strategic uses of political language, there are three problems with this hypothetical counter-argument. First, it assumes that labourists were socialists in secret who only used moderate language to hide their true political views. This assumption rests on a very weak evidential basis, at least in the towns and cities considered in this study. Second, there is a major theoretical problem with this view, as it fails to consider the constitutive rather than the merely reflective power of political language.[74] And finally, it does not explain why labourists articulated a labourist rather than a socialist perspective in environments where they were not electioneering or seeking to win over a hostile audience, such as at trade union conferences.

Conferences of this kind brought together like-minded individuals for the purpose of discussing the political, industrial and intellectual issues of the day. Consequently, reports of these gatherings offer an invaluable resource for those interested in teasing out the ideological differences between labourists and socialists. One such example is the 1894 conference of the NUBSO, a union that had come to represent 43,154 male and female workers, most of whom lived and worked in the towns and cities discussed in this book.[75] A discussion about collectivism began when William Inskip, the Leicester-based general secretary of the union and the prospective parliamentary candidate for Northampton, expressed his discomfort with his colleagues' views on the collective ownership of the means of production. For Inskip, collective ownership meant 'confiscation' and would, if introduced, inhibit the 'ability, thrift [and] energy' of the workman. Perhaps unsurprisingly, Inskip's views were challenged by socialist delegates, who had come to form strong minorities in several union branches (see Figure 2).

Crucially, Inskip also faced opposition from labourist delegates who sought to downplay the idealistic undertones of the demand. As a delegate from the Northamptonshire town of Rushden explained, many trade unionists favoured the principle of collective ownership because it was a good example of a 'practical' rather than an 'ideal' form of socialism. Daniel Stanton of the Northampton branch agreed with this view. Rather than focusing on the long-term implications of the demand, Stanton believed that the government should own and control certain industries because it would help to mitigate the 'uncertainty of unemployment'. The Post Office and the education system had proved that workers in government-controlled industries had better conditions, greater job security, higher wages and shorter hours than their counterparts in the private sector.[76] This was a neat summary of the labourist view of collectivism made by an activist who had served his political apprenticeship in the working-class radical movement and who refused, throughout his life, to become a subservient member of either the Liberal Party or one

Radicalism, socialism and labourism

Figure 2 'Rather more than he can swallow', *The Wyvern*, 25 May 1894

of the plethora of socialist organisations established in Britain during the late nineteenth century.

Conclusion

There were strong continuities between working-class radicalism and labourist forms of politics, identity and ideology. Over the course of the 1880s and 1890s, labourists played a crucial role in forming local 'labour parties', as either political organisations or unorganised tendencies, which exerted a minor influence on local political life during this period. Like their predecessors, labourists saw themselves as spokespersons for the working class and articulated a class-based, non-adversarial view of class relations. Their rejection of the theory of the class struggle survived the new unionist strike wave intact and continued to inform labourist assumptions into the twentieth century.

Labourism was the dominant ideology among labour activists. Throughout the 1880s, working-class radicals, like many liberals and socialists and even some conservatives, began to believe that the state could be used to improve the lives of the working class. In conceptual terms, this change signified the movement of the state to a more central position in working-class radical morphology – an important development that, for the sake of clarity and to remain consistent with political discourse at the time, could be described as the emergence of labourism. The growing importance of the concept of the state affected the interpretation of other concepts at the heart of working-class radical/labourist ideology, including democracy, liberty, individuality, progress, equality and the general interest, while the concepts of class and trade unionism added workerist inflections to labourist demands.

But labourism was not socialism. While the concept of the state added a collectivist tone to labourist demands, there were important conceptual differences between labourism and the various forms of socialism that experienced a revival in the 1880s. Labourists and socialists aired their differences during national- and local-level public discussions where they debated the practicality of socialist demands, the theory of the class struggle, the desirable extent of state intervention in the economy and the propriety of violence as an instrument of social and political change. Whereas socialists took 'a few steps forward' and embraced a new conceptual framework for understanding the world around them, labourists' embrace of the state only served to modify their pre-existing ideology.[77] While labourists and socialists found common ground on several contemporary issues, particularly in towns and cities where socialism took on a workerist character, their conflicting views on questions of a theoretical nature often had serious political and electoral consequences, not only in the short term but also in the longer term.

If the origins of labourism can be traced to a class-conscious rather than a populist radical tradition, then it is easier to account for subsequent developments in British popular politics. For one thing, it makes the emergence of labour politics in the 1880s and 1890s and the formation of a national Labour Party in 1900 look less like sharp disjunctures in British history and more like the renewal of an older political tradition. At the same time, by emphasising the class orientation of the working-class radical and labour movements, we minimise the danger of grouping all sections of progressive opinion under a single, populist heading. Appreciating the political and ideological differences between the labourist, liberal and socialist traditions is especially important if we wish to understand the tensions that arose between them during the early twentieth century and which, to a certain extent, remain with us today. It also helps to explain divisions in the progressive ranks during the final general election of the nineteenth century, when the governing Liberal Party sought to fend off challenges from both its right and left flanks.

Notes

1 For examples, see Webb and Webb, *The History of Trade Unionism*, pp. 362–375, 387; Cole, *British Working Class Politics*, p. 7; Harrison, *Before the Socialists*, p. 3; Hobsbawm, *Worlds of Labour*, pp. 156–157, 196, 200, 207; Kirk, *Change, Continuity and Class*, p. 14.
2 For examples, see Biagini and Reid, *Currents of Radicalism*, pp. 1–19; Biagini, *Liberty, Retrenchment and Reform*; Joyce, *Visions of the People*, pp. 8, 13, 34, 79.
3 Cole, *British Working Class Politics*, p. 81. See also Wolfe, *From Radicalism to Socialism*, p. 70.
4 Emy, *Liberals, Radicals and Social Politics*, p. 18; Freeden, *Ideologies and Political Theory*, pp. 194–198.
5 Advertisements for meetings often included invitations for 'Discussion & Criticism'. University of Leicester Special Collections, Leicester (hereafter LUSC), MS 81 27–35, political memorabilia collected by Archibald Gorrie, of Leicester (hereafter GOR), 'Anarchists on Anarchy! Co-operative Hall, High Steet'.
6 Emy, *Liberals, Radicals and Social Politics*, p. xiii.
7 Freeden, *Ideologies and Political Theory*, p. 78.
8 For general histories of these organisations, see M. Crick, *The History of the Social-Democratic Federation* (Keele, 1994); Bevir, *The Making of British Socialism*.
9 *Northampton Mercury*, 12 June 1886; *Norfolk News*, 13 March 1886; *Norfolk Chronicle*, 18 August 1888; *Leicester Chronicle*, 13 July 1889; 16 November 1889.
10 *Northampton Mercury*, 24 September 1887.
11 Principally because of its centuries-long reputation as a hotbed of political and religious radicalism. Wolfe, *From Radicalism to Socialism*, p. 104.
12 *Northampton Mercury*, 21 August 1886.
13 *Northampton Mercury*, 4 September 1886. Annie Besant, at that time a member of the SDF, offered a good-natured response to Bradlaugh's arguments a fortnight later. *Northampton Mercury*, 18 September 1886.

14 For examples, see *Norfolk News*, 31 January 1885; *Leicester Chronicle*, 16 October 1886; 8 October 1887.
15 Letter 'J. Hayward' to *Bristol Mercury*, 16 June 1886.
16 Letter 'Robert. S. Gilliard' to *Bristol Mercury*, 12 June 1886.
17 Letter 'T. W. Bishop' to *Northampton Mercury*, 22 January 1887.
18 Freeden, *Ideologies and Political Theory*, p. 447.
19 BRO, 32080/TC1/2A, BTC M, 1 March 1888.
20 *Leicester Chronicle*, 8 October 1887; LRO, DE1655, LAHU M, 19 November 1887.
21 *Northampton* Mercury, 6 July 1889.
22 Letter 'D. Irving' to *Bristol Mercury*, 30 October 1888. For examples of labourists making similar arguments, see *Leicester Daily Mercury*, 19 October 1889; *Northampton Mercury*, 6 October 1888; 13 October 1888.
23 For examples, see *Eastern Evening News*, 13 February 1883; *Eastern Daily Press*, 24 February 1883; *Bristol Mercury*, 18 March 1886.
24 Cunningham, 'The language of patriotism', pp. 8–9, 20, 27.
25 P. Ward, *Red Flag and the Union Jack: Englishness, Patriotism and the British Left, 1881–1924* (Woodbridge, 1998), pp. 59, 75.
26 P. Ward, 'Socialists and "true" patriotism in Britain in the late 19th and early 20th centuries', *National Identities*, 1:2 (1999), pp. 180–184; Readman, *Land and Nation in England*, pp. 182–187.
27 MRC, 547/P/1/6, NUBSO MR, August 1887; September 1887; December 1887; Letter 'The Workmen's Committee' to *Northampton Mercury*, 13 August 1887. See also *Leicester Chronicle*, 7 November 1885; LRO, DE1655, LAHU M, 24 June 1890; letter 'Robert G. Tovey, Sec. Bristol Trades' Council' to *Bristol Mercury*, 3 May 1888.
28 *Bristol Mercury*, 30 October 1888.
29 BRO 32080/TC1/2A, BTC M, 5 March 1885; D. Large and R. Whitfield, *The Bristol Trades Council, 1873–1973* (Bristol, 1973), p. 5; Bryher, *Labour and Socialist Movement in Bristol: Part 1*, pp. 32–33.
30 Bryher, *Labour and Socialist Movement in Bristol: Part 1*, pp. 32–38.
31 *Bristol Mercury*, 12 April 1886.
32 Large and Whitfield, *The Bristol Trades' Council*, p. 6; *Bristol Mercury*, 10 June 1886; 19 June 1886; 9 July 1886.
33 Hill, *Victorian Lincoln*, p. 238.
34 Cherry, *Doing Different?*, p. 5.
35 *Northampton Mercury*, 3 November 1888.
36 Lancaster, *Radicalism, Cooperation and Socialism*, p. 98; *Leicester Chronicle*, 10 December 1887.
37 For examples, see *Leicester Chronicle*, 15 September 1888; *Leicester Daily Mercury*, 8 October 1889.
38 *Leicester Chronicle*, 5 May 1888: emphasis added. Similar sentiments were expressed in October 1889 when a Liberal ward meeting refused to adopt the nominee of the Leicester Trades' Council as municipal candidate. See *Leicester Chronicle*, 26 October 1889.

39 *Leicester Chronicle*, 10 December 1887.
40 *Bristol Mercury*, 12 April 1886.
41 MRC, 547/P/1/5, NUBSO MR, January 1886; a transcript of the speech was also published in the *Northampton Mercury*, 9 January 1886.
42 *Norfolk News*, 22 January 1887.
43 LUSC, MS81 21 (Box 1), GOR, newspaper report of a debate between a social democrat and an anarchist in Leicester, 1892.
44 LUSC, MS81 34 (Box 1), GOR, 'What is Anarchy?', undated.
45 Clegg, Fox and Thompson, *A History of British Trade Unions since 1889*, pp. 55–57; 63; 82.
46 S. Bryher, *An Account of the Labour and Socialist Movement in Bristol: Part 2* (Bristol, 1931), pp. 6, 34; Kelly and Richardson, 'The shaping of the Bristol labour movement, 1885–1985', pp. 213–215.
47 Lancaster, *Radicalism, Cooperation and Socialism*, pp. 93–99; 121.
48 Cherry, *Doing Different?*, pp. 5, 28–33; MRC, MSS.524/4/1/13, Trades' Councils annual reports (hereafter TC AR), Lincoln, 1894; MRC, MSS.524/4/1/24, TC AR, Ipswich, 1892; Kettering, 1893; MRC, 547/P/1/7, NUBSO MR, December 1889.
49 For examples, see Hobsbawm, *Worlds of Labour*, pp. 156–157; E. Hobsbawm, 'The "new unionism" reconsidered', in W. Mommsen and H. Husung (eds), *The Development of Trade Unionism in Great Britain and Germany, 1880–1914* (London, 1985), pp. 15–17; I. Taylor, 'Ideology and policy', in C. Cook and I. Taylor (eds), *The Labour Party: An Introduction to Its History, Structure and Politics* (London, 1980), p. 5; Kirk, *Change, Continuity and Class*, p. 156.
50 Clegg, Fox and Thompson, *A History of British Trade Unions since 1889*, pp. 289–290; 302–303.
51 MRC, MSS.524/4/1/13, TC AR, Leicester, 1893; 1894.
52 Lancaster, *Radicalism, Cooperation and Socialism*, pp. 123–125.
53 *Lincolnshire Echo*, 15 October 1894; MRC, MSS.524/4/1/13, TC AR, Lincoln, 1894.
54 MRC, 547/P/1/7, NUBSO MR, February 1890; D. Howell, *British Workers and the Independent Labour Party, 1888–1906* (Manchester, 1983), p. 101.
55 Questions regarding the candidate's working-class credentials and the refusal of some 'weak-kneed Liberals' to vote for a labour candidate ensured his defeat. See *Norfolk News*, 7 November 1891; 13 August 1892; *Eastern Evening News*, 8 July 1892.
56 Cherry, *Doing Different?*, p. 15; *Eastern Evening News*, 5 November 1892.
57 For example, see MRC, MSS.524/4/1/6, TC AR, Norwich, 1894.
58 MRC, MSS.524/4/1/13, TC AR, Lincoln, 1892; letter 'E. C.S'. to *Western Daily Press*, 14 November 1892.
59 There are too many examples to list here, but the following offer a representative sample: MRC, MSS.192/GL/4/1, National Union of Gasworkers and General Labourers annual reports, 1894; letter 'W. Whitefield, Miners' Agent' to *Bristol Mercury*, 12 December 1895; *Lincolnshire Echo,* 12 March 1895; MRC, MSS.524/4/1/6, TC AR, Norwich, 1894.

60 MRC, MSS.524/4/1/6, TC AR, Norwich, 1893.
61 *Eastern Evening News*, 15 August 1884.
62 Freeden, *Ideologies and Political Theory*, pp. 448–449.
63 *Western Daily Press*, 27 October 1893. The Bristol Labour Electoral Association was formed during the strike wave by members of the Bristol Trades' Council and socialist activists. Bryher, *Labour and Socialist Movement in Bristol: Part 2*, pp. 6–7; 18; 50. See also *Lincolnshire Echo*, 2 November 1893.
64 *Bristol Mercury*, 12 January 1892; 16 January 1892.
65 Lawrence, 'Popular politics and the limitations of party', pp. 78–79.
66 *Norwich Mercury*, 18 January 1891; *Lincolnshire Echo*, 20 August 1894; 13 May 1895; MRC, MSS.524/4/1/13, TC AR, Leicester, 1893; Northampton, 1895. This was certainly not limited to the constituencies covered in this book; see Emy, *Liberals, Radicals and Social Politics*, pp. 69–70; J. R. Moore, 'Progressive pioneers: Manchester liberalism, the Independent Labour Party, and local politics in the 1890s', *The Historical Journal*, 44:4 (2001), p. 991.
67 Freeden, *Ideologies and Political Theory*, pp. 458–459.
68 Freeden, *Ideologies and Political Theory*, pp. 425–435, 438.
69 MRC, MSS.21/1846, Labour and Socialism: bound volume of pamphlets, 1886–1902, 'Debate on Socialism, by Labouchère and Hyndman, Northampton Branch of Social Democratic Federation', 1894: emphasis added. Labouchère was giving voice to an emerging intellectual current that could be seen as a precursor of 'new' liberalism.
70 *The Policy of Labour. Reprinted from the 'Labour Elector,' and issued by The Executive Committee of the National Labour Electoral Association* (London, 1889), pp. 3–19.
71 Emy, *Liberals, Radicals and Social Politics*, p. xiii.
72 *The Policy of Labour*, pp. 3–19.
73 MRC, 547/P/1/10, NUBSO CR, 1894.
74 G. Stedman Jones, 'The determinist fix: Some obstacles to the further development of the linguistic approach to history in the 1990s', *History Workshop Journal*, 42 (1996), pp. 20; 27; Lawrence, *Speaking for the People*, p. 102.
75 MRC, 547/P/1/10, NUBSO CR, 1894.
76 MRC, 547/P/1/10, NUBSO CR, 1894.
77 *Northampton Mercury*, 22 September 1893.

4

Splits in the progressive party

A split in the 'progressive' vote was just one of the reasons why the Liberals lost the 1895 general election.[1] In addition to Conservatives, Liberals and Liberal Unionists, the election was contested by 'Independent Liberals', 'Progressives', 'Radicals', 'Socialists', 'Labour-Liberals' and 'Liberal-Labour' men. Political labels were just as diverse in the towns that form the basis of this book. An 'independent Labour' candidate challenged a Liberal in Bristol East, two Conservatives and two 'Liberal and Radical' candidates contested Norwich, Lincoln saw a straight fight between a Liberal Unionist and a Liberal, and two Liberals, a Conservative and a member of the ILP stood in Leicester. The situation was even more complicated in Northampton, where a 'modern radical', a 'Labour Radical', a 'Bradlaugh Radical', a 'Social Democrat' and two Conservatives competed for two seats. The complex nature of progressive politics during this period even confused astute political operators such as the president of the Bristol Liberal Association, who, during a by-election contest in March 1895, spoke of 'Radical working men, or, if they liked to call them so, Labour candidates'.[2]

This statement was indicative of a broader discursive evolution in which 'labour' replaced 'radical' as a political descriptor. With the revival of socialism in the 1880s, the term 'radical' lost some of its sting, a trend likely accelerated by its appropriation by members of the Liberal Party. Still, the core principles of radicalism, if not the word itself, continued to exert a strong influence on progressive politics. Progressives often positioned themselves as the legitimate heirs of the English radical tradition while simultaneously claiming to offer novel solutions to problems that had entered the realm of practical politics. Socialists were particularly keen to root themselves in indigenous forms of radicalism, and often tried to establish a connection between the modern socialist movement and earlier forms of reformist or revolutionary politics. Labourists also took pride in their radical origins, and in some places used the terms 'radical' and 'labour' either together or interchangeably. At the same time, Liberal-inclined newspapers tried to claim that the modern-day 'labour parties', like the radicals of old, were spiritually if not politically part of the Liberal Party.

Establishing connections between older and newer forms of progressive politics becomes easier when we untangle party labels, identities and ideologies. Doing so reveals that the fragmentation of party politics in 1895 masked some of the political and ideological differences that divided progressives at the time. Ideological divisions did not always map onto party-political affiliations, and electoral alliances did not always reflect ideological alignments. By looking beyond the personal and organisational aspects of election contests, it is possible to uncover some of the major identities and currents of thought that shaped the political landscape of late Victorian England. And by interrogating the speeches and literature of the rival progressive candidates, it becomes possible to define with a reasonable degree of accuracy the ideological structures of liberalism, socialism and labourism.

This chapter focuses on three electoral battlegrounds where divisions in the progressive camp contributed to the defeat or near defeat of Liberal candidates. Although the electoral contests in Northampton, Norwich and (to a lesser extent) Bristol East have largely been neglected in previous research, they all help to reveal the splintered nature of the English radical tradition in the years leading up to the birth of the Labour Party. They also demonstrate the electoral significance of local peculiarities. For the *Pall Mall Gazette*, the contest in Northampton was essentially a squabble 'as to the title of [Charles] Bradlaugh's political property'.[3] Disagreements between labourists and socialists in Bristol East over the candidature of a 'Unionist Socialist' served to highlight the radical and anti-conservative roots of Bristol labour politics. Similarly, the failure of labourists or socialists to stand a candidate in Norwich exposed both the weakness of organised labour in the city and the enduring popularity of a lib–lab tactical alliance.

For proponents of the continuity thesis, the final decade of the nineteenth century served as a crucial bridge that connected popular radical or popular liberal traditions with 'radical liberal elements' in the early Labour Party.[4] But as several studies have shown, in their attempt to construct a narrative of continuity, scholars may have overlooked some of the important tensions within progressive politics during the late Victorian period. The 1895 election contests in Northampton, Bristol East and Norwich all add weight to this counter-argument, as they draw attention to differences between the radical, liberal, socialist and labour movements. The enduring strength of labourism, in particular, challenges the idea that progressive politics was wholly populist or 'plebeian' in tone. Like their working-class radical predecessors, labourists exhibited a strong sense of class, a preference for cultural autonomy if not political independence, and a distinctive understanding of themselves and their place in the social order. They also propagated a distinctive ideology that was, in many ways, a collectivist version of working-class radicalism. While labourists had come to believe that the state should intervene in certain areas of the economy, they refused to embrace the totality of the socialist programme. Instead, they preferred to offer a unique interpretation of political concepts that set them apart from socialists, liberals, conservatives and, crucially, popular radicals. By acknowledging the distinctiveness of labourism as an ideology and seeing it as the direct offshoot of a *working-class* rather than *plebeian* form of radicalism, it is possible to emphasise long-term continuity in popular ideas and language without devaluing the uniqueness of rival progressive traditions.

Labour radicalism in Northampton

Charles Bradlaugh's legacy cast a long shadow over politics in Northampton. After his death in January 1891, progressives of all persuasions attempted to claim that they, and not their rivals, were Bradlaugh's true heirs.[5] Not surprisingly, Bradlaugh also loomed large over the 1895 general election contest. To capture the working-class and trade union vote, the Northampton Liberal and Radical Association (LRA) selected Edward Harford, the general secretary of the Amalgamated Society of Railway Servants, to run alongside Henry Labouchère, who had represented the town since 1880. Not satisfied that a trade unionist was being run under the auspices of the Liberal Party, the SDF, which had established a strong, trade union-orientated branch in the town, put forward a 'working man's' candidate of their own, Frederick George Jones. To complicate matters even further, John M. Robertson, Bradlaugh's 'disciple', entered the contest as the candidate of the Bradlaugh Radical Association, an 'ultra Radical' organisation that had broken away from the LRA in early 1892.[6]

The willingness of the LRA to accommodate the demands of the Northampton 'labour party' was partly responsible for causing the fragmentation of what the *Northampton Mercury* called the 'progressive party'.[7] Recent events in the industrial sphere also shaped the tone of the contest. Just weeks before the polls opened, shoemakers in Northampton and across the country were engaged in a bitter industrial conflict with manufacturers in what the local press described as the 'shoe war'.[8] The nationwide lockout, which involved around 46,000 workers and lasted for five weeks, was the culmination of growing socialist militancy in the NUBSO and tensions between the union and the Manufacturers' Association over the introduction and use of machinery, the centralisation of operations in factories and workshops, and the gradual erosion of the shoemakers' autonomy in the workplace.[9] While both sides claimed victory when the lockout ended, the Terms of Settlement allowed manufacturers to limit trade union interference and enforce tighter discipline in their factories.[10] Shoe manufacturers had finally achieved mastery over their workshops and, with the subsequent surge in mechanisation, the disciples of St Crispin were well on their way to becoming semi-skilled factory operatives.[11]

One shoemaker who had entered the trade at the age of seven later reflected that this was the 'greatest change [the trade had] experienced since it was an industry'.[12] Still, despite the rapid pace of change in Northampton's staple industry, most trade union leaders refused to modify their political strategy. For SDF activists, the shoe war was a class war that proved the futility of cross-class collaboration in the political and industrial spheres. Consequently, during the 1895 election, the SDF emphasised the importance of political independence and urged working men to abandon their faith in 'Tory and Whig capitalists, landlords, lawyers, bankers, brewers, and Society fops'.[13] This analysis struck a chord with shoemakers who felt a sense of bitterness towards employers and trade union officials who, in their view, had betrayed the workers. But it failed to win over most of the leading figures in the local labour party, who remained hostile to the SDF's tactics and who continued to see value in maintaining an alliance with the LRA.[14]

Maintaining an alliance with an organisation that, in the words of one trade unionist, had always been more willing than the Conservatives to 'listen to the cry of the workers' was entirely in keeping with the conduct of working-class radicals in the 1870s and 1880s who had also established broad but fragile alliances with middle-class radicals and liberals.[15] And as in the 1870s and 1880s, this strategy was not the product of defeat or demoralisation. The LRA–labour alliance had proven to be a mutually beneficial arrangement that had helped the labour party achieve one of its central demands, namely representation on local governing bodies. For example, in the years leading up to the lockout, 'Labour Radical' candidates had obtained representation on the town council for the first time by working alongside the LRA.[16] Moreover, it was internal wrangling among local socialists and labourists rather than resistance from the LRA that had prevented the NUBSO's general secretary from standing in (and likely winning) the by-election contest held after Charles Bradlaugh's death in 1891.[17]

Still, the relative success of the LRA–labour alliance should not lead us to lose sight of the fact that, at root, it was a strategic alliance that rested on fragile foundations. As both sides made clear, it was an alliance of convenience rather than a populist movement in which class tensions were absent. Trade unionists justified the arrangement on the grounds that it allowed them to achieve their electoral ambitions more quickly than if they had to work independently or alongside less popular organisations such as the SDF. LRA leaders, on the other hand, considered it to be electorally advantageous for their organisation, with one leader admitting in the aftermath of the 1895 election that the LRA had only backed a trade union candidate 'to secure the working-man vote.'[18] The *Northampton Mercury* was also aware of the calculated nature of the agreement, writing in early 1895 that the 'real force of the Radical party of Northampton' could be found in its 'recognition of the right[s] of Labour'.[19]

As in all alliances, tensions were never far below the surface. Such tensions can be found in the discussions that took place between trade unionists and LRA leaders. For example, it was common for trade unionists to warn LRA leaders that unless they accommodated the demands of the labour party, trade unionists would run independent candidates or encourage working-class voters to withdraw their support from LRA-backed candidates, a threat that they followed through with on several occasions.[20] Tensions were also evident in the way activists, politicians and journalists spoke of the existence of a labour party despite the fact it was nominally subsumed within a broader political formation.[21] This suggests that there was a general acknowledgement in Northampton that the labour party had its own concerns and interests that were similar to, but not identical with, those of other political forces. This was consistent with the view of those who had identified tensions in the Northampton radical movement in the 1860s and 1870s despite the insistence of its leaders that such divisions were either irrelevant or non-existent.

While the local Liberal press tried to downplay divisions in the progressive party, it was clear that members of different sections held widely conflicting views about politics and society. During the 1895 election campaign, the SDF candidate and his supporters described England as a deeply class-ridden country in which the 'working classes', or the 'overworked and ill-paid toilers', stood in opposition to and 'at the mercy of the landlord and capitalist classes'. According to one of his handbills, the SDF candidate was the delegate of 'a great and noble cause' that sought the 'defeat of capitalism', 'the triumph of Socialism' and 'emancipation for the toilers'.[22] Henry Labouchère and his supporters, on the other hand, offered a thoroughly populist view of the social order, suggesting that society was divided into the industrious and the idle rather than the workers and the capitalists. Many of the songs that Labouchère's supporters circulated during the campaigns touched on this theme. 'Down with the Lords' carried an unequivocally democratic message, criticising the 'House of Peers', 'proud Bishops' and 'privileg'd paupers' while insisting that 'our rulers' should be 'men chosen by us'. 'The Liberal March' described an ongoing struggle between two opposing forces: 'Men and Liberals' inspired by the 'Honest principles' of 'freedom, life, and glory', and the 'lordly foe' of 'Peers and priv'lege' and 'Lords and Dukes'. And while 'Rouse Rads.! And Rally!' condemned 'rich paupers' and 'gluttons' guilty of 'grinding us for greed', it directed its appeal to 'Britons', 'True Rads' and 'Townsmen all' rather than to a specific social class.[23]

Edward Harford, the 'Labour Radical' candidate, appeared in some of these songs as Labouchère's loyal working-class sidekick. In 'Two, Worthy of our Choice!', voters were encouraged to vote for Harford because of his class background:

Support is due to Harford too –
The Railway Servants' Friend!
And, – from his past, – the Working class
Can well on him depend.

A British Workman! every inch,
Esteem'd by workman too;
He knows just where the shoe does pinch –
And, – *who* would 'pinch the shoe.'[24]

It is telling that the song made no mention of Labouchère's class background, preferring instead to emphasise his political acumen and experience. Such a combination of class-based and non-class-based themes reflected the duality at the heart of liberal politics in Northampton, a duality that not all activists were comfortable with. This is in contrast to labourists, who were entirely comfortable with idea of introducing class into the campaign. Harford admitted that he emphasised his class background to win votes, telling the LRA executive committee before the election that he would 'make a special appeal to labour voters in the town'.[25] According to the *Northampton Mercury*, he liked to open his speeches with a short summary of his social and educational background before expressing pride in having 'sprung from the ranks of Labour'.[26] He then moved on to discussing topical issues, always making sure to give priority to 'labour questions' such as the Employers' Liability Bill and the length of the working day while claiming to approach other questions from the workers' point of view. He was also keen to remind voters that he was uniquely qualified to represent working men because had known 'what it was to work for his livelihood ever since he was fourteen years of age'. For Harford, 'the man who knew the pinch of want, knew, probably, what was best fitted for the working classes'.[27]

Although Harford promised to represent all classes if returned to Parliament, he admitted that 'the working-classes would have his first consideration'.[28] Such sentiments were common among labourists at this time, just as they had been among working-class radicals in previous decades. Equally as central to the labourist perspective was a rejection of the notion of the class struggle. On one occasion, responding to a question from a socialist, Harford stated bluntly that 'he did not recognise a class war: he believed all their difficulties and grievances could be settled without war'.[29] By adopting a class-centred but non-confrontational approach to industrial relations, labourists could privilege the claims of their class while also expressing their hope for closer political and industrial co-operation. Labour activists in Northampton were particularly adept at doing this, perhaps because they had long experience of organising along class lines in the industrial sphere while seeking accommodation with middle-class politicians in the political sphere. While labourists were not averse to adopting an antagonistic tone in certain contexts, this was rare even during the shoe war of 1895. As a leading member of the local NUBSO explained, while the interests of workers and employers were 'not identical', both sides could achieve their respective goals by engaging in patient discussion and mutual deliberation.[30]

This strong sense of class added a social dimension to labourist interpretations of concepts such as democracy, liberty and equality. Interrogating the way candidates and their supporters defined these concepts allows us to tease out some of the ideological differences that distinguished them from each other. Though the four 'democratic candidates' had similar perspectives on the House of Lords, old-age pensions, the nationalisation of the railways, labour representation and Irish Home Rule, there were key differences in the way they presented and prioritised these issues. For example, Frederick George Jones, the SDF candidate, was the strongest advocate of state intervention, proposing, alongside a list of 'palliatives', the 'common and collective ownership of the land and the various instruments of wealth-production'.[31] Labouchère thought that this went too far, though he did promise voters that he would 'insist on the State legislating for the collective benefit of all its citizens'.[32] This view was shared by the Bradlaugh Radical Association candidate, John

M. Robertson, who believed that modern radicals should spend more time focusing on the issue of economic inequality and less time on 'secondary' causes such as temperance or Irish Home Rule.

John M. Robertson's non-socialist version of collectivism, which he developed in an 1892 pamphlet titled *Practical Radicalism*, echoed the views of labourists, who had also come to favour state intervention as a way of reducing unemployment and limiting working hours.[33] These similarities between labourism and 'practical radicalism' can best be understood by seeing them as members of the same ideological family. Democracy, liberty, individuality, progress and rationality formed the core of both ideologies, while adjacent concepts such as equality, rights, the general interest and the state added certain meanings to these core concepts. These structural similarities help to explain both the close relationship between labourists and radicals in towns such as Northampton and the broad similarities between labourist and radical programmes across Britain during this period.

But while there were significant conceptual overlaps between the two, the presence of class and trade unionism in labourism and their absence from 'constructive' forms of radicalism gave rise to disagreements over proposals such as labour representation.[34] Local SDF activists strongly supported this principle and claimed that they were the true labour party. They refused, however, to support Harford, a bona fide trade unionist, because he did not work directly for the nationalisation of the land and 'the means of wealth production, distribution, and exchange'.[35] Labouchère paid lip service to the principle of labour representation, especially when sharing a platform with Harford, but believed that voters should ultimately vote for candidates because of their principles rather than their class.[36] And while Robertson claimed to be a 'Labour Candidate in the true sense of the term', this was not because he was a working man or a trade unionist but because his programme had supposedly been 'framed in the interests of the workers'.[37]

Labourists had a different understanding of labour representation. The assertion of the importance of the principle, to paraphrase Michael Freeden, could be decoded as including a strong belief in democracy, understood to mean the rule of the people, attached to the adjacent concepts of rights, equality and the general interest, understood as the right of all members to be represented in a democratically elected Parliament; class, which added a sectional quality to labourist demands; trade unionism, regarded as 'influencing the economic distributionary patterns' of society 'towards greater equality of opportunity or need'; and peripheral concepts linked to institutions (such as Parliament) and ideas (such as the constitution).[38] The interconnection between these concepts bred a decidedly workerist notion of labour representation. For labourists, a labour candidate was not merely someone who had an advanced programme, even if that programme had been 'framed' in the interests of the workers. Nor was it someone who promised to work for the collective ownership of the means of production. It was someone who had 'sprung from the ranks of Labour' and who continued to serve their class as a trade union official. Because Harford fit this description perfectly and had received the endorsement of his 'brother workers', labourists, according to the NUBSO's Daniel Stanton, should be 'true to [their] own class' and vote for him.[39] Unfortunately, not everyone heeded this advice and a seat that had only recently belonged to one of the most famous radicals in the country passed into the hands of a Conservative.

Tory socialism in Bristol East

By 1895, Bristol radicalism had fractured into a number of different movements. Some activists had joined the Bristol Socialist Society (BSS), an ideologically diverse organisation that contained both 'practical politicians' and 'idealistic comrades' in its ranks.[40] Others worked alongside a new generation of activists in the Bristol and District Trades' Council Labour Electoral Association (BLEA), a representative body that comprised a committed band of delegates from the BSS and a larger contingent of what one member called 'thoroughly independent manual workers', many of whom were licking their wounds after an employers' counter-offensive in the aftermath of the new unionist strike wave.[41] Members of the 'Labour Party in Bristol', as commentators described the BLEA, continued the struggle of their radical predecessors by seeking to achieve labour representation on local and national bodies.[42] Though their election record before 1895 was modest at best, they had managed to establish a small but vocal presence on the School Board, the Board of Guardians and the city council, which represented a marked step forward for the local labour representation movement.[43]

An opportunity to achieve representation at the parliamentary level presented itself in March 1895 when the Bristol East seat fell vacant after the death of the sitting Liberal MP, Sir Joseph Dodge Weston. Though the Bristol Liberal Association had considered running a trade unionist candidate in what was an overwhelmingly working-class constituency, they eventually settled on William Wills of the wealthy Bristol tobacco family. Labour and socialist activists were not surprised by this decision, and it merely confirmed what they and their radical predecessors had long felt, namely that the Liberal Association was an elitist and out-of-touch organisation that had no interest in sending working men to Parliament. Refusing to be disheartened, they began searching for a candidate of their own, seeking advice and support from national-level personalities such as Keir Hardie, who had recently helped to establish the ILP. With financial support failing to materialise, Hardie and others urged activists to support the candidature of Hugh Holmes Gore, a popular local solicitor and a self-described Christian socialist.

Hardie's advice exacerbated tensions in the Bristol labour and socialist movements. For some, Gore was the ideal candidate. As well as being popular, he had a record of winning elections on explicitly socialist platforms. By early 1895, though, he was out of favour with leading figures in the BLEA and the BSS, primarily because he had rejected the appointment of a female Jewish teacher on religious grounds while serving as a member of the School Board. Moreover, while labour and socialist activists tended to be nonconformists who campaigned for a secular education system, Gore was an Anglican supporter of church schools. It was also not clear where he stood on the issue of Irish Home Rule, though he admitted privately to Hardie that he wished to run in the by-election as a 'Unionist Socialist'. These views raised questions about Gore's relationship with the Conservative Party, as did the refusal of the Bristol Unionists to nominate a candidate of their own.[44]

Gore came within 132 votes of ousting the Liberals in a constituency that they had held since its creation in 1885.[45] The Liberal press and the leaders of the ILP considered this a moral victory for socialism. Many activists in Bristol, however, were concerned that the wounds opened by Gore's conduct would take a long time to heal. While Hardie and other ILPers may have considered the result a great moral victory, local activists such as W. H. Spencer thought that it would spell 'disaster, disorder and confusion'.[46] The ILP, Spencer told Hardie, was guilty of 'complete trickery' for not revealing the origins of Gore's money, an oversight that had 'considerably shaken the confidence of the real Labour Party here'. And though Gore received support from people who used the socialist movement 'for what it can do for them personally', Spencer advised Hardie that he had not received support from 'any bona-fide trade unionist or labour man'.[47] As well as providing a neat summary of the tensions generated by the contest, this statement demonstrates how the politics of class could be employed to delineate the fault lines between those whom Spencer called 'Socialists and Labourites'.[48]

The few historians who have written about the Bristol East by-election have tended to consider it an 'extreme case' that that tells us little about popular politics at the time or as evidence of the electoral viability of a 'Tory-socialist' strategy.[49] To some extent, both perspectives are valid. 'Tory-socialist' is certainly an accurate description of Gore's programme.

His views on Ireland, Welsh disestablishment, church schools and the drink question all served to endear him to Conservative-leaning voters, while his desire to implement socialist economic measures, not to mention his class-based attacks on the Liberal Party, tapped into sentiments that Bristol-based socialists had long sought to exploit. A twin emphasis on socialist reconstruction at home and maintenance of the integrity of the British Empire abroad was far from unusual at this time, as a cursory glance at the works of Robert Blatchford, arguably the most influential socialist writer of the period, will testify. When seen in this light, Gore's views seemed to be representative of a distinctive strain of socialism whose proponents shared a closer affinity with toryism than they did with liberalism. This tory-radical or tory-socialist tradition was one of several currents of radicalism that fed into the early Labour Party.

But as far as Bristol is concerned, Gore's campaign was an extreme case. The main political and ideological currents that fed into the Bristol Labour Party in the early twentieth century were not tory in origin: they were radical. To some extent, labourism's roots in radicalism and its ideological affinity with liberalism can be understood by examining labourist attitudes to Irish Home Rule. The historical 'conversation' between Irish nationalism and English radicalism dated back to the late eighteenth century and continued via the Labour Party in the early twentieth century.[50] While Ireland had never been an straightforward question for non-conservatives, Gladstone succeeded in bringing the bulk of British radicals with him when he 'converted' to Home Rule in 1886.[51] 'Justice for Ireland' was a common slogan among members of the Norwich Electoral Organization of the Working Classes, the Lincoln Working Men's Liberal Association, the Northampton Radical Association and the Bristol Working Men's Reform Association, as well as among members of the Bristol, Leicester, Lincoln, Norwich and Northampton Liberal Associations. In 1886, radicals in Lincoln and Bristol also vented their anger at renegade MPs such as Joseph Ruston and Lewis Fry, both of whom opposed Gladstone's Home Rule plan.

For these activists, 'Justice for Ireland' was always part of a broader programme of universal democratic reform. While working-class radicals had used the issue to criticise vacillating Liberal MPs or avowed Liberal Unionists, there was always a sense that, for them, other issues were more important. This was even more the case for labourists and socialists. Though the question remained a highly contentious one at the 1895 election, concern for the fate of Ireland was simply not strong enough to bring liberals, labourists and socialists together.[52] In Bristol, for example, labourists sought to achieve their objectives by working against the local Liberal Association, despite its strong support for Home

Rule. And though the Liberal Association selected a candidate who was also favourable to Home Rule, labourists, even those who could not bring themselves to support Gore, wanted to stand an independent labour candidate. In the weeks leading up to the contest, John Curle, the BLEA's secretary, wrote to Hardie to confirm that the seat could be won 'easily' if they selected 'a candidate of the right stamp'. E. H. Jarvis advised Hardie that while the leaders of the BLEA and BSS could not endorse Gore, there was a 'strong opinion' in favour of standing a 'true man' or a 'prominent Labour Man such as Tom Mann'. W. R. Oxley, a member of the BSS, also hoped that the ILP could convince Tom Mann or Will Thorne to stand, believing that it would be a 'vast pity' if the Liberal nominee was returned unopposed.[53] Even W. H. Spencer, who had initially expressed sympathy with Gore's candidature, bemoaned the fact that finance had prevented the BLEA from standing a labour candidate and expressed his concern that the Liberals would run a 'half-bred Liberal-Labour mongrel' who would, if elected, claim to speak for 'genuine Labour' while in reality representing the interests of the Liberal Party.

Still, if their desire to punish the Liberal Party was so strong, why did labourists in Bristol not back Gore? Personal animosity, suspicions of underhanded dealings and what one ILP activist described as 'local and personal issues' all played a role.[54] Ideological differences were also important. For Gore and his supporters, the by-election contest was a straightforward battle between collectivism and individualism. Gore's most vocal supporters, who included leading ILP figures such as Ramsay MacDonald and Keir Hardie, drew attention to Gore's advocacy of collectivist schemes such as state ownership of the means of production and state aid for the unemployed. They also characterised the contest as a straight fight between capital and labour and poured scorn on the Liberals for (once again) running a wealthy capitalist in a working-class constituency. In their view, this demonstrated the need for an independent, socialist party of labour that would provide constructive solutions to pressing social issues. As Keir Hardie told voters at one election rally, the interests of the Liberal Party and the labour party were 'in nine cases out of ten diametrically opposed', a statement that would have resonated with voters in Bristol East, where the Liberal candidate had expressed his disapproval of collectivist measures such as a universal eight-hour day.[55]

The Bristol East by-election gave the ILP the opportunity to emphasise the polarisation of British politics into two camps. Labourists and socialists in Bristol largely agreed with this view and, like Gore, believed that political divisions could be mapped onto class divisions. However, they were critical of Gore's apparent lack of independence.[56] In fact, their anger at Gore over his views on the Irish question was not so much because they disagreed with him as because they were a sign that he had received money from the Conservatives. And if Gore was to serve in Parliament as a labour representative, then he could not accept secret financial assistance from one of the major parties. Not only would this have been a dishonest and dishonourable act, but it would have cut across the democratic foundations of labourist and socialist ideologies. It would certainly not have been in keeping with the best traditions of the Bristol radical movement, whose members had fought tirelessly to democratise political life by taking decision-making powers out of the hands of insidious 'wire pullers'. While the terminology might have changed, the democratic impulse that lay behind such criticisms had not.

The correspondence that passed between local activists and Keir Hardie gives some indication of the strength of feeling on this subject. BLEA members were particularly angry at the ILP for campaigning on Gore's behalf despite knowing that he had failed to secure a mandate from the legitimate representatives of the Bristol labour movement.[57] Initially, members of the BLEA considered the local branch of the ILP, which Gore and his supporters had formed in the midst of the contest, to be a 'hostile labour organisation'.[58] This statement highlights the bitterness generated by the contest, but it also hints at some of the ideological motivations behind labourist hostility to Gore. Labour activists, wedded to a particular way of thinking about society in which democratic accountability was paramount, may have seen the ILP branch as a potential rival to the 'real Labour party', the BLEA, which could claim to derive its authority from the bulk of trade unionists in the city.[59] With this in mind, it is perhaps not surprising that the BLEA and the BSS refused to support the ILP's candidate for Bristol East at the general election held four months after the by-election contest.

Robust radicalism in Norwich

The Conservatives only managed to capture both of Norwich's parliamentary seats on one occasion between 1832 and 1895. This was due to the strength of liberal feeling in the city and, to a lesser extent, because radicals and liberals were able to form effective but fragile electoral pacts. These pacts stemmed the Conservative tide at a municipal level and, during 1880s, helped to ensure the election of several labour candidates to political office. The strength of a labour-orientated wing of the Liberal Party also convinced leaders of the Norwich Liberal Association to stand a trade unionist candidate at the 1892 general election, but doubts about the candidate's working-class credentials, a lack of enthusiasm for the candidate among some liberal voters and the 'constructive' campaign run by the Conservatives allowed Samuel Hoare, the sole Conservative candidate, to top the poll.[60]

By the 1895 general election, labourists and socialists in Norwich could be found in three rather different political organisations. Trade unionists who clung to the hope of reorientating the Liberal Association in a radical direction frequented the town's Working Men's Radical Clubs, home to what one Liberal leader referred to as the 'extreme section' of the Liberal Party.[61] Those who abandoned their faith in liberalism and who dreamed of constructing a new social order could be found in the small branches of the SDF and Socialist League.[62] More successful was the local branch of the ILP, formed in autumn 1894 when the Trades Union Congress was held in the city. Unlike in Northampton and Bristol, the Norwich ILP instantly attracted some of the city's most prominent trade union leaders and stood against both Conservative and Liberal candidates at municipal elections, without much success.

The Norwich Liberal Association nominated two candidates in anticipation of the 1895 election: Frederick Verney, a clergyman and barrister who had been educated at the elite Harrow School, and Thomas Terrell, a self-made man described by the Liberal press as a 'robust Radical'. During the election campaign, the *Norfolk News*, despite admitting that there were differences of opinion within the 'progressive party', urged 'weak-kneed Liberals' and 'ardent Radicals' to set aside their differences and back the two candidates with 'energy and enthusiasm'.[63] These pleas failed convince the ILP and SDF branches, whose members disrupted meetings and urged voters to abstain from the poll.[64] Liberals were more successful at winning over labour activists who remained aloof from the socialist parties, including members of the Norwich Trades' Council and the Working Men's Radical Clubs.[65]

However, early in the campaign, Thomas Terrell made several statements that damaged his standing among working-class voters. At a large public meeting in the Agricultural Hall, Terrell said that 'if it were not for ignorance, working men would know the history of their country and the interests of their class'. 'It was ignorance', he continued, 'which was the great stronghold of Conservatism'.[66] This may have been part of a clumsy attempt to educate working-class voters and to convince them that they would only further their interests by sending radicals or liberals to Parliament. To many voters, though, Terrell's statements came across as elitist and patronising. The Conservative candidates immediately used Terrell's words against him and, as in previous contests, portrayed themselves as the true friends of the workers.[67] During their campaign meetings, they praised workers for their intelligence and criticised Terrell for his snobbery. They also reminded voters that the Liberal Association had selected strangers as its candidates, men who had 'come down to Norwich to teach Conservatives what they ought to do and to relieve them of the ignorance which they said they possessed'.[68] As election day drew near, Conservative posters asked voters if they appreciated being told by strangers that they were an ignorant group of people. This line of attack continued after the results had been announced and when it had become clear that the Conservatives had captured both seats. 'The electors that voted ... might be very ignorant', one of the victorious candidates said to rapturous laughter from his audience, but they had proven themselves to be 'very good and sober citizens'.[69]

For the *Norfolk Chronicle*, the 1895 election contest was 'one of the most severe political contests that Norwich ha[d] ever seen'.[70] It also reveals a great deal about popular politics at the time. For instance, it shows how the Conservative Party could use a politics of class to attack their Liberal opponents, many of whom still thought that their party was the natural home for working-class voters. The willingness of Conservatives to incorporate class-based themes into their appeals also suggests that such rhetoric had a certain level of electoral purchase. Though it would be impossible to determine the extent to which Terrell's comments pushed voters towards the Conservative candidates, it is certainly true that Liberal leaders considered the comments to be electorally damaging. If the Conservatives' use of class was indeed a factor in their victory, then it makes the example of Norwich even more intriguing for historians. While Norwich was an overwhelmingly working-class constituency, it was not home to a strong trade union movement, it lacked heavy, large-scale industries and it did not yet have a unified political labour movement.[71] In short, it did not contain the political and economic ingredients that one would expect to find in a town whose voters were seemingly swayed by appeals to class sentiment and who, just eleven years later, would elect one of the first Labour MPs in English history.

Terrell's supporters attempted to downplay the episode by claiming that he had been misquoted. But it would not have been entirely surprising if he had made the comments. Populist radicals in Norwich were not averse to expressing opinions tinged with a sense of paternalism or condescension towards sections of the working class. For instance, in the immediate aftermath of the contest, the radical *Norfolk News* argued that the Conservatives only won because their appeals resonated with 'the very lowest classes of the population'. The colours of the Conservative candidates 'showed a decided preponderance in some of the poor-class thoroughfares', while the Liberal colours were far more prevalent in the 'better-class artisan districts'.[72] George White, a leading member of the Norwich Liberal Association, made a similar argument several months later when addressing the Norwich Radical Club. During his speech, White told listeners to avoid 'the worst yards of St. Martin's and Pockthorpe' and focus on winning over those who lived in 'the more respectable working class districts such as Catton and North Heigham'. It was there, he argued, that they would find 'men who [had] raised themselves from the lower strata' and who 'formed the real backbone of the Liberal party'.[73]

While labourists also drew distinctions between 'better-class' artisans and 'the lower strata', they tended to deem poorly paid working men worthy of consideration. It was no coincidence that when trade unionists opened a new Radical Club in early 1896, they chose as their venue a building on Cowgate Street, one of the 'poor-class thoroughfares' that the *Norfolk News* had identified as a stronghold of working-class toryism. This was a sign that progressives took very different approaches to the thorny question of class. Furthermore, it showed that these approaches cut across party lines. The trade unionists who supported the Liberal candidates in 1895 articulated a sense of class that was in many ways indistinguishable from that held by those who joined the recently formed ILP branch. By reading their speeches and writings, it is possible to identify themes that also appeared in labourist statements in Bristol, Northampton and elsewhere, such as expressions of pride in one's social status, promises to prioritise the needs of the working class, an emphasis on the dignity of manual labour and a rejection of the notion of a class war.[74] This multi-layered identity set labourists apart from liberals and populist radicals, but also from revolutionary elements in the SDF and the Socialist League.

A defensive and conciliatory sense of class fed into and shaped labourist attitudes to contemporary political issues. Like their counterparts in other towns and cities, labourists in Norwich articulated a democratic and class-centred view of political change that, if realised, would have brought political institutions into line with the representative principles of the English constitution. The emphasis, then, was on the *restoration* of the civil, political and economic rights of the working class, a notion that had a long history in English radical thought. And because of their loyalty to the underlying principles of the constitution, labourists were vocal in their commitment to strategies that involved working within legal parameters. Their demand for a 'a fair and honest representation of the working classes' on local and national governing bodies, their endeavour to turn trade unionism into a 'mighty power' and their support for workers who engaged in strike action to counter the 'ever-increasing encroachments upon [their] rights and privileges' were all demonstrations of what one local activist called a 'peaceful but firm assertion of their rights'.[75]

Labourists' desire to attain their goals peacefully sometimes led them into alliances with other political forces. Co-operation with a local Liberal Association was particularly seductive at times when labour activists considered their own organisations to be too weak to sustain independent electoral campaigns, as was the case in Norwich during the early to mid-1890s. At the same time, the centrality of class to their conception of the political order shaped their perspectives to such an extent that these alliances, however long-lasting and electorally successful, always exhibited signs of conditionality. This was even evident in Norwich, a city where radical trade unionists had worked with the Liberal Association since the 1880s and where a lib–lab alliance had yielded some notable successes. The essential fragility of the lib–lab alliance can be seen in several ways, not least in the dogged refusal of labourists to abandon their identity as members of 'the labour party' despite local commentators describing them as little more than the 'extreme wing of the Liberal party'.[76]

Labourists' support for candidates who were not 'real labour representatives' incurred the wrath of those who held a very different understanding of political independence.[77] The small branch of the SDF, for example, adopted a vehemently independent stance, while the Socialist League followed William Morris in repudiating electoral politics altogether.[78] Members of the ILP were just as fervent in their commitment to political independence and, at the 1895 election, placed 'no confidence in either political party'.[79] The ILP's commitment to socialism, which placed it outside the boundaries of what leaders of the Norwich Liberal Association deemed acceptable, was partly responsible for this attitude. But as we have seen with the Bristol example, an impulse to form a party of labour separate from the Liberal Party flowed just as naturally from a labourist perspective as it did from a socialist one. In fact, when ILPers in Norwich defended their decision to sever their connection with the Liberal Party, they often used the same arguments that labourists in Bristol had been using since the 1880s.

At the time of the 1895 general election, the Norwich ILP's unwillingness to form alliances with other progressive forces stopped key labourist figures from joining it. Some labourists also refused to join the ILP because of its commitment to securing the collective ownership of the means of production. After listening to a lecture by an ILPer in

February 1895, Frank Delves, the chairman of the Norwich Trades' Council, condemned the theories as 'unpractical':

> It was better to attempt something practical than to aim at too much and fail. He believed in progress, but he could not think it was possible to jump all at once from the present competitive system to the ideas of Socialism.[80]

H. A. Day, a Fabian, offered a similar riposte to the ILP in a lecture delivered at the Radical Club in October 1897.[81] Plainly titled 'Why I do not belong to the I. L. P.', the lecture encapsulated the labourist view of socialism. While he did not believe in a 'hedgehog' policy of 'treating everyone as an enemy', Day insisted that:

> [He] thoroughly believed in the direct representation of labour, and had little faith that the average Liberal or Tory politician sprung from the capitalist or middle class understand and advocate all the needs of the workers.

This sentence contained all the ingredients of the labourist perspective, including an emphasis on direct as opposed to indirect labour representation and the assumption that members of other classes could not truly understand the needs of the working class. Day's speech also included other elements of the typical labourist viewpoint, including a fear that a socialist equality of provision would allow the 'loafing tramp' to be treated in the same manner as 'an honest steady workman'. Eschewing the millenarian tone of much socialist oratory, Day expressed a typically vague and conciliatory vision of the future in which 'every class and every interest [would be] fairly represented in the councils of empire'. Only then, he believed, could all sections of the community 'work together for the common welfare'. Day considered this to be a form of 'true socialism'.

Conclusion

Examining the way local activists used certain terms and concepts during the election contests of 1895 offers key insights into the nature of popular politics at this time. Even the ostensibly straightforward campaign in Norwich helped to shed light on the endurance of localist sentiments, the relationship between populist radicals and working-class voters, and the ability of the Conservative Party to tap into voters' sense of class. In some places election contests forced political actors to defend their alliance with those with whom they disagreed, while in others it encouraged activists to justify their opposition to candidates who, in the eyes of some people, were their natural political allies. Such discussions had important political consequences, causing rifts between socialists and labourists in some towns and lending a sense of fragility to lib–lab alliances in others.

These discussions are of value for scholars, as they uncover some of the ideological variations that occurred within ostensibly unified political movements. The fragmentation of the radical tradition as suggested in this chapter complicates the idea that there was an underlying unity to late Victorian progressive politics. Shifting the focus to the local level helps to uncover ideological and discursive differences within the 'progressive party'. During the 1895 general election contest in Northampton, progressives could be found on four different platforms. In Norwich, labour and socialist activists either voted for the 'Radical' and 'Liberal' candidates or abstained from the poll. And at the 1895 by-election in Bristol East, local circumstances caused a situation in which the socialist candidate may have received more support from conservatives than from labourists.

But fragmentation along political lines did not always correspond to ideological divisions. Regardless of which platform they stood on, socialists, liberals, labourists and populist radicals offered competing understandings of political demands and the concepts from which they flowed. By studying the political language of local activists, it is also possible to identify variations *within* as well as *between* these traditions. Suggesting that we contain the activists and politicians discussed in this chapter within a broad progressive party would only serve to minimise these variations. After all, this 'party' would have to include not only socialists, liberals and labourists, but also tory socialists and revolutionary socialists, 'old' and social radicals, and classical and 'new' liberals. A case could be made for seeing these variants as part of a broad political and intellectual tradition, but it is only by appreciating the differences between them that we can fully understand the tensions that erupted within the progressive party, not only during the late Victorian period but also in the years following the formation of the Labour Party in 1900.

Notes

1 While 'progressive' has often been used to describe late nineteenth-century socialists, labourists and collectivist liberals, Emily Robinson has recently shown that the term was well established by 1889 and that it was most strongly associated with, among other things, the idea of 'a self-guiding market economy'. E. Robinson, *The Language of Progressive Politics in*

Modern Britain (London, 2017), p. 68. For the 1895 general election, see P. Readman, 'The 1895 general election and political change in late Victorian Britain', *The Historical Journal*, 42:2 (1999), pp. 467–493.
2 *Western Daily Press*, 12 March 1895.
3 *Pall Mall Gazette*, 16 July 1895.
4 Biagini and Reid, *Currents of Radicalism*, p. 1.
5 For example, see Henry Labouchère's election address: NCL, 198–781/1895, NEE, 'To the Electors of Northampton', 1895.
6 Emy, *Liberals, Radicals and Social Politics*, p. 4; *Northampton Mercury*, 5 February 1892.
7 *Northampton Mercury*, 27 September 1895.
8 *Northampton Mercury*, 8 March 1895; MRC, 547/P/1/11, NUBSO MR, March 1895.
9 Clegg, Fox and Thompson, *British Trade Unions since 1889: Volume 1*, pp. 199–202.
10 Some manufacturers in Northampton even prohibited swearing, singing and shouting on their premises. MRC, 547/P/1/11, NUBSO MR, May 1895.
11 The defeat severely weakened the union in Northampton and elsewhere. Fox, *A History of the NUBSO*, pp. 244–245; MRC, 547/P/1/10, NUBSO MR, November 1894; MRC, 547/P/1/17, NUBSO MR, November 1901.
12 Saxton, *Recollections of William Arnold*, p. 79.
13 NCL, 198–781/1895: SDF campaign literature.
14 Discussions had taken place between labourists and members of the SDF about forming a 'united Labour party', but these quickly broke down amidst dissension and disagreement. See MRC, 547/P/1/9, NUBSO MR; May 1893; July 1893; MRC, 547/P/1/10; NUBSO MR, November 1894.
15 *Northampton Mercury*, 12 August 1892.
16 *Northampton Mercury*, 7 November 1890; 28 October 1892.
17 MRC, 547/P/1/7, NUBSO MR, February 1890; Howell, *British Workers and the ILP*, p. 101.
18 *Northampton Mercury*, 13 September 1895.
19 *Northampton Mercury*, 11 January 1895.
20 For example, see *Northampton Mercury*, 22 August 1890.
21 For example, see *Northampton Mercury*, 17 October 1890; 12 August 1892; 19 August 1892; 17 October 1890; 28 October 1892; 11 October 1895.
22 NCL, 198–781/1895, NEE, 'Social-Democratic Federation. General Election, 1895. To the Electors of the Borough of Northampton.', 1895. See also *Northampton Socialist*, 16 October 1897.
23 NCL, 198–781/1895, NEE, 'Down with the Lords'; 'The Liberal March'; 'Rouse Rads.! And Rally!', 1895.
24 NCL, 198–781/1895, NEE, 'Two, Worthy of our Choice!', 1895.
25 *Northampton Mercury*, 28 June 1895.
26 *Northampton Mercury*, 18 January 1895; 5 July 1895.
27 *Northampton Mercury*, 5 July 1895.
28 *Northampton Mercury*, 22 February 1895.

29 *Northampton Mercury*, 18 January 1895.
30 MRC, 547/P/1/11, NUBSO MR, May 1895.
31 NCL, 198–781/1895, NEE, 'Social-Democratic Federation. General Election, 1895. To the Electors of the Borough of Northampton.', 1895.
32 NCL, 198–781/1895, NEE, 'To the Electors of Northampton' (Labouchère), 1895.
33 J. M. Robertson, *Practical Radicalism* (London, 1892).
34 M. Pugh, *The Making of Modern British Politics, 1867–1939* (Oxford, 1982), p. 32.
35 NCL, 198–781/1895, NEE, 'Social-Democratic Federation. General Election, 1895. To the Electors of the Borough of Northampton.', 1895.
36 *Northampton Mercury*, 12 July 1895.
37 NCL, 198–781/1895, NEE, 'To the Electors of Northampton' (Robertson), 1895.
38 Freeden, *Ideologies and Political Theory*, pp. 81; 451.
39 *Northampton Mercury*, 12 April 1895.
40 W. W. Young, *Robert Weare of Bristol, Liverpool and Wallasey, Born: 1858, Died: 1920: An Appreciation, and Four of His Essays* (Manchester, 1921), pp. 34; 81.
41 BRO, 32080/TC1/4/5, Bristol Trades' Council annual reports (hereafter BTC AR), 1894; R. Whitfield, 'Trade unionism in Bristol, 1910–1926', in I. Bild (ed.), *Bristol's Other History* (Bristol, 1983), pp. 71–73; LSE, ILP/4/1895/48, Independent Labour Party correspondence (hereafter ILP C), W. H. Spencer to K. Hardie (Bristol). Bristol East, 10 March 1895.
42 *Bristol Mercury*, 26 April 1890; *Western Daily Press*, 16 June 1890.
43 Large and Whitfield, *The Bristol Trades Council*, pp. 11–12.
44 Bryher, *Labour and Socialist Movement in Bristol: Part 2*, pp. 55–56; LSE, ILP/4/1895/41, ILP C, H. H. Gore to Hardie (London). Bristol East, 7 March 1895; LSE, ILP/4/1895/53, ILP C, Hardie to Gore (London). Bristol East, 14 March 1895.
45 Bryher, *Labour and Socialist Movement in Bristol: Part 2*, p. 56; Howell, *British Workers and the ILP*, p. 386.
46 LSE, ILP/4/1895/59, ILP C, Spencer to Hardie (Bristol). Bristol East, 18 March 1895.
47 LSE, ILP/4/1895/64, ILP C, Spencer to Hardie (Bristol). Bristol East, 21 March 1895; LSE, ILP/4/1895/66, ILP C, Spencer to Hardie (Bristol). Bristol East, 24 March 1895.
48 LSE, ILP/4/1895/48, ILP C, Spencer to Hardie (Bristol). Bristol East, 10 March 1895.
49 Howell, *British Workers and the ILP*, pp. 385–388; Pugh, *Speak for Britain!*, p. 45.
50 L. Marley, 'Introduction', in L. Marley (ed.), *The British Labour Party and Twentieth-Century Ireland: The Cause of Ireland, the Cause of Labour* (Manchester, 2016), pp. 1–2.

51 G. Ó Tuathaigh, 'A tangled legacy: The Irish "inheritance" of British Labour', in L. Marley (ed.), *The British Labour Party and Twentieth-Century Ireland: The Cause of Ireland, the Cause of Labour* (Manchester, 2016), p. 24.
52 Readman, 'The 1895 general election', pp. 471–475.
53 LSE, ILP/4/1895/45, ILP C, J. Curle to Hardie (Bristol). Bristol East, 9 March 1895; LSE, ILP/4/1895/46, ILP C, E. H. Jarvis to Hardie (Bristol). Bristol East, 9 March 1895; LSE, ILP/4/1895/48, ILP C, Spencer to Hardie (Bristol). Bristol East, 10 March 1895; LSE, ILP/4/1895/49, ILP C, W. R. Oxley to Hardie (Bristol). Bristol, 10 March 1895.
54 LSE, ILP/4/1895/56A, ILP C, S. G. Hobson to Hardie (Bristol), Bristol East, 17 March 1895.
55 *Western Daily Press* 14 March 1895; 21 March 1895.
56 W. H. Spencer criticised Gore for working with 'the brewer and the publican' and for his links with the 'High Church Party': LSE, ILP/4/1895/64, ILP C, Spencer to Hardie (Bristol). Bristol East, 21 March 1895; LSE, ILP/4/1895/66, ILP C, Spencer to Hardie (Bristol). Bristol East, 24 March 1895.
57 LSE, ILP/4/1895/60, ILP C, R. Gilliard to Hardie (Bristol). Bristol East, 19 March 1895.
58 *Bristol Mercury*, 5 April 1895.
59 LSE, ILP/4/1895/64, ILP C, Spencer to Hardie (Bristol). Bristol East, 21 March 1895.
60 The *Eastern Evening News* blamed 'half-hearted Liberals' for the defeat. *Eastern Evening News*, 7 July 1892.
61 *Norwich Mercury*, 16 June 1894.
62 Cherry, *Doing Different?*, p. 113. Cherry notes that some members left the Socialist League after it veered off in an anarchist direction.
63 *Norfolk News*, 6 July 1895.
64 *Norwich Mercury*, 13 July 1895; *Norfolk Chronicle*, 20 July 1895.
65 *Eastern Evening News*, 15 July 1895.
66 *Eastern Evening News*, 2 July 1895; 5 July 1895; *Norwich Mercury*, 3 July 1895.
67 For examples, see *Eastern Evening News*, 30 June 1892; *Norfolk Chronicle*, 2 July 1892.
68 *Norfolk Chronicle*, 13 July 1895.
69 *Norwich Mercury*, 20 July 1895.
70 *Norfolk Chronicle*, 20 July 1895.
71 Cherry, *Doing Different?*, pp. 9–11.
72 *Norfolk News*, 20 July 1895.
73 *Eastern Evening News*, 1 January 1896.
74 For example, see MRC, MSS.524/4/1/6, TC AR, Norwich, 1893; 1894.
75 MRC, MSS.524/4/1/6, TC AR, Norwich, 1892; 1895.
76 *Norwich Mercury*, 29 June 1895.

77 Quote by a member of the Norwich Trades' Council, reported in *Eastern Evening News*, 28 October 1892.
78 Cherry, *Doing Different?*, pp. 18–23.
79 *Norwich Mercury*, 13 July 1895.
80 *Norwich Mercury*, 16 February 1895.
81 *Norfolk News*, 23 October 1897.

5

Labour and the nationalisation of politics

> Although there have been Labour members in individual constituencies ... there has been no united Labour movement in the country, advocating systematically the political claims and ideals which naturally supplement the economic claims and ideals of the working class and Trade Union movements. There have been men, but there has been no movement.[1]
>
> *Labour Representation Committee statement on the 1900 general election*

The unification of most labourist and socialist forces under a single party umbrella was a significant development in British political history. The extent to which the pre-First World War Labour Party achieved this aim has been well documented and passionately argued, as have questions regarding its electoral performance, its relationship with the Liberal Party, its apparent lack of ideology, and, more broadly, its wider social, cultural and ideological significance. But the way in which Labour contributed to the 'nationalisation' of British political culture has remained largely unexplored. For Daniele Caramani, this was a historical phenomenon that saw a 'highly localized and territorialized' form of politics give way to 'national electoral alignments and oppositions'.[2] Scholars who have explored this trend have uncovered a diverse range of phenomena that, in their view, marked turning-points on the road to a modern political system.[3] One such phenomenon was the professionalisation of party politics, a process in which the two major parties of the late Victorian era, the Liberals and the Conservatives, began to organise themselves on a national basis.[4] Scholars such as Kathryn Rix have since added additional layers to the argument by exploring, among other things, the professionalisation of electoral agents.[5] Almost twenty-five years after the publication of H. J. Hanham's influential work on the topic, Martin Pugh, writing in *The Making of Modern British Politics*, found little fault with the idea that the modern political system, which reached its zenith in the period after the Second World War, evolved from its origins in the period between the 1860s and the turn of the century.[6]

Other work has centred on patterns of electoral behaviour and determinants of political allegiance. For Pugh, the organisation of parties on a national basis coincided with an evolution in the way political parties conducted election campaigns. In contrast to the 'sporadic, localized contests' of the early to mid-Victorian era, during which a small minority of men were asked to vote for candidates based on their personalities, religious beliefs and views on local issues, elections from the 1870s onwards were marked by attempts to mobilise voters around key national figures, such as Disraeli and Gladstone, and important 'national' subjects such as Irish Home Rule. In this view, the rise in importance of national issues coincided with the emergence of class as the primary determinant of political allegiance. Socio-economic changes and the willingness of political actors to adapt to such changes have been used to explain a range of political developments, including the electoral success of the Conservative Party between 1886 to 1906, the Liberal 'renaissance' in the years before the First World War and the eventual replacement of the Liberal Party by the Labour Party as the main progressive force in British politics.[7]

The nationalisation thesis has not been without its detractors. Since the 1980s, an ever-expanding body of work has served to challenge the chronology of the dominant narrative by suggesting that national-level issues and party-political allegiances had been crucial factors in election contests long before the 1870s.[8] Some of the most important work, at least for the purposes of this book, is that which has taken issue with not only the chronology of the nationalisation thesis but also the central assumptions upon which it is based. Influenced to varying degrees by the 'linguistic turn', these studies have called into question the idea that there was an automatic link between economic-induced phenomena, such as a rise in 'class consciousness', and political developments, such as changes in electoral behaviour. Collectively, this work has encouraged scholars to take a greater interest in the way political parties and politicians 'defined and have been forced to redefine the social identities and audiences to which they belong'.[9] Duncan Tanner's extensive study of the early Labour Party was one such work, as it aimed to show how Labour's success and failures during the Edwardian and wartime periods were largely based on the party's ability to present practical and relevant ideas to its chosen audience.[10] And as numerous local studies have shown, there were marked regional variations in the way voters understood these ideas.[11]

The aim of this chapter is to explore the process of nationalisation from the perspective of the local political activist. These were individuals who served on the frontline of the political struggle, establishing and maintaining organisations, organising and chairing public meetings, producing and distributing political literature, writing letters, canvassing and standing for local political office. The activists that form the basis of this book performed tasks that political agents carried out for the Liberal and Conservative parties, but, unlike the increasingly professional and paid agents of the two major parties, they tended to work on a voluntary basis and had to fit their activism around other commitments. By 1914, many of their activities were being organised under the auspices of the Labour Party, founded as the LRC in 1900, which had finally come around to the idea of appointing paid organisers.[12]

The centralisation and growth of an official Labour politics helped to popularise the idea that a candidate's social class was more important than their character, their views on political and religious questions, and even their place of birth. Labour candidates, most of whom were funded by national trade unions, often claimed that, if elected to political office, they would represent a particular class or section of that class in addition to (and sometimes over and above) a geographic constituency. As illustrated in previous chapters, local peculiarities and localist sentiments were still important factors in election campaigns. But the Labour Party and its precursors always attempted to mobilise voters around a principle – direct labour representation – which challenged localised and territorialised notions of politics. Labour activists' role in breaking down this old idea of representation was not always intentional, as the poor financial state of their local parties and the fact that Members of Parliament did not receive a salary until 1911 often forced them to look outside their own constituencies to find a suitable candidate.

Whether intentionally or not, the pre-war Labour Party and its leading figures made a strong contribution to the nationalisation of political culture. The presence and activities of a small body of Labour MPs in the House of Commons provided activists in constituencies with an example to follow. This was as true for activists in areas where Labour was initially weak or non-existent as it was in areas where the party was strong. The party, its MPs and leading spokespersons acted as poles of attraction towards which labour and some socialist activists could navigate. By trying to force issues such as unemployment, trade union rights and old-age pensions to the frontline of politics, Labour helped to inculcate a sense of loyalty even among lib–labs and non-affiliated socialists who felt little need to adopt the party's strategy at a local level. Late Victorian labour activists were not without their heroes and political role models, but the novelty of the Labour Party lay in the fact that its leading personalities were members of a single party that intended to be truly national in scope. This was particularly the case after the 1906 general election, when twenty-nine candidates endorsed by the LRC were returned to the House of Commons.

The very existence of a national Labour Party promoted the idea that the party was a co-ordinating centre that could draw together previously disconnected trade unionists and socialists. This, in turn, served to impose a degree of order on labourist and socialist politics that had been lacking before 1900. This is not to say that all trade unionists and socialists, let alone all working-class voters, were avid supporters of the Labour Party. Nor is it to suggest that Labour MPs and members were in agreement on all questions, or that party leaders were successful in creating a disciplined, well-oiled party machine in the pre-war period. But the success of the party in at least popularising the idea that a national-level co-ordinating centre now existed was a novel and historically important development. Letters sent by local activists to the party's head office and circulars sent out by the party's secretary and organising secretary reveal the prevalence of this idea. Local activists demonstrated that they were keen to take advice and direction from party leaders, while party leaders, who produced and distributed pamphlets, formulated model rules and resolutions for local bodies and sometimes disciplined those who contravened party rules, seemed more than happy to play this role.

Labour's presence on the national stage also contributed to the standardisation of labourist discourse across Britain. Prior to 1900, there were important discursive and ideological similarities between political labour movements and, before them, working-class radical movements, which existed in towns and cities across England. To establish these connections, it is necessary to tease out subtle similarities or differences by conducting a close reading of speeches, letters, trade union reports and other materials associated with a diverse range of often ephemeral political and industrial organisations. Carrying out a similar analysis of their Edwardian successors, however, is a far easier task. In part this is because the evolution of formerly localised, disconnected and semi-autonomous organisations into local LRCs helped to ensure the preservation of materials, such as newspapers, election leaflets, handbills, trade union reports and other literature, which had only existed in scattered and sporadic form before 1900. But it is also because members of LRCs and trade union branches began to address similar topics, including the activities of the Labour Party, in a broadly consistent manner. Even those trade unionists and socialists who organised outside the party still engaged in discussions and often expressed their gratitude to Labour MPs who had, in their view, helped to further the cause of labour in Parliament. Among committed members, lukewarm sympathisers and even hostile critics, there was a growing sense that Labour, despite its faults, was their party.

Building the party

There were several signs before the First World War that Labour was developing into a co-ordinated, national movement. Ramsay MacDonald and James Middleton were particularly influential in encouraging this development. As secretary and assistant secretary of the party respectively, they were responsible for receiving and responding to correspondence from local activists, which involved offering advice about forming local parties, selecting candidates, running election campaigns and dealing with Liberal Associations. They also provided local groups with centrally produced leaflets, handbills, posters and conference reports, and devised model rules and resolutions for local groups to adopt to ensure that they were eligible for affiliation to the party.[13] At times, they even advised activists when and where to exhibit election posters so that they kept their 'freshness' during election contests.[14] By opening these lines of communication, MacDonald and Middleton were able to provide activists with a consistent interpretation of the party's role and objectives.

It was not their intention to run the party in an entirely top-down manner. Initially, as MacDonald admitted, they were happy to work with pre-existing bodies rather than try to establish a 'uniform system of organisation for the whole of the country'.[15] Still, activists at a local level expected MacDonald, Middleton and the party's executive committee to provide them with guidance and support. This was especially the case after the party's impressive performance at the 1906 election, which saw their representation in the House of Commons increase to twenty-nine. In the weeks and months following the election, Labour head office was inundated with requests for pamphlets, model rules, sample ballot papers, draft resolutions, annual conference reports and any other literature that activists could use to convince their societies to affiliate with the newly renamed Labour Party. Some activists simply wanted guidance on how to win over sceptical colleagues, while others sent draft copies of rules and constitutions to ensure that their local LRCs conformed with the party's regulations. It was also increasingly common for activists to ask head office for advice on the question of running local candidates, though, as a frustrated James Middleton reminded one member, this was a matter that rested with local organisations.[16]

The way in which activists responded to the development of the Labour Party depended on the political climate of their respective towns. This was clear in Norwich, which was one of the first cities to elect a Labour MP to the House of Commons. Labour's success in Norwich owed much to the activities of a local ILP branch of which George Roberts, the successful Labour candidate in 1906, was a leading member. Between 1900 and 1904, the Norwich ILP appointed a paid officer, convinced the Norwich Trades' Council to affiliate to the national Labour Party and resolved to stand its own candidate at the forthcoming general election.[17] The death of the sitting Conservative MP in December 1904 gave the ILP the opportunity to test its strength, and Roberts duly stood in a three-way contest against a Liberal and a Conservative. Although Roberts finished bottom of poll, an informal arrangement with the Norwich Liberal Association helped to secure his return to Parliament alongside the Liberal nominee a year later.

In his study of the Norwich labour movement, Steve Cherry suggests that the events surrounding these contests demonstrated the national party's influence on local political organisations.[18] This is true to the extent that party leaders deemed Norwich to be suitable for a 'one plus one' lib–lab arrangement. But local considerations also both facilitated and hindered the progress of the Norwich ILP. As Cherry himself noted, secret deals were struck between non-ILP trade unionists and local Liberals at the 1904 by-election, 'Liberal and Radical disagreements' over Roberts' candidature in 1906 threatened to disrupt the lib–lab arrangement, and Liberal–Conservative pacts helped to stem the tide of Labour at a municipal level.[19] Furthermore, according to Cherry, the Liberal Party only stood one candidate during the 1910 general elections, which left the way clear for Roberts, because they were fearful of a revitalised local Conservative Party that had achieved a string of successes in municipal elections.[20]

Situating these developments in a longer trajectory of popular politics in Norwich makes it easier to explain the popularity of a local lib–lab alliance. As noted in previous chapters, electoral alliances between different sections of the 'progressive party' had been commonplace in Norwich since at least the mid-1870s. From the 1880s, trade unionists had also achieved representation on local governing bodies by forming pacts with the Liberal Association, and in 1892 they even managed to convince the Liberals to run a labour candidate at a general election. The emergence of a nominally independent political labour movement in the late 1890s seemed to mark a decisive turning-point in popular politics, but even this view must be tempered somewhat. The Norwich ILP only achieved parliamentary success in 1906 because it came to an understanding with the Norwich Liberal Association. There was still a strong inclination among voters, and also among several leading trade unionists, that a tactical alliance between different progressive organisations would be the most effective way of achieving labour representation and other labourist goals. The decision of the ILP to run a candidate against the Liberal Party at the by-election in 1904, then, seems more like an aberration than the new norm.

The Norwich example highlights the important role that a committed band of ILP activists could play in shaping the history of local labour politics. It also shows how the ILP attempted to overcome parochialism in the labour and socialist movement. By 1900, Norwich-based activists were well versed in the business of national politics. The 'culture and consciousness' of the rural labourers who lived in the surrounding countryside, however, was 'local as opposed to national' until the early 1920s. In his study of rural radicalism in Norfolk, Alun Howkins suggests that the process of nationalisation in which party allegiances became 'a matter of class' was an urban process. The concerns of the three major parties remained dominated by urban and industrial matters, and work-based animosities arising in the countryside continued to be local and personalised, particularly in the isolated county of Norfolk.[21]

But from 1900, there were signs that Norwich-based activists were starting to take a greater interest in the concerns of the rural poor. Clarion cyclists ventured into surrounding villages and towns to spread the gospel of socialism, and the ILP, boosted in 1906 by the return of Roberts in Norwich, started to establish branches in semi-industrial towns throughout Norfolk. Leading ILPers and socialists such as John Bruce Glasier, George Lansbury and Keir Hardie visited these towns to address local labourers, and socialist speakers came to dominate on the platforms of the Eastern Counties Agricultural Labourers' and Small Holders' Union, renamed the National Agricultural Labourers' and Rural Workers' Union (NALRWU) in 1910. These developments helped to bring rural labourers into contact with urban-based trade unionists, and by 1914 the NALRWU had affiliated to the Labour Party. Roberts also played a crucial role in blurring the boundaries between the urban and the rural, and despite the fact that he represented an urban constituency, his attempts to establish a wages board for agriculture and his part in drawing up the ILP's rural programme in 1913 established him as the unofficial 'labourers' MP'.[22]

In many ways, labour politics in Leicester followed a similar pattern. In 1900, the overwhelmingly working-class ILP branch used its influence in the trade union movement to convince the Leicester Trades' Council, which was then dominated by delegates from the NUBSO and the LAHU, to affiliate to the national LRC.[23] It had also campaigned for Ramsay MacDonald at the 1900 election, but, as in Norwich, the official candidate of the LRC came bottom of the poll in a three-cornered contest. And as in Norwich, the presumed strength of the Labour vote convinced the local Liberal Association to seek what one activist described as an 'honourable' but 'unofficial arrangement' with the local LRC whereby each party would stand just one parliamentary candidate in what was then a double-member constituency.[24] The formation of a progressive alliance (or a 'mongrel coalition' as one Conservative politician called it) ensured the success of MacDonald and the nominees of the Liberal Association in 1906 and in both election contests in 1910.[25]

It is not surprising that the national Labour Party played such an important role in shaping the course of developments in Leicester during this period. As secretary of the party, it was in MacDonald's interest to ensure that Labour organisations in Leicester became models for others to follow, which may explain why he wrote the Leicester LRC constitution himself. His dual role as party secretary and local MP also meant that he had to defend the actions and inactions of the national party to local voters and activists. Some activists expressed discomfort with MacDonald's close relationship with the Leicester Liberal Association and the national party's refusal to contest by-elections in 1906 and 1913, which serves as a useful reminder that the views of local activists, elected representatives and party leaders were not always in harmony.[26] Indeed, in Leicester, there was little sign that activists wanted to extend the lib–lab pact to the municipal level. After gaining a foothold on local bodies with the tacit endorsement of the Liberal Association, the Leicester LRC broke free from the alliance in 1904 and made steady progress thereafter in elections to the city council and Board of Guardians. And in another departure from MacDonald's conciliatory strategy and appeal, local activists often attacked their Liberal and Conservative opponents in strong class terms, claiming, for example, that both operated in practice as two wings of a single party of 'capitalists and employers'.[27] Like their Victorian predecessors, Labour activists in Leicester emphasised the distinctive class character of their movement even as they formed tactical alliances with broader political organisations.

The national party's impact was also felt in towns and cities where local LRCs failed to make an electoral breakthrough. By the time the national LRC was formed in 1900, Bristol's own independent and trade union-based party, the Bristol Labour Electoral Association, had almost entered its tenth year of existence. Although local activists welcomed the formation of a national party, they initially saw little need to refashion the BLEA on a new basis. It was only the poor financial position of the BLEA, which had prevented it from standing a parliamentary candidate in 1906, that convinced leading activists to work with the city's

ILP branch to form a more financially viable organisation, the Bristol Labour Representation Committee, in 1907.[28]

The Bristol LRC embraced the independent spirit of local radical and labourist traditions and continued to direct its anger at the 'conservative' Bristol Liberal Association.[29] In the January 1910 election, it challenged the Liberals in their historical stronghold of Bristol East by running Frank Sheppard, a local member of the NUBSO, against the Eton-educated aristocrat Charles Hobhouse. Sheppard finished last in a three-horse race, but, for Duncan Tanner, the party was stronger than the results suggested.[30] In any case, the wave of industrial unrest that shook Bristol and other urban centres between 1910 and 1914 reinvigorated the political and industrial sides of the local movement, and in 1914 the Bristol LRC commenced its campaign in Bristol East for the anticipated general election.[31]

The decision to run a local man in January 1910 suggests that a degree of 'parochialism', as one local ILPer called it, continued to endure in Bristol labourist and socialist circles.[32] Still, it is possible to identify nationalising tendencies at work in Bristol. The Bristol ILP branch was particularly influential in this regard. Reorganised in 1906 after its dissolution during the Boer War, the Bristol ILP quickly became the political home for those who favoured bringing the local movement in line with the national Labour Party.[33] And judging by their correspondence with party head office, ILP activists were fully aware that they were exerting a nationalising influence on local politics. As well as complaining of the parochialism of local organisations, one member asked national leaders to 'gently intervene' to help him and his colleagues disrupt the relationship between the Bristol Trades' Council and the SDF-affiliated BSS, a move that would pave the way for the reorganisation of local bodies 'in harmony with the Labour Party'.[34] After succeeding in this endeavour, which delighted both ILPers and James Middleton, the ILP established itself as the main driving force behind the Bristol LRC and tried, but failed, to find a 'national man' to stand in the January 1910 election instead of Sheppard.[35]

The impact of the Labour Party on local affairs was more subtle in towns where it failed to establish a base. In Northampton, a local LRC did not come into existence until 1914, largely because of the attitude of the Northampton Trades' Council, which had been under the control of an unholy alliance of SDF and lib–lab activists since the 1890s. Following the advice of their national leaders, SDF activists initially made no attempt to establish a broad-based organisation that would work in conformity with the Labour Party. Conversely, for lib–labs, the relatively accommodating nature of the Northampton LRA, which was far more progressive in inclination than its counterpart in Bristol, meant that there was no need to establish an independent party at a local level.

But this did not mean that they were opposed to the efforts of the Labour Party. While they showed little interest in forming a local LRC before 1910, lib–labs in Northampton often spoke approvingly of the party and its small band of MPs. For example, the 1906 annual report of the Northampton Trades' Council praised Labour MPs for their actions on the Trades' Disputes Bill and expressed pleasure that Northampton's Liberal MPs had 'voted with the Labour Party':

> The thanks of all Trade Unionists are due to the Labour Members for the way in which this and other questions appertaining to Labour politics are being forced upon the attention of the House.[36]

Over the next four years, and despite remaining under the control of the SDF/lib–lab duopoly, the trades' council continued to pass resolutions endorsing the action of Labour MPs (and criticising the actions of the Liberal government) on issues such as pensions, unemployment and national insurance.[37] And while they also passed resolutions criticising the inactions of the Labour Party, these were always worded in a way that revealed activists' sense of disappointment with *their* party rather than an outright rejection of the principles for which it stood.

Spreading the party message

The existence of a national Labour Party helped to impose a sense of interregional unity on political bodies that had operated independently of one another before 1900. The party's existence also served to influence the tone and subject matter of labourist and socialist messages. This influence was exerted in both direct and indirect ways. Its indirect influence can be seen in the evolution of monthly and quarterly trade union reports that union leaders prepared and circulated to members. Initially, the purpose of these reports was to keep union members informed of the state of their trade and the activities of both their executives and members in other parts of the country. During the 1870s and 1880s, these reports had tended to focus almost exclusively on trade matters and only briefly touched on subjects of a political nature. Changes in the content and scope of the reports during the 1890s reflected the increasing politicisation of trade unionism in the aftermath of the new unionist strike wave. By the end of the decade, the reports had come to include not only information on wage rates, branch matters and union expenditure, but also news about other union organisations in Britain and across the world. Some reports even attempted to expand the horizons of trade union members by featuring educational elements such as poetry, inspirational quotes, and extracts from both fictional and non-fictional books.

Shifts in the tone of trade union reports after 1900 reveal something more than a change in the political allegiance of a handful of union leaders. For one thing, they reveal just how quickly the Labour Party established itself as part of the political consciousness of trade union activists. The monthly reports of the NUBSO are a case in point. The NUBSO was an 'old' union that represented male and female operatives in a trade that was experiencing a surge in mechanisation and the consolidation of its operations into factories. Before 1900, and to a lesser extent throughout the Edwardian period, there was disagreement among NUBSO members as to the best method of achieving their political and industrial objectives. A sizeable portion of influential activists, including many of those in Northampton, were members of the SDF who hoped to see the union become a fighting organisation committed to obtaining direct labour representation and the eventual socialisation of the means of production. The union's ILP contingent, which was particularly strong in Leicester, shared the SDF's commitment to these two objectives but hoped to achieve them by working through the Labour Party, which the NUBSO had affiliated to in 1900. A third group, whose members generally accepted the need for a Labour Party but who believed that it should work in close partnership with the Liberals, remained influential on the union's executive body and among the rank and file.

The latter group found its principal advocate in Edward Poulton, a Northampton-based activist who became the union's general secretary in 1908 and who occupied a midway point between 'the old Lib-Labs ... and militant Socialists'.[38] As general secretary, Poulton used his influence to accelerate changes in the scope and content of the union's monthly reports. From 1908 onwards, there was a noticeable increase in items about the international boot and shoe trade, particularly news about the trade in the United States and 'the colonies', and an increase in the number of poems, songs and newspaper extracts on non-industrial topics such as foreign trade, education, consumption, the poor law, women's suffrage and the growing threat of war. Crucially, and despite Poulton's enduring sympathy for the Liberal Party, there was also an increasing prioritisation of political matter focusing on the activities of the Labour Party. Monthly reports began to include contributions from Labour MPs, reports of the activities of Labour members in Parliament, personal and official accounts of party conferences, extracts from Labour-initiated bills and party leaflets, and, more generally, items about issues that the party considered to be of primary importance. By the end of 1911, one branch secretary even complained that 'nearly all the news that is published [in the monthly reports] is all for one political party'.[39]

The not untypical case of Edward Poulton, a self-proclaimed socialist who sympathised with the Labour Party despite working in harmony with the Liberals, reminds us of the fluidity of political identities at this time. So does the sheer variety of opinions expressed by NUBSO members in the correspondence pages of the monthly report. From 1907, and with the sanction of their executive, union activists from different parts of the country began to engage in heated political debates through an organ that, prior to 1900, had simply been a tool that union leaders used to disseminate information of a strictly non-party-political character. Discussions of this kind helped to further break down the formerly rigid boundary between trade unionism and party politics, which was precisely the intention of the early leaders of the Labour Party. The apparent success with which this attitude penetrated a union that was far from united in its support for Labour demonstrates just how much indirect influence the party wielded on the trade union world.

This influence can also be seen in the annual reports of local trades' councils. Initially, trades' councils used these reports to summarise their activities over the previous year and to provide trade unionists with useful information about their union branches and elected officials. Throughout the 1890s, many of these reports evolved into quasi-educational booklets that sought to inform and educate trade unionists about the world beyond their immediate vicinities. For example, it was not uncommon for reports to include an eclectic range of quotes by historical figures, writers and philosophers, such as Aristotle, Shakespeare, Milton, Mill, Byron and Cobden, as well as contemporary writers such as William Morris, Edward Bellamy and Robert Blatchford.[40] There was also a noticeable increase in overtly political content, a trend that continued and accelerated after the formation of the LRC in 1900. From this time on, annual reports, including those written by trade unionists who were not enthusiastic supporters of the party, began to include accounts of the activities of Labour leaders both inside and outside of Parliament.[41]

Of course, Labour Party leaders could not rely on these reports alone to ensure that their messages reached trade unionists. It was partly for this reason that an official Labour paper, the *Daily Citizen*, began publication in 1912, just months after the launch of an unofficial Labour paper, the *Daily Herald*.[42] But the enduring enthusiasm for localised newspapers suggests that the process of nationalisation was far from complete by 1914. So, too, does the evolution of local and regional Labour newspapers that had been in circulation long before the *Daily*

Citizen. While many of these papers operated outside the control of the national Labour Party, it is still possible to detect the party's indirect and perhaps unintended influence on their development. One such example is the *Leicester Pioneer*, which began life as a politically eclectic and locally orientated newspaper in the 1890s but which evolved into a nationally orientated, loyal Labour mouthpiece by the eve of the First World War. Set up initially by Tom Barclay, a supporter of Charles Bradlaugh and a founding member of the Leicester Socialist League, the *Pioneer* started life as a broad-based 'progressive' journal before coming under the influence of the ILP and the Leicester Trades' Council. Intended as a primarily political outlet, the *Pioneer* sought to build a mass appeal by interlacing serialised extracts from political and historical works with jokes, inspirational quotes, sports reports, remedies for ailments, housekeeping tips, poetry and train timetables alongside songs, poems and quotes about England's radical past. The paper also included advertisements for local events and businesses, regular reports of local political meetings and extracts from speeches by local Members of Parliament. This was a diverse range of topics to fit into just four pages, but there was just enough room for a single column titled 'Here, There, and Everywhere' that featured news on national and international events.[43]

The *Pioneer* only survived because it was taken over by the Leicester Pioneer Publishing Society, a consortium of trade union branches and other political organisations that relaunched the paper in June 1901. Its new owners insisted that the *Pioneer* remain an ideologically diverse paper that would seek to encourage understanding among all local reformers, but many of its new contributors, including Ramsay MacDonald, were members or fellow travellers of the ILP. And, once again, the involvement of the ILP played a vital role in breaking down parochialism. While many of the *Pioneer*'s local segments remained, the revised paper devoted more column inches to national developments, including reports of industrial disputes in different parts of the country, reports of meetings of bodies such as the Trades Union Congress, extracts from national newspapers on topics such as the Boer War, and a regular column written by MacDonald himself. It also introduced a new 'Parliamentary Notes' section that scrutinised the activities of parliamentarians in dealing with social questions such as housing, factory conditions, compulsory vaccination and the hours of labour. This was all part of a conscious plan to remind readers that the *Pioneer* aimed to represent 'more than a local movement'. As the paper's editor explained in June 1901:

> Leicester is but a unit of a host, a link in a chain, a part of an organic social whole; and its vital throb keeps time with the pulse of humanity at large.[44]

The *Pioneer* also provided a vehicle through which activists could establish links between their own movement and older radical traditions. After its relaunch, the paper introduced a regular column written by 'an Old Rad' to teach 'young "labour" men' about their nineteenth-century ancestors, including William Cobbett, Samuel Bamford, John Ruskin, John Stuart Mill, Robert Owen, William Morris and a variety of leading Chartists.[45] Other writers placed a greater emphasis on local historical episodes and sought to highlight how the experiences of older radicals in Leicester, and, in particular, their relationship with local Liberal organisations, provided a valuable lesson to contemporary activists about the importance of independence, especially in the aftermath of Ramsay MacDonald's election victory in 1906.[46]

Comparing their own activities with those of their ancestors could also cultivate a sense of local pride. James Gribble, a 'thorough-bred Northamptonian', NUBSO member and SDF/BSP (British Socialist Party) activist, liked to tell the story of how, as a baby, he had been held in the arms of Charles Bradlaugh, who prophesied that Gribble would grow up to be a fighter for the people's cause. Gribble also invoked the memory of Bradlaugh when standing as a candidate in the January 1910 general election, during which he stated that Bradlaugh would be 'working on the side of the Socialists' if he were alive.[47] Similarly, when the ILP held its annual conference in Norwich in 1915, the local branch distributed a pamphlet that portrayed the recent success of the local Labour Party as the next chapter in a long history of 'digression' and 'outburst'. Norwich's radical tradition reached back to Boudicca, 'the British Queen who withstood the military power of Rome' and who had lived in a village just three miles south of the city. It also included men burnt in the Lollard's Pit, men and women who set sail for the New World in the seventeenth century, women's suffrage activists and Norwich's first Labour MP, George Roberts.[48]

Not everyone was interested in wallowing in nostalgia about former glories. While socialist activists were keen to emphasise the roots of the political faith, they also wanted to emphasise its novelty. As MacDonald put it in a lecture in Leicester in 1902:

> [The labour movement has been] called upon to hew a path for themselves, and must throw aside old shibboleths and watchwords of their past faith, and prove themselves worthy, not by doing the same as their fathers, but by doing something new, necessary, and better for their children, and in order to make England better than it was before.[49]

MacDonald expressed similar views at a public meeting several months later, when he told listeners that the Labour Party must separate itself from old traditions, 'just as the young shoot was parted from the old tree'. It would be futile, he argued, for them to try and pour 'new wine into old bottles'.[50] Still, just weeks after MacDonald's victory in 1906, the *Leicester Pioneer* drew a direct comparison between the radical and labour movements in the city:

> We Leicester people may well be proud that our town has had so great a share in the advent of Labour, just as in the last generation Leicester had a great share in the Radical movement when represented by Noble, Biggs, Walmsley, and P. A. Taylor.[51]

By this time, national developments in the labour world had changed the content and character of the *Pioneer*. In late 1902, there had been a growing sense in local labour circles that, in the aftermath of the Taff Vale judgment,[52] there had been a 'new awakening amongst the people for direct Labour Representation'. Consequently, by increasing the size of the paper, editors hoped to include 'more news of the trade union movement throughout the country ... in view of the important move towards direct Labour representation'.[53] This trend was accelerated in October 1903 when the ILP, the Leicester Trades' Council and the newly formed Leicester LRC relaunched the paper as 'the official organ of the Labour party in Leicester'.[54] In contrast to the ecumenical tone of the early *Pioneer*, writers now published stories from a narrow party perspective, attempting, above all, to rally support for the party's activities at a national and local level. It also became an effective campaigning tool for Ramsay MacDonald, the Labour candidate (and, from 1906, MP) for Leicester, and often devoted whole-page spreads to his speeches during election contests.

The most obvious sign that the *Pioneer* had become a nationally focused party organ was the marked increase in stories and opinion articles about Labour's activities in other parts of the country. By late 1905, the paper had introduced sections titled 'Nottingham Notes', 'Loughborough Notes', 'Notes from the Capital' and 'From Labour's Standpoint' (written by Philip Snowden), and had begun to publish weekly articles by an anonymous Labour MP.[55] Though it still featured reports on local sport and crime, the *Pioneer* was quickly becoming an effective filter through which official party messages that originated from party leaders in London could be passed down to activists and potential Labour voters at a local level. The *Leicester Pioneer*, in the words of the secretary of the Leicester LRC, had come to represent 'the interests of the *national* Labour movement'.[56]

Election time

Liberal and Conservative activists had long been able to mobilise voters around key national figures. Election campaign materials and songs often praised the personality of a candidate and made references to questions of a local nature, but they also tended to emphasise a candidate's views on the government, the opposition, rival parties, their own party, and issues of a national and international nature.[57] During the 1868 and 1874 campaigns, for example, candidates in the five towns that form the basis of this book used their election addresses to affirm their commitment to broad principles and state their support for or opposition to national-level proposals. The foreign policy of Benjamin Disraeli's administration was an important topic of debate during the 1880 general election, and opposition to 'imperialism' was the first item in the election addresses of Liberal candidates. The House of Lords and the disestablishment of the state church were key issues at 1885 election, Irish Home Rule dominated discussions in 1886, and the Local Veto, Home Rule, reform of the House of Lords and the limitation of the hours of labour animated the campaigns in 1892 and 1895.[58]

This suggests that the process of nationalisation was well underway by the 1880s. But while this may be true of mainstream Liberal and Conservative politics, it does not fully explain the tone of unofficial forms of politics during this period. Working-class radicals, labourists and socialists were more likely than their opponents to introduce personal and local matters into election contests. As noted in previous chapters, candidates who did not receive the endorsement of a major party often drew attention to the wealth or tyrannical employment practices of rival candidates, the political moderation of their opponents or the refusal of the local Liberal Association to accommodate the demands of local labour parties. At the 1886 general election, for example, the Bristol Labour League put forward a candidate against Lewis Fry, the MP for Bristol North, who had 'violated the trust reposed in him' by opposing Irish Home Rule. While some activists saw the campaign as a chance to strengthen Gladstone's hand in Parliament, others stressed the importance of local factors in the contest. For the League's organising secretary, it was a perfect opportunity to challenge the power of 'upper-class men' in the Bristol Liberal Association, an organisation that wished to put forward its own candidate and which had failed to live up to its 'fine promises'.[59] For another supporter, it was a chance to send a 'local working man' to Parliament rather than Fry, a lawyer, or the Liberal candidate, a 'London surgeon'.[60]

The formation of a national Labour Party went some towards nationalising the focus of local activists. Localist sentiments and class-based attacks on rival candidates remained commonplace during election contests, but, from 1900 onwards, these became part of a broader strategy that attempted to situate local concerns, rivalries and organisations within a national context. Labour candidates played a key role in contributing to this development. The 1906 election address of George Roberts, for example, included a list of proposals that had long featured in socialist programmes, including secular education, collective ownership and control of 'the means of life', and a set of political reforms that would lead to the 'democratisation of our Government'. But unlike labour and socialist election addresses from the Victorian period, Roberts could now begin his address by declaring his allegiance to a national Labour Party that, in his view, was 'one of the most hopeful factors in modern politics'.[61] In an article on unemployment printed just weeks before the election, Roberts again drew attention to the actions of the national party, this time for its 'insistent agitation' on the unemployment question and for 'disposing of the fallacious idea' that it was 'merely seasonal'. Though he admitted that the problem had long existed, Roberts expressed his pleasure that the question was finally 'forcing itself into people's minds' and that, due to the growth of the new Labour Party and the acceptance of newer social and economic theories, 'the disinherited' had begun to 'cease meekly acquiescing in the merciless conditions which manacle and scourge them'.[62]

Ramsay MacDonald's address to the electors of Leicester in 1906, which placed primary emphasis on the causes of temperance, free trade, anti-vaccination and Chinese slavery, was undoubtedly part of his plan to strengthen his supposedly unofficial ties with the Leicester Liberal Association. But this was not typical of Labour addresses at the time, and it drew condemnation from some sections of the local Labour movement. On the eve of the election, one member of the Leicester Trades' Council challenged MacDonald's perspective by arguing that 'they must leave out the fiscal and all other questions in face of the serious position of trade unionism to-day'.[63] This is not an isolated example. A Labour song written especially for the contest highlighted MacDonald's plans for the unemployed and depicted him as the 'poor man's friend', while local activists distributed centrally produced posters, including the famous 'Labour at the Gate' poster, which emphasised the Labour party's unique social character and focus. Even the *Leicester Pioneer*, which subscribed to MacDonald's idea of establishing progressive unity, still liked to point out how Labour differed from the Liberals. One article from December 1905 explained that there were 'two chief aspects' of the political

Labour movement that set it apart from the Liberal Party: its insistence on political independence and its aim to secure the return of men to Parliament who 'approach national problems with the experience of the wage-earners behind them and the interests of the wage-earners in their hearts'.[64]

For the *Leicester Pioneer*, the existence of a strong parliamentary Labour group was necessary to 'raise the temperature' in the House of Commons and 'stiffen the backs and guide the hazy vision' of progressive Liberals. Similar references to the efforts of Labour MPs in Parliament were made by candidates who, while sympathetic to the party, did not stand under its auspices. Dan Irving, the SDF candidate for Accrington, admitted that some Labour MPs were among 'the most sterling Socialists he had ever known'.[65] Supporters of Harry Quelch, the SDF candidate for Southampton, informed voters that he would go to Parliament to support work of Labour MPs despite not being endorsed by the LRC, and even described him as the 'Labour Party' candidate in newspaper advertisements.[66] In Northampton, the SDF distributed leaflets that included complimentary quotations about one of their candidates from 'Prominent Men in the Labour Movement' such as Keir Hardie and Pete Curran, both of whom were key figures in the Labour Party. In fact, despite the fact that it was not affiliated with the Labour Party, the secretary of the Northampton SDF asked Labour head office whether his branch could use the party's famous 'Labour at the Gate' poster during its campaign.[67]

There was a palatable sense of euphoria among Labour supporters in the weeks that followed the declaration of results in 1906, and Labour head office was inundated with requests for more information about the party. Local activists were particularly optimistic about not only the benefits that Labour MPs could bring to their respective towns and cities but also the influence that they could wield at the national level. For example, though Liberal candidates were the major winners in Bristol, the leader of the Bristol Miners' Association thanked 'the advanced Labour minds of the country' for pressuring the new Liberal government into adopting 'the most advanced [programme] that had ever been presented to the nation'.[68] The *Leicester Pioneer* expressed similar sentiments and hoped that the presence of Labour MPs in the Commons would serve to 'arouse' and 'infuse fresh vigour' into the national trade union movement. Still, while the 'indirect influence' of Labour MPs on legislation could not 'fail to be immense', the *Pioneer* reminded trade unionists that they must now 'range themselves behind their representatives and loyally uphold their actions'.[69]

Labour candidates and their supporters also conducted their campaigns in a manner that highlighted the class-based orientation of their party and its ideological divergence from the Liberals. They did so by emphasising the importance of questions that, in their view, were of special interest to trade unionists and working-class voters, such as unemployment, poverty and the Osborne judgment.[70] Perhaps unsurprisingly, references to the ideological distinctiveness of the Labour Party were made more frequently in contests where Labour candidates were pitted against Liberals. This was the case in Bristol East during January 1910, when Frank Sheppard, following the example set by the pioneers of radical and labour politics in the city, adopted an antagonistic posture towards his 'very conservative' Liberal opponent, Charles Hobhouse.[71] For Sheppard, the questions of unemployment and the introduction of machinery 'were far more important ... than the question as to whether they should mend or end the House of Lords'.[72] They were also more important than the Irish question, a topic that Sheppard, like other Labour candidates, barely mentioned during his campaign.[73]

Unlike in previous attempts to win the seat, Sheppard and his supporters could now use the activities of Labour MPs to hold their opponents to account. Class, as ever, was a crucial part of this strategy. The *Bristol Labour Herald*, an election news-sheet published during the contest, frequently drew attention to the social differences between the shoemaker Sheppard and the Eton-educated Hobhouse, 'the gentleman; the land squire; the man of education, the product of ages of public school influence'.[74] But labourists also analysed their opponent's 'bad record' as an MP by judging the extent to which he supported proposals brought forward by Labour MPs.[75] While it may not have had 'old traditions' or 'great names to conjure with', the Labour Party, as one activist put it, 'had begun to create new traditions'.[76]

Conclusion

Mapping the organisational trajectory of labour politics from its origins in the working-class radical traditions of the 1870s through to the eve of the First World War sheds light on important aspects of the nationalisation phenomena. In the aftermath of the 1867 Reform Act, locally initiated radical organisations sprang up across England to challenge the moderation and undemocratic nature of Liberal politics. In the 1870s and 1880s, many Liberal leaders agreed to reorganise their organisations on the 'Birmingham model', which involved the establishment of broad-based, inclusive and nominally democratic Liberal Associations.[77] At the same time, radicals who sought to maintain their independence or semi-independence from organised liberalism helped to establish socialist societies and labour parties, some of which were part of larger national organisations but all of which were still shaped by their local environments. During the Edwardian period, though, many of these individuals became affiliated to a national Labour Party through their membership of national-level trade unions or national-level socialist societies. As John Bruce Glasier explained in 1912, Labour 'was not a federation of branches; it was a federation of national organisations'.[78]

This was a novel development. By facilitating the growth of an 'official' Labour politics that privileged the universal principle of labour representation, Labour helped to challenge localised conceptions of politics that had long privileged more personal factors, such as a candidate's character and their links to a particular constituency. The activities of Labour MPs on the national stage offered local activists a crucial example to follow, and party head office helped to bring previously detached political forces closer together by offering advice, formulating coherent messages, and presenting itself as a national-level co-ordinating centre for local activists and sympathisers. These developments encouraged the standardisation of labourist discourse, an evolution which can be traced by studying minute books, election posters, pamphlets, and other party and trade union literature.

Political parties had been producing their own literature long before 1900. What made Labour's literature so important was that it offered a consistent message to trade unionists and socialists who, before 1900, had engaged in the political process as part of autonomous local parties, loose political networks, one of the two major parties or one of a myriad of national but numerically weak socialist parties. The process through which these disparate forces evolved into a single, national movement was by no means simple or free of personal, political or ideological conflict. Nor was this process complete by the First World War. But when we compare labourist and socialist discourse in 1914 with that of twenty years earlier, it is evident that a marked shift had taken place. Above all, this shift is noticeable in the way Labour activists, as well as lib–labs and non-affiliated socialists, used the example set by Labour MPs to justify their local activities and demonstrate the value of electing working men to Parliament.

The evolution of local newspapers and trade union reports in particular demonstrates how Labour exerted a nationalising influence on British politics. While it is not clear whether the minimisation of localist sentiment was part of a premeditated plan or an unintentional side effect of building a national organisation, there is plenty of evidence to suggest that local activists expected guidance from head office about the party's message, especially during election contests. This may have been because party leaders, guided by the decision of party conferences, refused to adopt a comprehensive party programme before 1918. Still, the lack of a programme did not stop party leaders from authorising the publication of centrally produced pamphlets, leaflets, handbills, posters and other literature that served to reveal the political and ideological orientation of key party thinkers. And judging by their letters to head office, MPs and local activists found these materials to be extremely useful in ensuring that they presented the 'correct' messages to local voters both during and between election campaigns.[79]

Notes

1 Labour History Archive and Study Centre, Manchester (hereafter LHA), LP/LRC/1/285, general correspondence to and from LRC head office (hereafter LRC GC), printed draft of statement regarding Labour Representation and the Elections, November 1900.
2 Caramani, *The Nationalization of Politics*, p. 1.
3 For an overview of the debate, see Blaxill, 'Elections', pp. 400–416.
4 H. Hanham, *Elections and Party Management: Politics in the Time of Disraeli and Gladstone* (London, 1959).
5 K. Rix, *Parties, Agents and Electoral Culture in England, 1880–1910* (Woodbridge, 2016).
6 Pugh, *Making of Modern British Politics*, pp. 1; 22; 295.
7 J. Cornford, 'The transformation of conservatism in the late nineteenth century', *Victorian Studies*, 7:1 (1963), pp. 37; 65–66; Clarke, Lancashire and the New Liberalism, p. 406; Pelling, *Popular Politics and Society*, p. 120.
8 For example, see G. W. Cox, 'The development of a party-orientated electorate in England, 1832–1918', *British Journal of Political Science*, 16:2 (1986), pp. 187–216; F. O'Gorman, *Voters, Patrons and Parties: The Unreformed Electoral System of Hanoverian England 1734–1832* (Oxford, 1989); J. A. Phillips and C. Wetherell, 'The Great Reform Bill of 1832 and the rise of partisanship', *Journal of Modern History*, 63:4 (1991), pp. 621–646; F. O'Gorman, 'Campaign rituals and ceremonies: The social meaning of elections in England, 1780–1860', *Past and Present*, 135 (1992), pp. 79–115.
9 J. Lawrence and M. Taylor, 'British historians and political sociology', *Politix*, 81 (2008), p. 33.
10 Tanner, *Political Change and the Labour Party*, p. 442. See also D. Tanner, 'Class voting and radical politics: The Liberal and Labour parties, 1910–31', in J. Lawrence and M. Taylor (eds), *Party, State and Society: Electoral Behaviour in Britain since 1820* (Aldershot, 1997), p. 106.
11 Worley, *Labour inside the Gate*, p. 2. For an example, see M. Roberts, '"Villa Toryism" and popular conservatism in Leeds, 1885–1902', *Historical Journal*, 49 (2006).
12 R. McKibbin, *The Evolution of the Labour Party 1910–1924* (Oxford, 1983), p. 22; LSE, JN1129.L3, LP CR, 1914.

Labour and the nationalisation of politics   149

13 LHA, LP/LRC/2/190, LRC GC, Leicester Trades' Council, 1 May 1901; LHA, LP/GC/2/132–7, general correspondence to and from Labour Party (post-1906) head office (hereafter LP GC), drafts of model rules for trade unions, undated.
14 LHA, LP/LRC/1/237i, LRC GC, leaflet regarding return of candidates; draft of resolution regarding socialist consolidation, 1900; LHA, LP/LRC/13/367, LRC GC, correspondence regarding 1904 Norwich by-election, February 1904.
15 LHA, LP/LRC/1/269, LRC GC, amended draft report of committee appointed to consider what organisation the LRC could promote, signed Edward Pease and Ramsay MacDonald, 1900.
16 LHA, LP/GC/4/95–7, LP GC, correspondence with Coventry LRC, May 1906.
17 LSE, ILP/4/1899/98, ILP C, R. Smart to J. Penny (Norwich). Report on Norwich, 20 September 1899; MRC, MSS.524/4/1/6, TC AR, Norwich, 1901; 1902.
18 Cherry, *Doing Different?*, p. 67.
19 Cherry, *Doing Different?*, pp. 63–77.
20 Cherry, *Doing Different?*, p. 83.
21 A. Howkins, *Poor Labouring Men: Rural Radicalism in Norfolk 1870–1923* (London, 1985), pp. xii; 60.
22 Howkins, *Poor Labouring Men*, pp. 105–106, 111–112; Readman also notes how leading ILPers kept the issue of land nationalisation to the fore during the Edwardian period. Readman, *Land and Nation in England*, pp. 20–21, 190–191.
23 D. Cox, 'The Labour Party in Leicester: A study in branch development', *International Review of Social History*, 6:2 (1961), p. 203; Lancaster, *Radicalism, Cooperation and Socialism*, pp. 126, 155, 173.
24 LHA, LP/MAC/08/1/3, J. R. MacDonald office correspondence, Sir J. Rolleston MP and G. E. Hubbard (Leicester LRC), March–April 1905.
25 *Leicester Pioneer*, 6 January 1906.
26 *Leicester Pioneer*, 6 January 1906; 13 January 1906; 20 January 1906; LHA, LP/GC/3/184–5, LP GC, Leicester LRC, 20 April 1906; 25 April 1906; LHA, LRC/31/183, LRC GC, T. Furborough, Leicester, 11 January 1906.
27 Lancaster, *Radicalism, Cooperation and Socialism*, pp. 168–169.
28 LHA, LP/LRC/7/108, LRC GC, Bristol Trades' Council to J. R. Macdonald, 19 February 1903; LSE, 37/28, material collected by Arthur Ebenezer Cooke, 1886–1936, notes on formation of LRC in Bristol.
29 Tanner, *Political Change and the Labour Party*, p. 291. For similar case studies see G. L. Bernstein, 'Liberalism and the progressive alliance in the constituencies, 1900–1914: Three Case Studies', *The Historical Journal*, 26:3 (1983), p. 618.
30 Tanner, *Political Change and the Labour Party*, pp. 298–299.
31 Labour representation on the city council grew from four in 1910 to eight in 1913. *Western Daily Press*, 2 May 1914.

32 LHA, LP/GC/8/88, LP GC, Cooke to Middleton, 29 September 1906.
33 Howell, *British Workers and the ILP*, p. 386; LSE, FILM 86, Independent Labour Party – Bristol branch. Minute books for the period 11th December 1906 to 13th November 1918 (hereafter BILP M), 11 December 1906.
34 LHA, LP/GC/13/141, LP GC, Cooke to Macdonald, 23 March 1907.
35 LHA, LP/GC/18/56, LP GC, Cooke to Middleton, 28 August 1907; LHA, LP/GC/21/66, LP GC, reply to F. Freeman, 28 November 1907; LSE, FILM 86, BILPM, 29 November 1907; LSE, ILP/5/1912/8, monthly report of the Bristol ILP General Secretary, Walter H. Ayles, 4 November 1912.
36 Northamptonshire Record Office, Northampton (hereafter NHRO), 1977/44/NTC1, Northampton Trades' Council Annual Reports (hereafter NTC AR), 1906.
37 NHRO, 1977/44/NTC1, Northampton Trades' Council minute book (hereafter NTC M), 19 June 1907; 6 March 1908; 15 April 1908; NHRO, 1977/44/NTC2, NTC M, 20 July 1910; 19 October 1910; 25 July 1911.
38 Fox, *A History of the NUBSO*, p. 327.
39 MRC, 547/P/1/27, NUBSO MR, December 1911.
40 See MRC, MSS.524/4/1/13, TC AR, Lincoln, 1893; 1894; 1896.
41 See MRC, MSS.524/4/1/24, TC AR, Ipswich, 1900; 1901; MRC, MSS.524/4/1/26; TC AR, Bath, 1903.
42 L. Beers, *Your Britain: Media and the Making of the Labour Party* (London, 2010), pp. 24–26.
43 Lancaster, *Radicalism, Cooperation and Socialism*, pp. 113, 172; *Leicester Pioneer*, 19 January 1895; 2 February 1895.
44 *Leicester Pioneer*, 22 June 1901.
45 *Leicester Pioneer*, 21 September 1901; 28 September 1901.
46 *Leicester Pioneer*, 20 January 1906.
47 *Northampton Independent*, 5 January 1910.
48 LSE, ILP/5/1915/76, ILP pamphlets and leaflets, report of the Norwich Conference, April 1915.
49 *Leicester Pioneer*, 27 December 1902.
50 *Leicester Pioneer*, 30 May 1903.
51 *Leicester Pioneer*, 27 January 1906.
52 In the aftermath of a railway strike in South Wales, the House of Lords decided, in July 1901, that the Taff Vale Railway Company could sue the Amalgamated Society of Railway Servants in a corporate capacity for damages caused by the action of its officers. The union thus had to pay £23,000 to the affected company to cover damages and costs.
53 *Leicester Pioneer*, 27 September 1902.
54 *Leicester Pioneer*, 17 October 1903.
55 *Leicester Pioneer*, 11 November 1905.
56 *Leicester Pioneer*, 9 December 1905: emphasis added.
57 For examples, see LRO, 10D64/1, Leicester Liberal Songsheet, 1880; NCL, 198–781/9/1880, NEE, 'War Song', 'The Death of the Tories', 1880.

58 For examples, see *Norwich Mercury*, 27 September 1884; NCL, 198–781/9/1886, NEE, 'To the Electors' (Hasting Lees and Richard Turner), 1886; *Lincolnshire Chronicle*, 21 June 1892; 12 July 1895. Paul Readman has argued that the land question was also an important political issue between the early 1880s and the First World War. Readman, *Land and Nation in England*, pp. 23–39.
59 *Bristol Mercury*, 12 June 1886.
60 *Bristol Mercury*, 22 June 1886. Marshall eventually withdrew from the contest, supposedly due to financial difficulties.
61 LSE, ILP/6/20/17/2, ILP parliamentary election addresses (hereafter ILP PEA), 'Norwich Parliamentary Election, 1906. To the Electors' (G. H. Roberts), 1906.
62 LSE, ILP/6/20/17/2, ILP PEA, 'Reprint of Article on Unemployment contributed by G. H. Roberts, Labour Candidate for Norwich', 1906.
63 *Leicester Pioneer*, 6 January 1906.
64 *Leicester Pioneer*, 23 December 1905; 6 January 1906.
65 *Northern Daily Telegraph* 29 January 1906.
66 *Southern Echo*, 9 January 1906; 10 January 1906; 12 January 1906.
67 LHA, LP/LRC/29/344, LRC GC, Northampton SDF, January 1906.
68 *Bristol Weekly Mercury*, 10 March 1906.
69 *Leicester Pioneer*, 27 January 1906.
70 The Osborne judgment of 1909 ruled that trade union expenditure for political purposes was beyond the unions' lawful authority.
71 Tanner, *Political Change and the Labour Party*, pp. 291, 299.
72 *Western Daily Press*, 7 January 1910.
73 E. O'Connor, 'British Labour, Belfast and Home Rule, 1900–14', in L. Marley (ed.), *The British Labour Party and Twentieth-Century Ireland: The Cause of Ireland, the Cause of Labour* (Manchester, 2016), p. 56, 61. While Daniel Jackson has recently challenged the idea that Edwardian Britain met the Irish question with indifference, he suggested that opposition to Home Rule was 'most virulent' in larger northern cities. D. Jackson, *Popular Opposition to Irish Home Rule in Edwardian Britain* (Liverpool, 2009), pp. 27–28.
74 *Bristol Labour Herald*, 4 January 1910.
75 *Bristol Labour Herald*, 13 January 1910.
76 *Crewe Guardian*, 12 January 1910.
77 Liberal Associations on the Birmingham model were formed all over the country, including in Bristol, Leicester, Lincoln, Northampton and Norwich. Pugh, *Making of Modern British Politics*, pp. 30–31.
78 LSE, JN1129.L3, LP CR, 1912; Pelling, *Popular Politics and Society*, p. 108.
79 For more on early Labour literature and visual imagery, see Beers, *Your Britain*, pp. 28–32.

6

Labourism, class and populism

The refusal of the Labour Party to recognise the class war disappointed those who believed society was divided into two irreconcilable classes.[1] If this refusal represented a true reflection of Labour opinion rather than a strategic attempt to maintain unity between diverse political and trade union forces, then one may be inclined to conclude that populist understandings of the social order were more prevalent than class-based perspectives in the early party. This argument has been put forward by an eclectic range of scholars who have drawn attention to the 'radical liberal' roots of the Labour Party and the enduring influence of cross-class perspectives on the party's early rhetoric and appeal. For Patrick Joyce, popular politics, including labour politics, was primarily concerned with 'the people' rather than the working class between 1840 and 1914. Joyce suggests that 'populism' is a more appropriate description than 'class' because it connotes inclusiveness, extra-economic categorisation, reconciliation and fellowship, all of which were prevalent themes in popular political discourse during this period.[2]

Contrary to the claims of some of his critics, Joyce did not proclaim the absence of class. Rather, he sought to bring to light alternative identities that were 'every bit as lusty as' or 'stronger' than class.[3] But while the search for non-class identities in modern Britain remains an important scholarly exercise, the argument for populism has downplayed the significance of workerist sentiments in early Labour discourse. At a local level, party activists and sympathisers articulated a conception of the social order that owed a great deal to older, exclusivist notions of class. This was certainly the case in the towns and cities covered in this book, where activists retained a strong sense of loyalty to the discursive frameworks that they inherited from the working-class radical movement. In public debates and in their election literature, labourists expressed pride in their working-class background and claimed that they sought primarily to represent their class in the corridors of power. When they discussed the merits of the Labour Party, they often drew attention to its class composition, the social background of its MPs and its proposals for dealing with problems faced by the workers. While inclusive concepts such as 'the people' and 'the nation' did appear in labourist discourse, activists tended to imbue these concepts with less inclusive meanings by using them in conjunction with, and sometimes as alternative descriptions for, 'the workers'.

At the same time, labourists rejected accusations that they subscribed to the theory of the class struggle. Though they adopted a class-centred approach to politics, they only did so as a way of making nominally democratic institutions more representative of society as a whole. Far from seeking to subvert what they considered to be the core principles of the English constitution, they advocated political reform and increased labour representation as a way of affording each section of the community its fair share of political representation. Similarly, in the industrial sphere, labourists favoured negotiation and arbitration over strike action, even during the 'Great Labour Unrest' of 1910–1914.[4] The spirit of 'defence not defiance', which had animated trade union discourse in the nineteenth century, remained alive and well in the early Labour Party.

The class-centred yet non-adversarial tone of labourist discourse confirms Joyce's argument that popular attitudes at this time were more 'ambiguous' and 'elusive' than scholars had previously thought.[5] But it does not fit into Joyce's rather narrow definition of class, which, as well as connoting inclusiveness, extra-economic categorisation and reconciliation, must also connote conflict. Refusing to apply the term 'class' to this view of social relations because it lacks one element of this rather narrow definition places an unnecessary boundary on a concept that, in the words of Neville Kirk, deserves to be 'open-ended, flexible, and pluralistic'.[6] Furthermore, to describe labourist discourse as populist would simply be misleading, at least in the towns covered in this book. Labourists did not emphasise 'social justice' and 'human fellowship' over and above more restrictive notions of social relations. By building on Joyce's suspicion that he was describing a form of 'class consciousness' in which 'class identity (but not class opposition) was strong' – a view that he disregarded because it 'had very little to do with class *as we would understand it*' – this chapter attempts to show how labourists rejected the inevitability of class struggle while embracing a notion of class in which a profound sense of separateness and social exclusion were both crucial elements.[7]

This was a period in which material and political changes threatened to loosen the boundaries of existing identities. Between 1900 and 1914, there was a marked growth in the number of women employed in certain sectors and a doubling of female trade union membership.[8] These developments, and the tireless work of both famous and little-known female activists, forced male trade unionists to pay more attention to 'the woman question'. The activities of women's suffrage campaigners had a similar impact, encouraging male labourists to confront and justify their preconceptions about women's role in society. But even as male labourists expressed sympathy with women workers, they still tended to marginalise them in both overt and subtle ways. Like their nineteenth-century counterparts, trade union leaders accused women of causing problems for 'the men' by increasing the chances of unemployment or by contributing to low wage rates across a particular industry. At political and trade union meetings, in their speeches during election campaigns, and in party and union literature, they continued to promote a gendered conception of work that served to reinforce stereotypes about women's place in society. And though they were more likely than their predecessors to direct appeals to women workers, they still couched them in terms that emphasised the otherness of women and that downplayed the shared interests between men and women workers.

The typical labourist of the Edwardian period was a male trade union official. In general, he was a white British resident of an urban town or city, a churchgoer and someone who was either employed or had previously been employed in a manual occupation. These were the building blocks of the labourist identity, and it was common for labourists to express pride in their nationality, their 'manliness', their commitment to hard work, their contribution to the prosperity of Britain and its empire, and, on occasion, their membership of the international white working class.[9] For labourists, the experience of political and social exclusion helped to nurture an inverted sense of class pride rather than a 'defeatist and fatalistic' mentality.[10] Their restrictive conception of the working class also served to reinforce boundaries between those who belonged to this group and those who did not. While there was a discernible shift in the way they spoke about agricultural labourers, urban-based labourists approached the land question from an urban-centric point of view, viewing their rural brethren as worthy of support but also a threat to the hard-won rights of better-organised and better-paid urban workers. And despite playing a key role in campaigns for the 'right to work', labourists continued to draw a sharp distinction between the 'deserving' unemployed who wanted to find work and the 'unemployables' who, presumably, did not.[11] As Jon Lawrence has argued, while Labour Party activists took a greater interest in the question of poverty during the Edwardian period, they often spoke for the poor and disadvantaged 'in the name of social justice, rather than class interest'.[12] Long-held assumptions about gender, place, work, nationality and race were hard to shake off even in the face of political and economic change.

'What its name implied'

Class-based terminology was an ever-present feature of labourist discourse in the years before the First World War. The language of class that was used by Labour MPs, councillors, candidates and activists included many of the elements that had featured in working-class radical discourse during the mid- to late Victorian period. For example, in their election speeches and literature, candidates continued to direct their appeals to the 'workers', 'working men' and 'wage earners' and urged members of these groups to abandon their old party-political ties and vote Labour 'in their own interests'. George Roberts expressed these sentiments during his by-election campaign in Norwich in 1904:

> [Labour] appealed to them, not as Liberals, or as Tories, but as working men with common interests – men whose needs and aspirations were identical, and he asked them to recognise that their interests lay with the working class party, and not be allowed to be led away by the catch-cries of Liberals and Tories.[13]

Appeals to class interest sometimes took on a more demanding tone. During the 1906 contest in Leicester, a leading member of the local trades' council and supporter of the lib–lab ticket of Ramsay MacDonald and Henry Broadhurst informed a group of trade unionists that:

> Those who did not support Messrs MacDonald and Broadhurst would be traitors to their trade union principles.[14]

As this quote suggests, labourists tended to reject universalist conceptions of political representation in favour of more exclusivist understandings, which led them to advocate the direct representation of the labour interest by 'bona fide' workers or, as was more often the case, by trade unionists. Essentially, this was because they thought that only working men and trade unionists could truly understand the needs of their class. For Charles Freak, the general president of the NUBSO:

> The feelings of the workers can never be properly understood by those who have never been at the bench. They are liable to make mistakes through ignorance as well as class interest … the workers must have men of their own kidney to represent them.[15]

Similarly, as another leading trade unionist from Leicester told a May Day rally in 1912:

> It was no use sending Duke this, and His Grace that, or Sir Tom, Dick, and Harry, to Parliament. They would not help them. They must flood the House with some good Trade Unionists.[16]

The argument that middle-class and upper-class politicians 'would not help' the workers did not necessarily stem from a feeling of antipathy towards these classes. Often, it derived from the assumption that it was simply not possible for members of other classes to understand the needs of the workers, not having experienced life from their perspective. As a Labour councillor told the *Leicester Pioneer* in 1902:

> I recognise among both parties some who are sympathetic and considerate of the workers' welfare; but in many cases their very social position prevents them from appreciating to the full the necessities of the workers.[17]

Trade unionists had a distinct advantage over other candidates because they had first-hand experience of working-class life, an experience that they were both proud of and happy to draw attention to in their speeches and literature.[18]

It was also common for labourists to emphasise the class composition and orientation of their organisations. The founders of the Northampton LRC, for example, hoped that the organisation would be of value to 'the whole of the workers' once it had weaned them from 'allegiance to the Radical and Tory Parties'.[19] This echoed the strategy of LRC activists in other places such as Bristol, where the Liberal Party retained the support of the bulk of working-class voters. LRC activists tried to drive a wedge between the Liberals and their working-class supporters by claiming that the Bristol LRC was in a 'better position to know, and to represent, the needs of the wage-earners' because it was composed of 'bona fide worker[s]'.[20] Keir Hardie had made similar remarks at a 'mass meeting' in Bristol several years earlier when he told 'the working men and women of Bristol' that:

> The Labour Party was what its name implied, the party with but one object – to be of service to the class to which they all belonged.[21]

As we shall see, not all Labour MPs agreed with this somewhat limited view of Labour's objectives. But Hardie's assertion that Labour wanted to be of service to one class was a common refrain among Labour activists, many of whom promised to prioritise the concerns of 'their class' if elected to political office. This they would do by approaching political and social questions from the workers' point of view. As a 1905 article in the *Leicester Pioneer* put it, one of 'chief aspects' of the Labour Party was that it aimed to secure the return to Parliament of men who 'approach[ed] national problems with the experience of the wage-earners behind them and the interests of the wage-earners in their hearts'.[22]

This privileging of the working class was one of the most distinguishing features of the Labour movement. This was certainly the case in Bristol, where the Labour Electoral Association, the forerunner of the LRC, only adopted 'wage workers unconnected with political parties' as candidates.[23] Exclusivist sentiments of this kind also played a role in Labour's campaign in Bristol East in January 1910. The *Bristol Labour Herald*, an election news-sheet published especially for the contest, attempted to convince working-class voters that Labour, in terms of its composition and focus, was a fundamentally unique political party.[24] It did so by pointing out the divergent backgrounds of Frank Sheppard, the Labour candidate and former shoemaker, and Charles Hobhouse, the Liberal candidate whom the *Herald* described as 'the gentleman; the land squire; the man of education, the product of ages of public school influence'.[25] Articles in the *Herald* sometimes appealed to voters on the basis of religion, but these were exceptions to the rule. As the penultimate edition of the paper exclaimed, 'Workers! [This Is] Your Battle!'[26]

Class-based appeals were not the preserve of labourists. Socialist activists, particularly those who were active trade unionists, were also comfortable introducing class into political discussions. The Northampton branch of the SDF/BSP, which was far more trade union-orientated than the party's national leaders, often placed as much emphasis on the class background of its candidates as it did on their political views.[27] The ILP branches in Lincoln, Leicester and Norwich were overwhelmingly working-class in composition and orientation, as were the two main socialist organisations in Bristol.[28] And like their labourist colleagues, socialist election candidates often avowed themselves as trade unionists and appealed to working-class voters' sense of social exclusion during their campaign speeches.[29] As an ILP municipal election candidate from Bristol explained in 1910:

> As a Labour party they did not venerate persons, but their cause, and they would find him on the workers' side in all cases. The workers' side was the right side always.[30]

Populism and the class war

Leading figures in the Labour Party were conscious of the need to find the most appropriate vocabulary to win over their chosen audience. On an annotated draft of a centrally produced leaflet discussing the Chinese slavery issue, for example, one reviewer crossed out the words 'free labourers' and suggested 'workmen' as an alternative, because 'the British workman uses the term "free labourer" as meaning blackleg'.[31] There is also plenty of evidence to suggest that Labour candidates and local-level activists tailored their verbal and non-verbal language according to context and audience. If a Labour candidate had the backing, or at least the acquiescence, of a Liberal Association, as Ramsay MacDonald and George Roberts had in Leicester and Norwich respectively, then it was more likely that the candidate would downplay the social and political differences between Labour and the Liberals. This helps to explain why Roberts placed such a strong emphasis on the class composition of the Labour Party in the 1904 by-election, in which he stood against a Liberal and a Conservative, while highlighting Labour's intention to promote the 'general well-being of *the people*' in the 1906 election when he stood as part of a 'one plus one', lib–lab arrangement.[32]

Ramsay MacDonald was far more astute at playing this game than Roberts. Indeed, if one were to compare a random selection of MacDonald's speeches and writings from this period without knowing their author, it would be hard to believe that they been written by the same individual. When MacDonald campaigned in Leicester before he came to an agreement with the Leicester Liberal Association, he delivered speeches and wrote articles for the *Leicester Pioneer* that underlined the class character of the Labour Party. For instance, at a meeting in May 1903 he told voters that he and the Labour Party wanted to elect only men drawn from 'the bench, the factory, and the mine, and [who] had a knowledge of Labour and Labour demands'.[33] He was also adept at blending class terminology with populist notions of the 'idle' and the 'industrious', including at a candidate selection meeting in 1902 when he described 'the Dukes, Lords, and Idle Ladies and gentlemen' as 'parasites', while also drawing attention to the moral divide between 'trade unionists' and 'landlords and capitalists'.[34]

But in the weeks leading up to the 1906 election, by which time MacDonald and the Leicester Liberals had established an informal progressive alliance, MacDonald was vocal in his condemnation of anyone who claimed that Labour was a one-class party. As he explained in an article in the *Leicester Pioneer*, Labour was a party 'striving for the common well-being' and guided by the principle that 'justice must be absolute and universal, and not partial and modified by class considerations'. He pursued this populist line of argument when addressing both trade union and non-trade union audiences. At a meeting organised by the Leicester Trades' Council, for example, he insisted that Labour sought 'fair play for the servant, and fair play for the master', while at a meeting at which the president of the Leicester Liberal Association was on the platform he admitted that he had always appealed for a 'catholic interpretation of the word Labour', believing that the party should 'open the doors wide' so that 'all intellectual democrats might come in, work inside, and help the people of England'.[35]

This last statement foreshadowed organisational changes in the Labour Party during the First World War. But in 1906, MacDonald's views on this question were out of step with those held by party activists, many of whom were far more relaxed about the idea that Labour was a class party. MacDonald appeared to be aware of this fact, which may explain why he adapted his communication style depending on his audience. There was very little populism in a speech that he delivered in support of Roberts' candidature in Norwich in 1904, during which MacDonald told voters that 'he came there that night to appeal to them, the working men of Norwich, to tell them that this organisation [the LRC] was their organisation'.[36] Similarly, while he conducted an unambiguously populist campaign in Leicester in January 1910, he used a language of class when speaking on behalf of the Labour candidate for Ince in Lancashire. Addressing voters on the eve of the poll, MacDonald said that the only university that he and his colleagues had attended was the:

> University [of] the fields, the mines, the factories, the workshops, and the benches – (hear, hear) – and [they] went into the House of Commons accomplished in nothing except in experience in life – (hear, hear) – and in that respect [they] were richer probably than anybody else in the House of Commons.[37]

The apparent ease with which Labour politicians could shift between different political languages has led some scholars, including Patrick Joyce, to suggest that Labour discourse was more populist than class-based. It is certainly true that Labour politicians used terms such as 'the people', 'the idle' and others that were more inclusive than, say, 'the workers'. But very often they used populist and class-based terms interchangeably and imbued terms such as 'the people' with exclusivist meanings. It is possible to find examples of this in centrally produced literature, including in the Labour Party's manifesto for the 1906 general election. 'The House of Commons', it begins, 'is supposed to be the people's House, and yet *the people* are not there'.[38] Presumably, for the author, 'the people' did not include 'landlords, employers, lawyers, brewers, and financiers', as they had already entered the Commons 'in force'. Instead, we are left to deduce that 'the people' were those who the author discussed in the remainder of the manifesto, such as 'Labour', 'the aged poor', 'the Trade Unions', 'shopkeepers and traders', 'underfed schoolchildren' and 'the unemployed'.[39]

The inclusion of shopkeepers and traders in this list is curious, as these groups rarely featured in labourist appeals in the towns and cities covered in this book. This is particularly true if we shift the focus away from politicians such as MacDonald and towards municipal election candidates, locally based journalists and ordinary party activists who were responsible for transmitting party messages to voters at the local level. When we do this, we find that these local-level political actors often used populist terms such as 'the people' as alternative descriptions to more exclusive terms such as 'the workers'. For example, while one of the chief writers for the *Leicester Pioneer* claimed that the paper was 'owned, worked, and controlled by *the People* in the interests of *all classes alike*', its editions were filled with workerist sentiments of which the following is typical example:

> At the head of this new journal is a stalwart workman, full seven feet high, with an axe raised in the air, fully bent on the business of making a new thoroughfare to a better future.[40]

After the paper became the official organ of the Leicester LRC, writers became less apologetic about the classist tone of their articles, and on the eve of the 1906 general election the paper's editor admitted that it was now run 'solely in the interests of the workers'.[41]

For those who subscribed to the labourist view of class relations, there was no contradiction between organising on a class basis and rejecting the notion of a class war. This non-adversarial view of class relations survived the intense and often-violent industrial unrest that engulfed many parts of Britain between 1910 and 1914. The strike wave encouraged a minority of trade unionists to embrace a more oppositional notion of class relations, which some, including workers in Liverpool and the South Wales coalfields, expressed in revolutionary terms.[42] By 1914, for example, the president of the Bristol Trades' Council had begun to speak of 'the class war' and 'the exploiters' and had come to believe that 'the fight between Capital and Labour was becoming more determined and more bitter'.[43] But there is little evidence to suggest that these views reflected those of the majority of trade unionists in Bristol or elsewhere.[44]

They certainly did not represent the views of the leaders of the Bristol LRC, the ILP or, to a lesser extent, the BSS, many of whom denied that they favoured a 'class war' or 'anything which put class against class'.[45] William Whitefield of the Bristol Miners' Association even wrote a letter to the *Western Daily Press* to challenge the views of the president of the Bristol Trades' Council and to reassure readers that they were not 'a true reflex of the desires and feelings of the Bristol workers of the L. R. C.'.[46]

This is not to say that labourists adopted a deferential posture when speaking about or to employers. They could be just as insistent in their demands as their more militant counterparts, particularly when they felt that the rights of the workers were under threat. It is not difficult to find examples of labourists and moderate socialists reiterating their commitment to constitutional action in an assertive and, at times, threatening tone. Consider, for example, the following statement made by Daniel Stanton, a long-time lib–lab in Northampton who predicted an upheaval in the boot and shoe trade in 1913:

> Although we do not want to force a fight any more than we did in 1887 or 1895 ... we shall be there, ready to meet them, if the necessity arises, and the fight will not be a one-sided one.[47]

This defensive posture and the Labour Party's official rejection of class-war politics irritated socialists who wanted Labour to become a fully fledged socialist party that recognised the class war. Election campaigns conducted by these militant socialists, many of whom were members of the SDF/BSP, served to highlight the tonal differences between moderate and more combative versions of socialism during this period. During the January 1910 general election, for example, the two socialist candidates for Northampton distributed a leaflet in which they promised to fight the battle of 'the working class against capitalism and landlordism', arguing that 'the real antagonism' in society was between:

> The two great classes into which modern society is divided: the 'Haves' and the 'Have Nots,' the propertied class and the proletariat; the workers and the shirkers.[48]

While members of the ILP often exhibited hostility to the SDF, some of them embraced similar notions of the class war. Before he became Labour MP for Norwich in 1906, for example, George Roberts had frequently articulated an antagonistic view of class relations, urging trade unionists in 1901 to stop 'crying peace when war is being openly waged against us'.[49] Still, Roberts and other ILPers were more inclined to subscribe to evolutionary forms of socialism, and, as MacDonald pointed out at the 1907 ILP conference, they rarely made '"the Social Revolution" a hackneyed shibboleth on [their] platforms'.[50] Indeed, MacDonald spoke for many at the 1909 ILP conference when he discussed how socialism was to come about:

> Is it to be a sudden change? A sudden change owing to force, or a sudden change owing to legislative action? To me, the first is quite unthinkable. We can cut off kings' heads after a few battles; we can change a Monarchy into a Republic; we can deprive people of their titles, and we can make similar superficial alterations, by force; but nobody who understands the power of habit and of custom in human conduct ... [and] the delicate and intricate complexity of production and exchange which keeps modern Society going, will dream for a single moment of changing it by any act of violence.[51]

Labour women, Labour men

Labourists, like all political actors, often departed from the definitional meaning of words and phrases. At times, they were explicit about who was and who was not a member of 'the working class'. More often, though, they left the task of definition to their listeners and readers. This may have been because labourists, feeling that the term was prevalent in ordinary political discourse, believed that audiences would understand who they were referring to. It may also have been why they rarely elaborated on their definition of social groups such as 'the people', 'our people', 'the democracy' and so on. But while they could stretch or contract the meaning of such words, there were limits to the elasticity of language. By using terms such as 'our people', labourists were making it clear that there were important differences between 'us' and 'them', whoever 'us' and 'them' might be. Despite their prevalence in the workforce, women were very rarely including in labourist conceptions of 'us'. This period witnessed a growth in the number of women employed in certain sectors, including in the textile trade, the boot and shoe industry in Northampton, and the food processing industry in Bristol, as well as a doubling of female trade union membership between 1906 and 1914.[52] These changes in the composition of the workforce, as well as the tireless work of women activists such as Miriam Daniell and Helena Born in Bristol, Rose Scott in Northampton and Mary Bell in Leicester, encouraged male trade unionists to pay more attention to 'the woman question'.[53] By the turn of the century, women had begun to play an important role in progressive political movements, and in some places had won election to local school boards and Boards of Guardians. They formed women's sections of local ILP branches, regularly attended and spoke at labour, socialist and anarchist meetings, and contributed to local labour papers. And, of course, they were active in women's suffrage campaigns, particularly from 1908 onwards.[54]

But male trade unionists and political activists continued to marginalise women. For example, trade union leaders continued to couch their appeals in terms that drew attention to the 'otherness' of women workers. Authors addressed their trade union and trades' council annual reports to 'fellow workmen' and the 'Trade Unionist and Labour Man' despite the fact that many of these organisations now represented male and female workers.[55] Similarly, though women had been able to vote in municipal elections since 1869, labourists and socialists directed their electoral appeals to the working men.[56] And on the rare occasion that they did make specific appeals to women, they appealed to them as wives and mothers rather than on the same basis as men. For example, an SDF leaflet for a municipal election contest in Northampton in 1904 notified male voters that their place was on the 'political barricades', from where they could 'carry the Red Flag of Socialist freedom'. The 'Women of Northampton', on the other hand, were asked to consider how capitalism had plunged them into 'untold domestic miseries' that had served to 'un-sex' them. Rather than telling women voters that they, too, could take up a position on the political barricades, the leaflet simply demanded that they use their 'gentle influences to nerve and stimulate' their husbands in '*their* fight' against '*your* bitter class enemies'.[57]

With a few notable exceptions, and despite passing resolutions of moral support, male labourists generally showed little enthusiasm for women's suffrage campaigns.[58] Something that did pique their interest was the question of the limited franchise bill which would have enfranchised women on the same basis as men. This proposal, which also drew condemnation from women's suffrage campaigners such as Margaret Bondfield, Mary Macarthur and Sylvia Pankhurst, worried many male activists who feared that it would increase the power of the propertied classes.[59] As one delegate to the 1905 ILP conference explained, the ILP, as 'a workingman's party' that recognised 'the great principle of human equality', could not in any logical sense support a proposal that would only enfranchise 'the well-to-do'. Statements of this kind did not go unchallenged. After reminding the speaker that the ILP was not just a 'working *man's* party', Teresa Billington argued that the bill was a 'practical, achievable step' towards the complete attainment of 'political equality before the law'.[60]

Billington's comments demonstrate that socialist women were far from passive in their dealings with their male counterparts. The same can also be said of women trade unionists. The National Federation of Women Workers, which, as Sarah Boston has shown, 'organised more women, fought more strikes and did more to establish women trade unionists than any other organisation' between 1906 and 1920, helped to improve conditions for its members and to inspire legislation that fixed minimum wages for women working in the 'sweated' trades.[61] There was also a general increase in female membership of mixed unions such as the NUBSO, which had strong branches in all the towns covered in this book. From 1906 onwards, women began to join the union in greater numbers after union leaders ran a dedicated recruitment campaign, and a small but vocal core of women activists began to form in Leicester, among other places. One of the key activists in Leicester was Lizzie Willson, a heel builder who, despite receiving little attention in official accounts of the union's history, was arguably the most influential female member of the NUBSO before the First World War. After becoming the first woman elected to the union's executive council in 1910, Willson travelled widely to encourage women to join the union, which they did in unprecedented numbers. But Willson's association with the NUBSO came to an abrupt end in September 1911 when she and other members of the Leicester women's branch, including the suffragette Alice Hawkins, left to form the Independent National Union of Boot and Shoe Women Workers after union leaders charged them with a variety of misdemeanours, including, among other things, violating agreements between the union and employers and making malicious charges against members of the union's executive. The secessionists rejected these accusations and claimed that the 'men's union' had simply not done enough to help women in their struggle for fair wages and fair treatment.

The task of rebuilding the decimated Leicester women's branch fell to Mary Bell, a long-time member of the union who embraced the militant spirit of the immediate pre-war era and helped to ferment discontent among shoe operatives across the country. The wave of trade union militancy between 1910 and 1914 led to some important gains for women in the industry, including wage advances and minimum wage agreements in certain areas. But many of the problems that women in the industry faced did not disappear overnight. Their wages remained relatively low, especially when compared with those of their male counterparts, and they still had to struggle against the deeply entrenched attitudes and practices of their male colleagues. For instance, male trade unionists and workers continued to believe that certain departments of the trade were off bounds for women, an assumption that Mary Bell did not, at this point, wish to challenge.

Who were 'the workers'?

What did labourists and socialists think about their rural counterparts? For one thing, there was a strong sense of nostalgia about England's pre-industrial past, particularly in towns and cities where workers retained some form of connection to surrounding rural districts.[62] Some of the leading trade union and socialist activists in these areas, from Ernest Bevin (Bristol) and Frank Sheppard (Bristol) to Daniel Stanton (Northampton) and George Roberts (Norwich), had been born in rural towns and villages and, in some cases, had worked as agricultural labourers in their formative years. For many socialists, agrarianism was central to their political project. In their view, the overthrow of capitalism would enable urban workers to rebuild rural England and reconnect with the cultural traditions of their ancestors.[63] Land nationalisation in particular would restore to the people their inheritance in the soil, something that had been taken away from them with the rise of modern capitalism and the end of a medieval 'Golden Age' during which a relatively collectivist social organisation had sustained a 'race of masterless men'.[64]

Sympathy with the rural poor surfaced during the 'rural rebellion' of the immediate pre-war years, when the NALRWU and farm workers' sections in the Workers' Union organised strikes across Lancashire, Somerset, Cheshire, Kent, Worcestershire, Northamptonshire and Norfolk.[65] Urban trade unionists welcomed these developments and provided both moral and financial support to the labourers' efforts. In his study of rural radicalism in Norfolk, Alun Howkins argues that this was a sign that farm labourers, who had once been by known for their 'localism' and distrust of national organisations, were being gradually integrated into the broader labour movement. There was certainly a shift in the way urban labourists and socialists spoke about their rural counterparts. Whereas trade unionists in the Victorian period had pointed to the distinctions between urban and rural workers, their successors were more willing to incorporate rural labourers into 'the working class'.

Norwich serves as a good example of this attitudinal shift. The agricultural unions of the late nineteenth century had little contact with unions based in Norwich, whose members feared that migration from the surrounding countryside would reduce their wages. During a strike of labourers in St Faith's, Norfolk, in June 1910, however, Norwich-based unionists praised 'those brave men, *their fellow workers*, [who] were fighting for the rights of freedom and justice'.[66] Such a shift in attitude was partly the result of the efforts of the Norwich ILP and its leading light, George Roberts. For Howkins, Roberts' election victory in 1906 'gave the Norfolk Labour movement, indeed the whole of the East Anglian movement, the sure and certain belief that they could win'.[67] By pressing the claims of labourers in the House of Commons and serving as chairman of the Labour Land Enquiry in 1912–1914, Roberts played a crucial role in strengthening the bonds between urban- and rural-based trade unionists[68] – so much so, in fact, that by the time of the strike in St Faith's in 1910, Norwich trade unionists were not only happy to support the strike through meetings and collections but were also comfortable in treating those involved in the strike as bona fide members of the working class.

A similar shift seemed to occur in Northampton, where the trades' council assisted in the organisation of farm workers across Northamptonshire.[69] But this shift was by no means complete by 1914. Urban trade unionists still believed that the depopulation of agricultural districts, and the consequent migration of rural labourers into towns and cities, posed a danger to their own rights and interests. Expressions of concern about the deleterious effects of rural-to-urban migration was particularly strong in Bristol, where, by 1911, over a third of inhabitants had been born outside the city. These concerns were so serious for Bristol-based activists that they formed a central part of Frank Sheppard's parliamentary campaign in January 1910. Sheppard promoted life in the countryside as a way of building up a 'sturdy manhood', a pastoral view that, as Mark Freeman has shown, was common in the 'popular nostalgic country literature' of the time.[70] But in one of his election leaflets, Sheppard also blamed 'the continued stream of our people from the country districts' for the 'congestion in our big cities'. As a solution to the problem, the Bristol LRC advocated the nationalisation of the land and proposed a 'vigorous' policy of 'back to the land', which foreshadowed the demands put forward by the national Labour Party in 1913.[71]

For Sheppard, the depopulation of agricultural districts was one of the causes of unemployment, an issue that Labour MPs and activists tried to push to the top of the political agenda. Between 1906 and 1910, Labour candidates gave unemployment a leading place in their manifestos, while many of those who became Labour MPs, including Ramsay MacDonald and George Roberts, were 'very zealous' in their efforts to pass a 'Right to Work' bill through Parliament.[72] Agitation (and unemployed violence) peaked in 1907–1908, when official figures suggested that 5.8 per cent of all trade unionists in Britain were out of work.[73] But this was only an approximate guide, and trade unionists often claimed that the situation was far worse than official figures suggested.

And yet, again, it is possible to identify continuities in the way labourists spoke about the unemployed. In particular, they continued to draw a sharp distinction between the 'deserving' or 'bona fide' unemployed who had temporarily lost their job through no fault of their own, and the 'loafers', 'unemployables' and men who would rather 'shirk' than work.[74] As G. E. Hubbard of the Leicester Trades' Council argued in December 1905, the unemployed could be divided into three classes: the 'seasonal unemployed, the permanently unemployed, and the unemployable'. For Hubbard, work could be found for the seasonal unemployed by reducing the hours of labour and abolishing overtime, while the creation of farm colonies would provide work for the permanently unemployed. But for the third and 'worst class to deal with', Hubbard believed that 'some compulsion would have to be applied' to ensure that they could become 'decent citizens'.[75]

Although the 'right to work' appeared regularly in Labour manifestos, Kenneth Brown believes that most trade unionists saw the cry as 'a sort of shibboleth, a declaration of faith rather than a genuine legislative proposal'.[76] The same could be said of their attitude to poverty. Activists tended to speak for the poor and disadvantaged 'in the name of social justice, rather than class interest', taking on the role of a sympathetic but detached observer who had been roused to take action on behalf of the poverty-stricken out of a sense of moral indignation rather than common experience.[77] This encouraged men and women to serve on local Boards of Guardians, but it also led many of them to adopt a way of speaking that only served to highlight their disconnect from those 'on the next rung ... below them'.[78] Condescending attitudes to the poor can be found in the pages of the *Leicester Pioneer*, which often adopted a moralistic tone when discussing the topic. In an article published in September 1902, for example, an anonymous writer asked why the poor of Leicester did not leave their 'fetid dens' and move to other parts of the city where they could find 'better places to let at little, if any, more rent'. Rather than asking a representative of 'the poor' to answer the question, the writer offered his own views and claimed that the poor stayed in their 'warrens' because their surroundings had produced such a 'deadening and degrading influence upon them that that they have no desire to change'. Still, there was hope for those who had been 'dragged up in filth and indecency', but only if labourists and other progressives worked to 'improve them'.[79]

While labourist conceptions of 'the working class' did not always include those at the margins of society, it did often include non-manual employees such as clerks, teachers, government employees and Post Office workers. Still, as in the case of rural labourers, early Labour leaders and activists often drew attention to the distinctiveness of non-manual workers and 'their status as somehow slightly apart from other workers'.[80] 'White-collar' workers were conscious of their ambiguous position in society and their distinctiveness from other workers. At the 1912 Labour party conference, for example, H. H. Elvin of the National Union of Clerks admitted that many of those in attendance would be surprised to hear 'a clerk advocating the right to strike' because 'it had always been considered that clerks were of the jellyfish order'.[81] Nevertheless, assumptions of this kind did not stop clerks from organising on an industrial basis and attempting to convince other trade unionists that they, too, were poorly paid and had to deal with poor working conditions.[82]

There was similar ambiguity in the way labourists and socialists dealt with race and nationality. As in the late Victorian period, they consistently reaffirmed their solidarity with the international working-class movement, especially during annual May Day rallies. Socialists also presented themselves as anti-militarists, particularly during times of mounting international tensions, and some even tried to downplay the importance of national boundaries altogether. Such views were not typical of labourists at this time, however, and behind gestures of international solidarity often lay assumptions about the cultural and technical superiority of the white working man. As we saw in Chapter 3, labourists had long articulated a form of patriotism grounded in the pragmatism of the English worker and the democratic nature of his nation's constitution. As they believed that they could achieve their objectives through existing institutions, labourists continued to reject proposals put forward by anarchists, revolutionary socialists and others inspired by the actions of their less patient European counterparts. At the same time, the labourist language of patriotism was far from inclusive, especially when compared with that of their liberal counterparts, who often referred to Britain's *national* character, rather than the character of its working-class population, in their speeches, election addresses and publications.[83] As George Roberts reminded listeners during the January 1910 election contest, it was no coincidence that 'John Bull was generally represented in caricature as the embodiment of the British nation – the working classes really comprising the British nation'.[84]

Labourists' views on nationality and race surfaced during debates about the Boer War, 'Chinese slavery', 'alien' immigration, the 1911 seamen's strike and the looming threat of an international war. When discussing these topics, activists often tried to untangle the notions of patriotism, nationalism, jingoism and imperialism. For some, including several writers for the *Leicester Pioneer*, patriotism was not the preserve of 'self-styled imperialists' and those caught up in the 'frenzy of Jingoism' but a noble sentiment that could animate the politics of those who wanted the British Empire to evolve into a looser network based on the principles of justice, mercy, toleration and self-government.[85] Others were keen to promote a civic form of patriotism rooted in the culture, geography and history of England without invoking notions of empire or militarism. While a 'sense of Imperialism refused to inflate' the writer of the *Leicester Pioneer*'s 'Woman's Column', she knew in her 'heart of hearts' that she loved her 'dear old England'.[86]

These discussions revealed that labourists and socialists had absorbed basic imperialistic assumptions about, among others, 'Asiatics', 'the white man', Jewish immigrants and 'Jewish financiers'.[87] Not surprisingly, sentiments of this kind were more common among labourists in areas such as Bristol where workers were more likely to come into contact with workers from other countries. In 1911, for example, Charles Jarman of the Bristol branch of the National Sailors' and Firemen's Union expressed his belief that international trade unionism was necessary to prevent ship-owners from 'putting the seamen of one country against the seamen of another' but, in the same year, also criticised ship-owners for having 'flooded the vessels with Chinamen' (or 'Ching-Changs', as he referred to them).[88] As Sascha Auerbach has shown, this depiction of Chinese labourers was common among trade unionists at the time, many of whom portrayed Chinese men as 'immoral, feminized, mutinous, sexually deviant and mercenary'.[89] It was also a deeply rooted attitude that, while surfacing in response to certain external stimuli such as a foreign war or fears about 'alien' immigration, had formed the core of the labourist identity since at least the mid- to late Victorian period.

Conclusion

The Labour Party was, from the outset, a party of urban trade unionists. Many of its MPs and activists felt a strong sense of pride in their craft or trade, especially those who worked (or had worked) in craft industries such as shipbuilding, shoemaking, engineering and typesetting. At the same time, they made a conscious effort to impose unity on these groups by using terms and phrases that served to minimise any distinctions between them. Terms like 'the working class', 'the workers', 'working men' and 'labour' were especially popular, as they suggested a commonality of interests between those (men) who worked. Furthermore, during this period, labourists became more amenable to seeing rural labourers and non-manual workers as fellow members of the working class.

These changes foreshadowed later developments when previously marginalised groups came to play a more central role in organised Labour politics, particularly after the First World War. But in the years before the war, terms such as 'working class' also continued to function as terms of exclusion by constructing invisible dividing lines between those who worked and those who did not.[90] And despite increased agitation on behalf of the unemployed, the poor and other groups that had traditionally been excluded from this conception of the working class, the labourist identity remained largely intact throughout the pre-war period. In particular, labourists continued to marginalise women by suggesting that they increased the chances of unemployment and contributed to a general decline in wages, and by using gendered language when discussing work, trade unionism and politics.

To demonstrate discursive continuities with older working-class radical traditions, this chapter has examined the way in which Labour activists articulated their understanding of the working class in the years leading up to the First World War. It has also drawn attention to the resilience of the working-class radical understanding of class relations. Labourists believed that the working class had unique grievances that could only be resolved if they organised on a class basis. At the same time, and like their Victorian predecessors, they strongly rejected accusations that they sought to encourage a class war. The prevalence of this non-adversarial sense of class partly explains the enduring popularity of the phrase 'defence not defiance' within trade union circles, as well as the frequency with which labourists blamed industrial conflicts on the actions of 'unjust' employers rather than on the industrial system itself. By making their organisations strong and engaging in constructive dialogue with employers and their organisations, labourists believed, workers could achieve many of their economic objectives without any 'unkindly action', 'unpleasantness', 'strife' or 'class war'.[91]

To some extent, this view corresponds with what Peter Clarke has described as 'the social democratic theory of the class struggle', whose advocates accepted the class dimension of democracy and worked within class parties while denying the necessity of class conflict. But while Clarke associated this view with early Fabians and the 'new liberals', it was also prevalent, in a far more exclusivist form, among labourists and their working-class radical predecessors.[92] Their commitment to this 'separate but equal' doctrine explains why they claimed to support the right of all classes to a fair share of political representation, as well as the right of employers to protect their interests in a legal manner, while privileging the claims of the working class in the political and industrial arenas. Theirs was a cry of indignation against the unbalanced nature of the social and political order, an imbalance that could only be rectified by increasing the number of working-class representatives on local and national governing bodies and establishing what one Leicester-based activist called a 'fair field' of industrial relations in which judges would no longer favour the claims of employers over trade unionists.[93] Despite the emphasis on conciliation rather than conflict, this was not a populist vision of the social order. Labourism remained a tradition in which class identity (but not class opposition) was strong.

Notes

1. A. Thorpe, *A History of the British Labour Party* (London, 1997), p. 13.
2. Joyce, *Visions of the People*, pp. 5, 56, 335. See also Vernon, *Politics and the People*, pp. 297, 310, 326.
3. Joyce, *Visions of the People*, pp. 1, 334–335; See also P. Joyce, 'The imaginary discontents of social history: A note of response to Mayfield and Thorne, and Lawrence and Taylor', *Social History* 18:1 (1993), pp. 81–85.
4. This challenges the view offered by scholars who see the pre-war industrial unrest as marking a turning-point in class relations. For example, see S. Todd, *The People: The Rise and Fall of the Working Class, 1910–2010* (London, 2014), pp. 13–14, 28.
5. Joyce, *Visions of the People*, p. 93.
6. N. Kirk, 'Decline and fall, resilience and regeneration: A review essay on social class', *International Labor and Working-Class History*, 57 (2000), p. 94.
7. Joyce, *Visions of the People*, p. 11; emphasis added.
8. Boston, *Women Workers and the Trade Union Movement*, p. 71.
9. J. Hyslop, 'The imperial working class makes itself "white": White labourism in Britain, Australia, and South Africa before the First World War', *Journal of Historical Sociology*, 12:4 (1999), pp. 398–421.
10. McKibbin, *Classes and Cultures*, p. 131; Belchem, *Popular Radicalism in Nineteenth-Century Britain*, p. 72.
11. P. Thane, 'Labour and welfare', in D. Tanner, P. Thane and N. Tiratsoo (eds), *Labour's First Century* (Cambridge, 2000), pp. 80–88.
12. Lawrence, *Speaking for the People*, p. 147.
13. *Norwich Mercury*, 9 January 1904.
14. *Leicester Pioneer*, 6 January 1906.
15. *Leicester Pioneer*, 18 October 1902.
16. *Leicester Pioneer*, 17 May 1902.
17. *Leicester Pioneer*, 27 September 1902.
18. For examples, see LSE, ILP/6/21/4, ILP municipal election addresses (hereafter ILP MEA), Belgrave Ward (Leicester), T. Adnitt, 1912; Newton Ward (Leicester), A. H. Reynolds, 1912.

19 NHRO, 1977/44/NTC3, NTC AR, 1914; NHRO, 1977/44/NTC3, NTC M, 7 January 1914; 22 April 1914.
20 *Western Daily Press*, 18 February 1913.
21 *Bristol Weekly Mercury*, 24 March 1906.
22 *Leicester Pioneer*, 23 December 1905.
23 LHA, LP/LRC/11/78, LRC GC, Bristol LEA (J. A. Cunnington, Sec) asks if LRC will support their municipal work, 10 October 1902.
24 *Bristol Labour Herald*, 2 April 1910.
25 BRO, 11171, papers of Alderman Frank Sheppard, Frank Sheppard's election card, January 1910; *Bristol Labour Herald*, 4 January 1910.
26 *Bristol Labour Herald*, 4 January 1910.
27 NCL, 198–781/1906, NEE, 'To the electors of Northampton' (J. Gribble and J. E. Williams), 1906.
28 Cherry, *Doing Different?*, p. 94.
29 LSE, ILP/6/21/1/11, ILP MEA, John James Milton (Bristol), 1912; LSE, ILP/6/21/1/13, ILP MEA, F. F. Clothier (Bristol), 1913.
30 *Western Daily Press*, 15 October 1910.
31 LHA, LP/LRC/13/256ii, papers regarding LRC Leaflet No. 11 'Slavery in the Transvaal', including manuscript draft and copies, some with manuscript notes by committee members, undated.
32 LSE, ILP/6/20/17/2, ILP PEA, 'Norwich Parliamentary Election, 1906. To The Electors' (G. H. Roberts), 1906; emphasis added.
33 *Leicester Pioneer*, 30 May 1903.
34 *Leicester Pioneer*, 26 April 1902.
35 *Leicester Pioneer*, 11 November 1905; 13 January 1906; 20 January 1906.
36 LHA, LP/LRC/13/165, LRC GC, correspondence with Councillor S. Flint (Leicester) with extract from *Eastern Daily Press* (12 January 1904), February 1904.
37 *Wigan Observer and District Advertiser*, 22 January 1910.
38 I. Dale (ed.), *Labour Party General Election Manifestos, 1900–1997* (London, 2000), pp. 10–11; emphasis added.
39 Dale, *Labour Party General Election Manifestos*, pp. 10–11.
40 *Leicester Pioneer*, 15 June 1901; 29 June 1901: emphasis added.
41 *Leicester Pioneer*, 2 December 1905.
42 B. Holton, *British Syndicalism 1900–1914: Myths and Realities* (London, 1976), pp. 80, 90; K. Morgan, 'The new liberalism and the challenge of labour: The Welsh experience, 1885–1929', in K. Brown (ed.), *Essays in Anti-Labour History: Responses to the Rise of Labour in Britain* (London, 1974), p. 171.
43 *Western Daily Press*, 6 February 1914.
44 M. Richardson, 'Bristol and the labour unrest of 1910–14', in D. Backwith, R. Ball, S. E. Hunt and M. Richardson (eds), *Strikers, Hobblers, Conchies and Reds: A Radical History of Bristol 1880–1939* (Newton Abbott, 2014), p. 237; Kirk, *Change, Continuity and Class*, p. 169.
45 LSE, 37/1, material collected by Arthur Ebenezer Cooke, 1886–1936, notes on experiences in Bristol, 20 March 1912; *Western Daily Press*, 3 November

1910; A. Bullock, *The Life and Times of Ernest Bevin, Volume One: Trade Union Leader, 1881–1940* (London, 1960), p. 15.
46 Letter 'W. Whitefield' to *Western Daily Press*, 2 March 1914.
47 MRC, 547/P/1/29, NUBSO MR, February 1913.
48 NCL, 198–781/1910, NEE, 'To the Electors' (J. Gribble and H. Quelch), 1910.
49 MRC, MSS.524/4/1/24, TC AR, Ipswich, 1901.
50 LSE, ILP/12/1/1, ILP annual conference reports (hereafter ILP CR), 1907.
51 LSE, ILP/12/1/1, ILP CR, 1909.
52 The number of women in trade unions rose from 166,803 in 1906 to 357,956 in 1914. Boston, *Women Workers and the Trade Union Movement*, p. 71; For Bristol, see. J. Lynch, *A Tale of Three Cities: Comparative Studies in Working-Class Life* (London, 1998), pp. 11–12, 33, 139.
53 For women's activism in Bristol, see E. Malos, 'Bristol women in action, 1839–1919', in I. Bild (ed.), Bristol's Other History (Bristol, 1983), pp. 97–128; M. Dresser (ed.), *Women and the City: Bristol 1373–2000* (Bristol, 2016); A. Tuckett, *Our Enid: The Life and Work of Enid Stacy, 1868–1903* (Salford, 2016); S. Rowbotham, *Rebel Crossings: New Women, Free Lovers, and Radicals in Britain and the United States* (London, 2016).
54 Bristol became the centre of Annie Kenney's highly successful attempts to build the Women's Social and Political Union in the West of England from 1908 onwards. Malos, 'Bristol Women in Action', p. 123.
55 BRO, 32080/TC1/4/13, BTC AR, 1906.
56 B. Griffin, *The Politics of Gender in Victorian Britain: Masculinity, Political Culture and the Struggle for Women's Rights* (Cambridge, 2012), p. 13.
57 NCL, 198–781/10/1904, NEE, 'Socialist Call to Arms!', 1904; emphasis added.
58 'The relationship between Labour and female suffrage was fraught with ambiguity and conflict'. M. Francis, 'Labour and gender', in D. Tanner, P. Thane and N. Tiratsoo (eds), *Labour's First Century* (Cambridge, 2000), p. 201. See also Charlotte Despard's address to the 1910 ILP conference: LSE, ILP/12/1/2, ILP CR, 1910.
59 LSE, JN1129.L3, LP CR, 1906.
60 LSE, ILP/12/1/1, ILP CR, 1905.
61 Boston, *Women Workers and the Trade Union Movement*, pp. 60–70.
62 Griffiths, *Labour and the Countryside*, pp. 25–50; Readman, *Land and Nation in England*, p. 191.
63 Howkins, *Poor Labouring Men*, pp. 106–107.
64 Readman, *Land and Nation in England*, pp. 12; 184–185.
65 R. Groves, *Sharpen the Sickle! The History of the Farm Workers' Union* (London, 1981), pp. 136–151.
66 *Norfolk News*, 18 June 1910: emphasis added.
67 Howkins, *Poor Labouring Men*, p. 105.
68 Readman, *Land and Nation in England*, pp. 191–192.
69 NHRO, 1977/44/NTC2, NTC M, 11 February 1912; NHRO, 1977/44/NTC3, NTC M, 2 November 1913; 19 November 1913; 30 November 1913; 17 December 1913.

70 M. Freeman, *Social Investigation and Rural England, 1870–1914* (Woodbridge, 2003), p. 171.
71 BRO, 11171, papers of Alderman Frank Sheppard, election handbill, January 1910; M. Tichelar, 'Socialists, Labour and the land: The response of the Labour Party to the land campaign of Lloyd George before the First World War', *Twentieth Century British History*, 8:2 (1997), p. 129. For similar sentiments, see LHA, LP/GC/1/172, LP GC, Jabez Chaplin (LAHU) correspondence, 21 February 1906.
72 *Leicester Pioneer*, 13 January 1906. The election song 'Ballad for the Leicester Electors' described MacDonald as the 'poor man's friend' for his views on unemployment.
73 K. Brown, 'The Labour Party and the unemployment question, 1906–1910', *The Historical Journal*, 14:3 (1971), pp. 599–616.
74 For example, see MRC, 547/P/1/20, NUBSO CR, 1904; LSE, ILP/6/20/17/2, ILP PEA, 'Reprint of Article on Unemployment contributed by G. H. Roberts, Labour Candidate for Norwich', 1906.
75 *Leicester Pioneer*, 2 December 1905.
76 Brown, 'The Labour Party and the unemployment question', p. 615. For a discussion of the Labour Party's attitude to the unemployed and pauperism, see Thane, 'Labour and welfare', pp. 80–88.
77 Lawrence, *Speaking for the People*, p. 147.
78 Letter 'Nomad' to *Leicester Pioneer*, 11 October 1902.
79 *Leicester Pioneer*, 28 December 1901; 27 September 1902.
80 Lawrence, *Speaking for the People*, pp. 144–146; J. Lawrence, 'Labour and the politics of class, 1900–1940', in D. Feldman and J. Lawrence (eds), *Structures and Transformations in Modern British History* (Cambridge, 2011), p. 254.
81 LSE, JN1129.L3, LP CR, 1912.
82 LSE, JN1129.L3, LP CR, 1911.
83 P. Readman, 'The Liberal Party and patriotism in early twentieth century Britain', *Twentieth Century British History*, 12:3 (2001), pp. 274–277.
84 *Eastern Evening News*, 4 January 1910.
85 *Leicester Pioneer*, 6 July 1901; 28 June 1902. A correspondent challenged this view: *Leicester Pioneer*, 5 July 1902.
86 *Leicester Pioneer*, 9 August 1902.
87 For example, see *Northampton Mercury*, 8 April 1904; LSE, ILP/12/1/1, ILP CR, 1905; 1907. See also P. Kaarsholm, 'Pro-Boers', in R. Samuel (ed.), *Patriotism: The Making and Unmaking of British National Identity, Volume I: History and Politics* (London, 1989), p. 120.
88 *Western Daily Press*, 11 April 1911; 15 June 1911; 19 June 1911; J. P. May, 'The Chinese in Britain, 1860–1914', in C. Holmes (ed.), *Immigrants and Minorities in British Society* (London, 1978), pp. 115–116; K. Lunn, 'Immigrants and strikes: Some British case studies 1870–1914', in K. Lunn (ed.), *Race and Labour in Twentieth-Century Britain* (London, 1985), p. 37;

L. Tabili, *'We Ask for British Justice'*: *Workers and Racial Difference in Late Imperial Britain* (London, 1994), p. 47.
89 S. Auerbach, *Race, Law, and 'The Chinese Puzzle' in Imperial Britain* (Basingstoke, 2009); pp. 3, 18, 32, 37.
90 'To be a worker was to be a member of a community, of a family, of a nation, as well as of a trade'. Joyce, *Visions of the People*, p. 93.
91 MRC, 547/P/1/21, NUBSO MR, October 1905; *Western Daily Press*, 12 May 1908.
92 Clarke, 'The social democratic theory of the class struggle', pp. 3–18.
93 *Leicester Pioneer*, 17 May 1902. For other examples, see letter 'Working Man' to *Western Daily Press*, 29 September 1903; NHRO, 1977/44/NTC2, NTC AR, 1912.

7

Labourism and the challenge of war

Since the 1980s, formerly dominant interpretations of British political, cultural and social history have been challenged by scholars who have drawn attention to the resilience of populism and the survival of non-class identities in early twentieth-century Britain. While these studies have provided a valuable corrective to stagist accounts of Britain's political development, they have not seriously challenged the view that the First World War and the political, industrial and intellectual changes which it brought about were crucial in explaining the realignment of party politics in the post-war period. With a few notable exceptions, proponents of the stagist and continuity models have argued that wartime developments, including splits in the Liberal Party, Labour's participation in the coalition government, a shift in popular attitudes towards the state and, in 1918, the expansion of the franchise, provided the necessary environment in which Labour could replace the Liberals as the dominant force on the British left.[1]

This chapter offers a fresh perspective on this debate by examining the ideological evolution of Labour activists in towns and cities that were at the forefront of this realignment. The examples of Leicester, Lincoln, Bristol, Northampton and Norwich, as well as other towns and cities across the East Midlands, East Anglia and the South West, strengthen the argument that a complex array of factors enhanced the electoral prospects of Labour among old and new voters. But the primary concern of this chapter is not to explain Labour's growing electoral strength but to explore the way local political actors responded to the political, economic and intellectual developments of the war years. If we wish to explain the post-war rise of the Labour Party, it is reasonable to suggest that we focus on the ideological journey of those who acted as the party's representatives and spokespersons, maintained the party machinery, kept the party together at a local level and, in many cases, went on to serve as Labour MPs and councillors in the interwar period.

One of the principal arguments of this chapter is that there were deep conceptual continuities between pre-war and wartime articulations of labourist ideology. As noted in the introductory chapter, this study is not the first to use the term 'labourism' to describe the dominant ideology of the early Labour Party. In fact, some of the elements that scholars have identified as 'labourist', including the centrality of parliamentarianism and a prioritisation of immediate over long-term goals, were present in local forms of labourist discourse. But the morphological analysis of ideology allows us to go further than this and uncover the conceptual framework on which these sentiments were based. Furthermore, seeing labourism as the logical outgrowth of working-class radicalism, a conceptually coherent ideology that differed in important respects from liberalism and socialism, goes some way towards rescuing labourism from the pejorative uses to which it has often been put. The concepts at the centre of working-class radical ideology – democracy, liberty, individuality, progress and rationality – remained at the heart of labourism, while adjacent concepts such as equality, rights, the general interest, class, trade unionism and the state served to provide the core concepts with particular meanings. Marginal concepts such as nationalisation added a vital gloss to the labourist core, while peripheral concepts such as Parliament and the right to work linked core and adjacent concepts to the 'real world'.

For scholars such as Selina Todd and Matthew Worley, Labour only displaced the Liberals by adapting to the changed post-war environment.[2] One of the aims of this chapter is to suggest that there was no need for labourists to adapt at all. The war certainly generated new labourist demands, but the conceptual framework on which they were based remained intact. If anything, labourists believed that the war simply validated their pre-war beliefs. The expansion of state power in previously untouched spheres of economic life, a development that many considered to be essential if the country was to win the war, only served to vindicate the arguments put forward by labourists and others in the Labour Party before 1914.[3] Labourist demands for representation on wartime committees also emerged from the same conceptual relationship that had created the demand for labour representation since the mid- to late Victorian period. And because of the interdependent relationship between the concepts of class, democracy, trade unionism and equality, these demands continued to take on a class inflection, with labourists contending, for instance, that the working class suffered and sacrificed more than any other during the course of the war.

The expansion of the state initially appeared to threaten the rights and liberties of trade unionists, which reawakened labourist suspicions that state power, if placed in the wrong hands, could be wielded against the workers.[4] It also gave labourists the opportunity to present themselves as the protectors of the hard-won rights of the workers at a time when the Liberal Party seemed to be abdicating its historical role as the guardian of civil liberties. But if this meant that local Labour parties were becoming 'attractive, contemporary, version[s] of the Liberal party', as Duncan Tanner argued, then this was not because labourists or socialists had cast aside their old beliefs.[5] Labourists, as the ideological descendants of a nineteenth-century tradition in which the notions of equal rights, civil liberty, and limited and constitutional government had a strong place, had always presented themselves as staunch defenders of the constitution and the British system of government. In any case, suggesting that local Labour parties were merely becoming contemporary versions of the Liberal Party downplays the distinctive contribution that labourists made to the intellectual landscape of pre-war and wartime Britain. Armed with a collectivist and class-inflected ideology, labourists were well placed to operate in an environment in which statist proposals were becoming more acceptable and the once-dominant Liberal Party was losing its hold over its working-class base.

Labourism before the war

Edwardian socialists, liberals and conservatives often expressed their support for the principle of labour representation. But due to the arrangement of concepts in their morphologies, they articulated this demand in different ways. As we saw in previous chapters, the liberal interpretation of democracy led many of its proponents to favour a qualified understanding of it that viewed the sectional rule of a specific group or class as potentially harmful to the pursuit of the general interest.[6] This may explain why so many Liberal candidates accused their Labour opponents of promoting a sectional view of politics that contravened the unwritten rule that politicians should represent the community rather than a class. As one Liberal alderman from Leicester put it in 1902:

> Working-men on the Council don't care how they run the rates up. They are always looking after the working-man; it is this for the working-man, that for the working-man ...[7]

Liberal candidates were often drawn into such discussions by their Labour opponents, who attempted to discredit Liberal and Conservative candidates by drawing attention to their wealth, tastes and educational backgrounds. During the 1904 by-election in Norwich, Louis Tillett, grandson of the former radical MP for Norwich, criticised the Labour candidate for bringing up his profession in election meetings:

> The fitness of anyone for Parliament was to be gauged by the principles that one professed, and not to be examined by a small tooth comb into his past career.[8]

George Roberts, Tillett's Labour opponent in 1904, disagreed, and urged voters 'not as Liberals, or as Tories, but as working men with common interests' to vote for 'the working class party'.[9]

Liberals could remain liberals while expressing reservations about the principle of labour representation. But because democracy was a core rather than an adjacent concept in labourist ideology, and because the adjacent concepts of class, trade unionism and equality helped to finesse and anchor this core concept, it would have been logically inconsistent for a labourist to express similar reservations. The specific configuration of concepts in labourism also led labourists to articulate this demand in strong class terms. For instance, they emphasised the benefit that increased labour representation would accrue to the workers first and foremost and justified their agitation on the question by pointing to 'widespread attacks' on workers' rights by the press, the law courts, traders' associations and the major political parties.[10] In the words of the *Leicester Pioneer*:

> The Labour party desires representation in the House of Commons in order to amend industrial law, and [to] use the power of legislation and administration to improve the conditions of the wage-earning and industrial classes.[11]

In the early 1900s, events in the political, industrial and legal worlds proved to be the catalyst for increased agitation on the labour representation question. But while the stimulus for action was new, labourists fell back on an older theoretical framework both to understand these events and to formulate their responses to them. Indeed, the Taff Vale judgement seemed to validate what labourists had been saying since the 1880s and what working-class radicals had been saying since the 1860s, namely that Parliament and other nominally democratic bodies should be constituted of different classes of society, that each class had a right to its fair share of representation, that the working class was the most numerous but least represented class on these bodies, and that the best representatives were those who had emerged from the class on whose behalf they claimed to speak.

The presence of trade unionism and class as adjacent concepts in labourist morphology helps to explain why labourists often prioritised the interests of the workers over the general interests of the community. Labourists were not opposed to the idea of effecting change for the benefit of all, but they believed that this could only happen when the immediate concerns of the working class had been considered and dealt with. Examples of labourists expressing such views are not difficult to find. A 1909 municipal election handbill from Ipswich argued that 'the welfare of the community generally *can only be secured* by an improvement in the conditions of the working classes'.[12] A handbill for a municipal election candidate in Leicester in 1912 stated that it was the candidate's aim to 'seek the welfare of the community, *but chiefly* ... to remember the great working class community to which so large a number of the residents in this Ward belong'.[13] And in another handbill from the same elections, a Labour candidate claimed that he would 'improve the conditions of life for the Workers *in particular* and the Citizens as a whole'.[14]

The labourist articulation of the demand for labour representation bore a striking resemblance to that of working-class radicals in the Victorian period. This is not to deny that there were differences between the working-class radical of 1870 and the labour activist of 1910. Rather, it is to suggest that the conceptual frameworks upon which their demands were based remained largely intact across a period of marked social, political and economic change. The arrangement of concepts in both morphologies produced the notion that all male members of the community were entitled to equal political and industrial rights. For both working-class radicals and labourists, progress meant strengthening the rights and liberties of the people, establishing a truly representative and democratic political system and creating the political conditions in which workers could achieve their own emancipation. The concept of class sharpened these notions and pulled them in a sectional direction. And even as they succeeded in achieving some of their demands, labourists continued to claim that the workers were unfairly treated and unrepresented. While they sometimes claimed that their prioritisation of working-class concerns was temporary, it was, in fact, an integral part of their thinking about politics and society.

The links between democracy, individuality and progress also led labourists to advocate a range of policies, including triennial Parliaments, the payment of MPs and the reform or abolition of the House of Lords, which they hoped would establish a sound democratic framework for all. The close connection between democracy, class, trade unionism and liberty, understood as the autonomy and self-determination of the individual, convinced labourists that the political system – which, despite its defects, was deemed to be a more representative system than those found in other countries – was the most effective means through which the workers could achieve their emancipation. It led them to give primacy to the liberties of the workers, which explains why songs such as 'Banners of Freedom' and 'Marching on to Liberty' retained their appeal in labourist and socialist circles.[15] It also explains why activists drew upon the themes of oppression and tyranny in their speeches during the pre-war industrial unrest when 'tyrannical masters' stood in opposition to those 'great fighters for liberty' who sought to protect 'those liberties [that] their forefathers [had] won for them'.[16]

Candidates for peripheral status in labourist morphology during this period include Parliament; the constitution; the empire; social order; patriotism; national self-determination; reform or abolition of the House of Lords; nationalisation of the land, mines and railways; old-age pensions; free trade; and traditional gender roles. These ideas, institutions, policy proposals and assumptions, though not vital for underpinning labourism's basis structure, helped to root the core and adjacent concepts in their historical, geographical and cultural context. This explains why activists rarely spoke about democracy, liberty and other concepts in a wholly abstract sense, and why they showed little enthusiasm for the campaign for women's suffrage despite having made formal commitments to the principle of universal suffrage. Not surprisingly, this left male labourists open to the charge of hypocrisy, and those who did take up the cause of women's suffrage often used labourists' own arguments against them.[17]

Labourist ideology was based on a system of core and adjacent concepts that, at their most abstract, could operate in different time periods and settings. But peripheral concepts such as the constitution helped to ground labourism in its immediate historical context.[18] Labourists continued to express their admiration for the English constitution, viewing it as the guarantor of rights and liberties that needed to be defended at all costs. Accordingly, they insisted that they were working to correct certain abuses that had 'entrenched themselves' in the constitution.[19] The constitutional crisis of 1909–1910, caused by the House of Lords' rejection of David Lloyd George's 'People's Budget', allowed labourists and progressives of all shades of opinion to present themselves as the rightful custodians of the radical tradition. During the two general elections of 1910, both of which were largely fought on the issue of the Lords and its powers, Labour candidates and their supporters drew upon the linguistic resources of the centuries-old English radical tradition, stressing, among other things, the sovereignty of the people through their representatives in the House of Commons and an almost limitless belief in the capacity of a reconstituted Commons to exert its authority over non-elected bodies. In the words of Arthur Henderson, Labour's official leader and candidate for Barnard Castle in County Durham:

> No longer content with resisting the people's will with regard to legislation, the Lords, by rejecting the Budget, have subverted the principles of the Constitution and usurped the rights of the Commons in connection with finance.[20]

Similarly, speaking after the contest, George Roberts, MP for Norwich and Labour's chief whip, praised 'Radicals, Socialists, and Labour men [who] utilised their full franchise for the freedom of popularly-elected representation and for democracy being predominant in a democratic constitution'.[21] Even socialists who operated outside the Labour Party, including the two Social Democratic Party candidates for Northampton, presented themselves as 'Socialists and Democrats' who stood for 'the completest form of democracy', 'Government of the People by the People for the People' and 'for the People ... against the Peers'.[22]

The peculiar nature of the 1910 election contests provided a context in which archaic terms could reappear in political discourse. The assumptions that lay behind these statements, however, were far from new. These assumptions also influenced labourist responses to the Great Labour Unrest of 1910–1914. Most labourists attempted to give rank-and-file initiatives a veneer of respectability and continued to exhibit what George Dangerfield called a 'theological reverence for the operations of Parliament' and a sense of dismay 'at the very mention of the word "revolution"'.[23] In fact, what seemed to anger them most was the action of government ministers who, in their eyes, had flouted the constitution by calling in the military during the national railway strike and by issuing a circular to local police authorities advising them to enrol special constables. Trade unionists across the country condemned these actions in a class-based language of rights and constitutionalism, claiming that they were 'violation[s] of constitutional liberty', 'unnecessary and illegal', 'a gross danger to civil liberty' and a threat to the 'ordinary civic rights of workmen'.[24] Even Daniel Stanton, a long-standing member of the Northampton Trades' Council and a staunch lib–lab in politics, criticised the actions of the Liberal government and likened Winston Churchill, the home secretary, to the tsar of Russia for enacting laws without passing them through the House of Commons. Looking back on the unrest in early 1914, Stanton remained convinced that employers and government officials had gone 'outside the law and any Constitution in order to crush at any cost, and with any weapon, the aspirations of the workers'.[25]

Socialism and the right to work

As a palliative for unemployment, the Labour Party introduced several 'Right to Work' bills into the House of Commons that would have given local authorities the necessary powers and funding to provide temporary employment to those who found themselves out of work. While these attempts were unsuccessful, they reveal just how relaxed labourists had become about using the state to improve the lives of the workers. Since the 1880s and 1890s, political, economic and intellectual developments had coalesced to shift the concept of the state to an adjacent position in the frameworks of labourism and new forms of liberalism. By harnessing some of the evolutionary theories that were in vogue at the turn of twentieth century, they also came to accept the inevitability of a slow and gradual march towards a future in which the state would play a significant role in the economic sphere. Evolutionary theories also altered labourist definitions of progress, which increasingly came to be identified with attempts to regulate the anarchy of the market, and the general interest, which would benefit from attempts to push society along an evolutionary path towards a more democratic social and political order.

Like the new liberals, labourists saw the state as 'the primary agent of a rational society' that could 'alleviate and repair some of the ills that dehumanized its members and incapacitated society as a well-functioning organization'.[26] After 1900, labourist manifestos included a wider range of statist proposals than ever before. But because of the presence of class and trade unionism in labourist morphology, labourists were primarily concerned with how the state could protect and extend the political and industrial rights of the workers. One of the consequences of the elevation of the state in labourist morphology, then, was a redefinition of the concept of rights, a concept that, for Michael Freeden, acts as a 'protective capsule' for the concepts 'most valued by the ideology promoting them'.[27] Whereas working-class radicals had once emphasised the right to a voice in the selection of candidates, the right to have a hand in the making of the law and the right to form and join a trade union, labourists added the right to work to the list. The old working-class radical notion of rights did not disappear in the Edwardian period; it simply evolved to take on a new meaning.

Labourists had become convinced that the state should assume responsibility for areas in which 'fundamental needs' were concerned.[28] This was a view that they shared with socialists who operated inside and outside the Labour Party. The ideological similarities between labourism and socialism led Michael Freeden to consider labourism a 'weaker British version' of socialism rather than an ideology in its own right.[29] It is true that some labourists pushed the boundaries of their ideology to near breaking-point. In some cases, it is incredibly difficult to determine where labourism ends and socialism begins. Concepts such as equality, democracy, liberty and the state can be found in all variants of labourism and socialism, and, due to the personal and organisational overlaps within the Labour Party, labourists and socialists often grappled with the same real-world practices and policy proposals. But just as in the late nineteenth century, there were important conceptual differences between labourism and its variants and socialism and its variants.[30] The most crucial differences between them were the contrasting positioning of concepts in their respective morphologies and, in particular, the location of equality (at the core of socialism but adjacent in labourism), liberty and democracy (both core in labourism and adjacent in socialism).

Labourists and socialists were well aware of the ideological differences that divided them and often engaged in discussions about the limitations of each other's approach. One such discussion took place through the pages of the *Leicester Pioneer* in late 1902 when a member of the Leicester branch of the ILP wrote a series of articles outlining the differences between 'the Labour man' and 'the Socialist'. For the writer, labourist and socialist ideas were 'distinct but not antagonistic'. The views of 'the Labour man' did not extend beyond an inarticulate feeling that 'something is wrong, and that something must be done to right it'. These ideas were not 'organised' and had no 'plan of campaign', but for that very reason they were perhaps 'more in harmony with the favourite policy of the English people, which is to "muddle through"'. The socialist movement, on the other hand, had its course 'definitely marked out, and the objects to be attained clearly defined'.[31]

There was a tone of disappointment in this article, which was not untypical of socialist (and socialist historians') attitudes to the ordinary 'Labour man'. The writer's analysis seemed to be vindicated several weeks later, when a letter sent by 'Labourite' thanked the writer and the ILP for their 'action and propaganda' over the previous few years but asked them to step aside so that 'the unions [could] work the matter out to the far end'.[32] The writer's response to this letter reveals some of the key differences between socialism and labourism at this time. In a guarded criticism of the supposedly narrow focus of the ordinary 'Labour man', the writer downplayed the significance of the Taff Vale decision and argued that the strike weapon, 'though once effective, [had] now become obsolete'. Rather than simply focusing on industrial topics, trade unionists, the writer argued, should work for the 'all-round betterment of the entire working-class' and follow the ILP's example in seeking a 'reformation in England' that would establish an 'industrial Commonwealth, founded upon the socialisation of the land and capital'.[33]

'Labourite' would probably have seen this as neither desirable nor practical. During this period, many labourists showed signs of distrust towards certain forms of state intervention, particularly when it threatened to encroach on the work of the trade unions and friendly societies.[34] They also expressed discomfort at the idea of nationalising the entire economy. Even when they did express support for limited state intervention, they tended to emphasise the immediate benefits that intervention would bring to the workers rather than seeing it as a stepping-stone towards a socialist commonwealth. They favoured the nationalisation of the coal mines, for example, because it would increase miners' wages and improve their working conditions.[35] They proposed old-age pensions because trade unions and friendly societies had tried but failed to provide them themselves.[36] And they wanted the government and local authorities to find work for the unemployed because voluntary organisations 'could do no more' without their assistance.[37] Labourists did not want the state to become the sole employer of labour, nor did they see it as the 'institutional manifestation of the socialist community'.[38] Instead, they believed that the state was an efficient and effective tool that workers could use to mitigate perennial problems which private capitalists had proven unwilling or unable to deal with.

Some labourists went further in stressing the importance of nationalisation, which serves as a useful reminder that labourism, like all ideologies, was capable of producing variations on its core themes. It is also more accurate to speak of English socialisms rather than a single English socialism. Many of the personal and ideological conflicts between (and within) the ILP, the Fabian Society, the SDF/BSP and other socialist bodies were often played out a local level. In Leicester, for example, it was not uncommon for members of the ILP to criticise the sectarianism and extremism of the SDF/BSP. In 1902, one writer for the *Leicester Pioneer* even disparaged the efforts of those who had been involved in the socialist revival of the 1880s, referring mockingly to the 'palmy days of William Morris' when 'every Socialist looked forward with eager expectancy to the "Social Revolution," and was prepared to name the date at which it might be expected to take place'.[39] On the other side, SDF/BSP members often criticised the ILP for their moderation. During Ramsay MacDonald's election campaign in December 1910, a self-described 'revolutionary marxist' accused MacDonald of trying to 'cover over' and 'hide the antagonism between capital and labour' and described him as a 'Liberal M. P.' who '[threw] dust in the eyes of the working-class'. The sooner MacDonald ceased to call himself a socialist, 'the better it [would] be for the working class'.[40]

Socialism of the latter type was especially popular among members of the SDF/BSP. Combining an emphasis on class war with a healthy dose of scepticism towards the Labour Party, SDF/BSP members were less concerned than their ILP counterparts about offending the sensibilities of liberals and labourists. James Gribble, a militant member of the NUBSO and an executive member of the SDF/BSP, acted as a thorn in the side of labourists in Northampton for much of this period, engaging in a variety of activities – such as fighting the police during an unemployment demonstration in 1901, striking a lib–lab councillor in the face after a heated council meeting in 1904 and, most famously, organising a march of striking bootmakers from the town of Raunds to the House of Commons in 1905 – which served to highlight the gulf between moderates and militants in the broad socialist movement. It is possible to detect a similar spirit of defiance in the BSP's campaign during the 1913 Leicester by-election, a contest that would decide who would serve as MacDonald's colleague in the House of Commons.[41] Controversy erupted before the campaign had even begun when the Labour Party executive refused to endorse the candidature of George Banton, the choice of the Leicester LRC. In another sign of the nationalising influence of the Labour Party, George Roberts, the party's chief whip, advised local activists against supporting Edward Hartley, the BSP candidate, and urged them to follow the lead of the executive, who '[possessed] the most intimate knowledge of what was best for the national movement'.[42]

But in spite of Roberts' advice, Hartley received the support of most members of the Leicester Trades' Council, several Labour councillors and aldermen, and an assortment of national-level personalities such as George Lansbury, Henry Hyndman and Robert Bontine Cunninghame Graham. Crucially, though, he did not receive the endorsement of the local LRC, and his chances were damaged even further when a manifesto purportedly written by MacDonald, Roberts and Arthur Henderson that suggested that MacDonald might sever his connection with Leicester if the actions of the Leicester LRC helped to return a Conservative candidate found its way into the hands of the Leicester Liberal Association.[43] Even if this was a factor in Hartley's defeat, it is also possible that the violent language he used during the contest alienated him from some of those who had previously cast their votes for MacDonald. To give one example of many, Hartley stated on one occasion that 'if he had an opportunity of cutting the throat of the moneylender he would be pleased to give him a happy despatch as quickly as possible'.[44] Ultimately, the Liberal candidate topped the poll and Hartley finished a distant third, which his organiser blamed on 'traitors within their camp'.[45]

But labourists were not necessarily 'traitors' for refusing to vote for a candidate like Hartley. As we have seen, they rejected the violent sentiments that often emanated from characters within the BSP. Rejecting the antagonistic notion of a class war, they gave expression to an ideology that was distinct from socialism, as well as from old and new forms of liberalism. By this time, many liberals had, like labourists, come to believe that the state should place constraints on the activities of some individuals in order to strengthen the freedom of a large majority of others. But labourism and new liberalism differed in terms of their internal conceptual morphology. This helps to account for the disagreements that arose between labourists and new liberals on policy issues such as labour exchanges and health and unemployment insurance. It also helps to explain why they tended to prioritise different issues and policies during election contests. Though liberals could also make direct appeals to working-class voters, they were more likely than their labour opponents to use a language of populism. While disgruntled socialists felt that they were almost indistinguishable from one another, the ideological differences that had divided labourists and liberals in the 1880s and 1890s continued to do so in pre-war period.

Attempting to distinguish between an individual's party-political affiliation and their political ideology is not an easy task, particularly in dual-member constituencies where ideological liberals voted for Labour candidates and ideological labourists voted for Liberal candidates. The enduring strength of lib–labism, a political current that is deserving of more scholarly attention and a more robust ideological analysis, also makes this a difficult task. There has been a tendency in the literature to define those trade unionists who continued to feel a sense of affinity with the Liberal Party as ideological liberals, thereby blurring the distinctions between ideology and political practice. But to tar all lib–labs with the same ideological brush, as if lib–labism was a distinct body of thought, is highly misleading. While many labourists were not opposed to the idea of a national Labour Party, and while they accepted the need for independent labour parties in localities where Liberal Associations were hostile to the labour interest, they resisted efforts to sever all ties with the forces of liberalism in their own towns for strategic rather than ideological reasons.

Such attitudes were prevalent in Leicester and Norwich, where Labour activists reached a political accommodation with local Liberal Associations. For example, William Hornidge, who had left Northampton for Leicester in the 1890s to take up his appointment as general president of the NUBSO, admitted that he 'allied himself to Liberalism' so that he could 'get out of it all he could for the good of Labour'.[46] Similar views were common in Northampton, where labourists and socialists refused to establish an LRC until the eve of the First World War. Most labourists, some of whom had been involved in the lib–lab alliances of the 1880s and 1890s, continued to favour an accommodation with the progressive Northampton LRA. In their view, the ability to work with minimal discomfort in a tactical alliance with the Liberals meant that there was no need, at a local level at least, for an independent party of labour. Some activists pointed to previous attempts to obtain political office on independent lines, most of which had ended in failure, as proof that trade unionists needed the backing of the Liberals to succeed. Still, when it seemed that the local Liberals were backing away from their promise to accommodate the demands of the 'labour party', labourists began to look for alternative methods of seeking redress for their grievances. In Northampton, the breaking-point came during the pre-war industrial unrest, when the actions (and inactions) of Liberal MPs and the Liberal government convinced formerly staunch lib–labs to work with the local BSP and ILP branches to form an LRC.[47] Daniel Stanton, who had resisted efforts to form an ILP in the town in the 1890s, who had become a town councillor with the backing of the local Liberals and who had convinced his national union, the NUBSO, to rescind its policy on political independence, now believed that trade unionists should 'drop [their] political parties and "isms" and go in strong for Labour'.[48]

Patriots and pacifists

By the time the Northampton LRC was founded in October 1914, Britain was at war with Germany. Political and industrial developments during war served to accelerate the professionalisation of labour politics in Northampton, as in other towns and cities. By the end of 1918, the experience of the war years had transformed what was essentially a fragile alliance into a unified, independent and ambitious electoral machine that sought to challenge the dominance of the Liberal Party at the municipal and parliamentary levels. To some extent, this was because the issue of the war brought labourists and socialists together. Although it is possible to identify anti-war attitudes among members of the local ILP branch, such sentiments were not universal. Most members of the Northampton Trades' Council interpreted the war as a defence of the 'rights of small nations' and supported the government's efforts to defeat 'Prussian militarism'. So, too, did members of the fiercely pro-war local

BSP, which followed Henry Hyndman into the unfortunately named National Socialist Party in 1916.[49] The decision of the Northampton Borough Labour Party to stand a member of the National Union of Railwayman (and an ILPer) rather than a member of the locally dominant NUBSO at the 'coupon election' of 1918 caused some dissension within the party's ranks, but the result, which saw the Labour candidate receive over 37 per cent of the vote, was generally regarded as promising in the circumstances.[50]

Conflicts between industrially minded trades' councils and politically minded LRCs were common during the war period.[51] There were also instances where leading Labour figures, including local councillors, former parliamentary candidates and, in some cases, sitting MPs, found themselves out of step with their local trades' councils and LRCs. Norwich is perhaps an extreme example of this. The strong local branch of the ILP officially opposed the war, believing that it was being fought 'in the interests of international financiers, capitalists, and armament manufacturers'.[52] This was in contrast to the views of George Roberts, the local Labour MP who had done so much to build the ILP in its formative years. Though 'a hater of war', Roberts 'never doubted that the Allied cause was right' and believed that the war '[had to] be continued until the conditions of a satisfactory and durable peace are won'.[53] Roberts' commitment to the war effort encouraged him to take up various posts in the wartime government, including that of Minister of Labour from August 1917. His elevation to a post of cabinet rank necessitated a by-election contest, and Roberts was returned without a contest with the endorsement of the Labour Party executive.[54] But he failed to receive the backing of the local ILP, the local LRC and the Norwich Trades' Council, all of which repudiated his candidature. After being forced to resign his membership of the ILP and his union, the Typographical Association, he stood successfully as a 'Coalition Labour' candidate in 1918 against a Liberal and an ILPer.

Despite notable exceptions, trade union and socialist leaders in Leicester also refused to take part in the recruitment campaigns, opposed military conscription and, in November 1916, urged the government to seek a negotiated peace.[55] But unlike in Norwich, their views on the conflict were in harmony with those of their local Labour MP. Despite resigning the party chairmanship at the beginning of the war, Ramsay MacDonald remained politically active during the conflict and spoke at numerous meetings across the country, sometimes in the face of threats of violence from the 'patriotic labour' British Workers' League, among other groups. When the general election came in 1918, the Leicester Labour Party put MacDonald forward as their candidate for the newly created constituency of Leicester West, but this time he did not receive support from the Leicester Liberal Association because, in the words of one of its leading members, it could not 'put [its] trust in his loyalty as a true Englishman'.[56] In a campaign that the *Leicester Daily Press* described as 'the most-talked-of contest in the country', MacDonald faced the combined might of the Leicester Liberals, the Leicester Unionists, the former editor of the *Leicester Pioneer* and two of the best-known trade unionists in the city, all of whom lent their support to MacDonald's coalition-backed opponent, Joseph Frederick Green of the National Democratic and Labour Party (formerly the British Workers' League).[57] MacDonald, along with the Labour candidates for Leicester East and Leicester South, lost heavily.

Anti-war and pacifist views were common in socialist circles in Lincoln, where in 1916 the police raided homes to confiscate literature produced by the ILP, the No-Conscription Fellowship and the Union of Democratic Control.[58] The local ILP branch also increased its hold on the local trades' council, which, by the end of 1918, had become what one rabidly anti-German member described as 'a Sub-Committee of the I. L. P.'. This was probably an exaggeration, as the Lincoln Labour Party selected Arthur Taylor, a long-time trade unionist and determined critic of the ILP's anti-war stance, as its candidate for the 1918 general election. As in other constituencies, Taylor distanced himself from the wartime activities of the ILP and, instead, tried to associate the Liberals with the pacifist and 'peace-by-negotiation' movement.[59] This strategy seemed to work, as Taylor, the first Labour parliamentary candidate in Lincoln's history, polled a respectable 28.5 per cent share of the vote and forced the Asquithian Liberal candidate, the city's MP since 1906, into third place.

The Labour Party in Bristol also enjoyed a period of growth during the war years. Whereas the Bristol LRC did not contest a single seat in the December 1910 election, the reorganised Bristol Borough Labour Party put forward candidates in Bristol East, Bristol Central, Bristol North and Bristol South at the coupon election of 1918. Still, there were disagreements between pacifist and pro-war elements in the local movement. Under the leadership of the devoutly religious Walter Ayles, ILP members distributed anti-conscription literature, held open-air meetings that were often met with physical violence and, in some cases, served time in prison.[60] As a result of these activities, and despite obtaining a strong presence on the leadership bodies of the LRC and the Bristol Trades' Council, the ILP branch saw its membership and financial contributions decline during the war years.[61] But the ILP's stance on the war was not representative of the movement as a whole, and many of the city's leading trade unionists, including the former parliamentary candidate Frank Sheppard, supported the war effort.[62] With this in mind, it was probably not surprising that all four Labour candidates at the 1918 general election attempted to distance themselves from the wartime activities of their pacifist colleagues.

These examples confirm Martin Pugh's view that Labour effectively entered the 1918 election contest as three parties: anti-war, belligerent patriots and moderate pro-war.[63] And yet not only did the party remain united, but it also stood over three hundred more candidates in 1918 than it had in December 1910. There are several reasons why this was the case. A considerable increase in trade union membership between 1914 and 1918 improved the finances and broadened the affiliated membership of the Labour Party and its local organisations.[64] The co-optation of Labour Party members onto national and local wartime committees also helped to give the party an influence that it had lacked in the pre-war years.[65] Arthur Henderson, George Roberts, J. R. Clynes and several other Labour MPs served in Lloyd George's wartime government, while, at a local level, members from all sections of the party joined Committees for the Prevention of Distress, War Pensions Committees, Food Control Committees, Naval and Military War Pensions Act Committees, and military tribunals. Labour representation on these bodies was particularly important in places where labourists and socialists had struggled to work together before the war. In Northampton, James Gribble, a former militant member of the BSP, helped to enhance the prestige of the local Labour Party by devising a scheme for raising money for various war-related causes.[66] The 'Gribble Scheme', which raised a total of £27,778 by the war's end, received praise from across the political spectrum, something that Gribble and his colleagues were not used to. Although Gribble had been 'preaching simple things to Northampton for 25 years', this was 'the first time he had been able to induce people to take any notice of them!'[67]

Labourism during the war

The demand for labour representation on wartime committees emerged from the same conceptual relationship that generated similar demands in the pre-war period. It flowed from a core belief in democracy, understood to mean the rule of the people; the adjacent concepts of rights, equality and the general interest, jointly decontested as the right of all members of the community to be represented on democratically elected bodies; the concepts of class and trade unionism, which added a workerist tone to labourist demands; and peripheral concepts such as Parliament, patriotism and the English constitution.[68] Consequently, both moderately pro-war labourists and belligerent patriots contended that as the war effort was a national concern that required the co-operation of employers, workers and all political parties, 'bona fide' representatives from all social and political groups deserved to be represented on wartime committees. While anti-war labourists refused to join many of these committees, this was because they were opposed to the conflict rather than because they had abandoned their faith in the principle of labour representation.

For Jose Harris, the model of equality envisaged by labourists before the war had been one in which 'manual workers would share the material security, educational standards and access to jobs and public offices enjoyed by the professional middle classes'.[69] In the context of the war, however, this notion of equality came to include the idea of an equality of sacrifice. Labourists often claimed that the working class had lost the most men in the trenches, had borne the brunt of price rises and rent increases, and had gone further than others in setting aside their rights and liberties in the interests of the nation.[70] Resentments at a perceived inequality of sacrifice led some pro-war labourists and socialists to make class-based attacks on the 'middle-class … fancy sock brigade', middle-class men who either opposed the conflict or refused to do their part in the war effort.[71] Labour candidates incorporated similar themes into their 1918 election campaigns, drawing attention to the sacrifices made by trade unionists and the benefits that increased labour representation would bring to the workers in the post-war era. Ernest Bevin (Bristol Central) promised voters that he would strive to give his class access to what 'the other class' had. Robert Jackson (Ipswich) urged the 'Workers of Ipswich' to 'Send [Jackson] to Westminster to continue the Fight to Victory for the Workers'. George Banton (Leicester East) told voters that he and his party stood for 'the workers' and 'organised labour' against 'the profiteers', 'lords and dukes', 'mineowners' and 'railway and brewery shareholders'.[72]

Events during the war period brought patriotism to the fore in labourist discourse. While belligerent patriots were more likely to make nationalistic and xenophobic statements, moderately pro-war and even anti-war activists were comfortable using the language of patriotism. Labourists continued to evoke the constitutionalist ethos of the English radical tradition and, with the continuation of the coalition beyond the end of the war, portrayed themselves as the standard bearers of a free and unfettered Parliament. The 1917 Bolshevik Revolution also encouraged them to reaffirm their commitment to constitutionalism.[73] At the 1918 election, Labour candidates denounced the 'violent and unjustifiable' methods of the Bolsheviks and condemned the 'outrages', 'anarchy' and 'bloodshed' with which they were associated.[74] While some candidates and activists generated controversy by claiming that Labour wanted to initiate a revolution, they were quick to clarify that revolution meant 'a change of mind' or a 'constitutional revolution' only.[75] A peaceful revolution was possible in a country like Britain because 'the democracy', in the words of the Labour candidate for Lincoln, 'had a constitutional means open to them of enforcing their will upon those who sit in the seat of power'.[76] 'Evolution', Bevin argued in late 1917, 'was the only possible method of securing emancipation for the working people'.[77]

The allegation that Labour candidates were secret revolutionaries who would 'hoist the Bolshevist banner' if given the reins of power were entirely unfounded.[78] As in the pre-war era, labourists did not see anything wrong with the underlying principles of the constitution. What they did criticise was the unrepresentative composition of the House of Commons and the existence of undemocratic bodies such as the House of Lords. In their view, the political task of the Labour Party was to strengthen the democratic elements of the constitution. Labour activists thus positioned themselves as the true defenders of the constitution, just as they had done during the constitutional crisis of 1909–1010 and as working-class radicals had done during the Bradlaugh case in the 1880s. Rather than posing a threat to the constitutional order, a strong Labour Party in the House of Commons would be 'the best antidote to Bolshevism and revolution'.[79]

Trade unionism also continued to have a significant bearing on the decontestation of labourism's core and adjacent concepts. Both during the war and throughout the 1918 election campaign, labourists used 'the workers', 'organised labour' and 'trade unionists' interchangeably when talking about labour representation. They associated the abstract notions of rights and liberty with the liberty of trade unionism and trade union rights and privileges and fought hard to protect these rights by ensuring that conscription and wartime restrictions on the right to strike were temporary measures only.[80] The theoretical tools that labourists used to make sense of these measures remained those that had proven useful in previous struggles against hostile legal rulings. Anti-war, pro-war and belligerent patriot views on these questions were very similar, and, by the time of the 1918 election, the strength of feeling on the subject ensured that Labour candidates from all sections of the party placed the restoration of civil and industrial liberties at the centre of their campaigns.[81]

For Herbert Witard, who stood against the renegade George Roberts in Norwich in 1918, the wartime government was guilty of destroying

'British liberty' and instituting a 'system of slavery' by introducing the Munitions of War Act.[82] This and other criticisms of the coercive actions of the government serve as useful reminders that labourists and socialists continued to express discomfort at the idea of an all-powerful state. Indeed, for many, the state's growth was both impressive and frightening.[83] The wartime government had fixed rents, introduced rationing and taken control of food prices. By the time the armistice was signed in November 1918, it was also in control of military enlistment, the output of munitions, civilian labour and all shipping, rail and canal transport.[84] Government intervention in industrial relations led to wider trade union recognition and national wage agreements, which brought more trade union members into previously poorly organised industries such as hosiery. As well as expanding the state's executive power, the war also expanded 'Labour's understanding of that power … in both a negative and a positive direction'.[85]

By the end of the war, there was a widespread feeling that state intervention in industry had helped Britain to victory. This feeling was particularly strong among socialists such as Sidney Webb, a key figure in the Labour Party during the war and one of the chief architects of its 1918 constitution and first-ever comprehensive policy document, *Labour and the New Social Order*.[86] The inclusion of the collectivist Clause IV in the new party constitution aligned with the forward-thinking, project-building desire of socialists in the party. Scholars have disagreed, however, about the overall significance of these changes. For Matthew Worley, they helped to clarify the distinctions between 'an emerging Labour socialism and a pre-established Liberalism', while for Jose Harris, the acceptance of Clause IV was 'an index of increasing hostility to private ownership of industry among the "Triple Alliance" of leading trade unionists'.[87] Ben Pimlott, on the other hand, felt that the new constitution was more successful at reducing socialist influence in the 'higher Party echelons', a view echoed by Ross McKibbin among others.[88] While trade unionists allowed ideologically charged resolutions to pass at the two party conferences in 1918, they were more interested in consolidating their dominant position in the party apparatus.[89]

What seems clear is that the 'socialist commitment' in the constitution and the proposals contained in *Labour and the New Social Order* were vague enough to allow party members and voters to invest them with their own meanings.[90] The 1918 election campaign is especially revealing in this regard. Most Labour candidates seemed to accept the principles if not the details of *Labour and the New Social Order*. In their election addresses, they advocated state provision for discharged soldiers and sailors, the retention by the state of all raw materials in its possession and the continuation of rent controls. While some went further and claimed that Labour wanted to abolish the present industrial system, most were content to work within the limits set by *Labour and the New Social Order*, which proposed the immediate nationalisation of the railways, mines, electrical power, canals, harbours, roads, postal service, telegraphs and health insurance, and the nationalisation of other 'main industries' when 'opportunity offers'.[91]

The popularity of such proposals brought labourists and socialists closer together than ever before, at least in an ideological sense. But there remained key conceptual differences between labourism and socialism. Rather than seeing the proposals as stepping-stones to a socialist 'co-operative commonwealth', labourists continued to see them as effective and, by the end of the war, proven methods of achieving their long-held goals. Their wartime experiences also convinced them that nationalisation would bring immediate benefits, such as fuller bargaining rights, better wages and improved working conditions, to the workers affected. And however much some labourists spoke of the *eventual* nationalisation of the 'main industries', they remained resistant to the idea of bringing certain industries, such as the boot and shoe trade, into public hands.[92]

Conclusion

During the election campaign in Northampton in 1918, Alfred Slinn, a local Labour councillor, admitted that he wanted to see 'reconstruction upon the basis of a Social Democratic Republic'. In the words of one of Slinn's colleagues, this would be a process in which 'the people in their collective capacity' would take over the 'whole means of life'. But Slinn acknowledged that 'some of those present did not want Socialism'. Instead, they wanted 'security of employment, better wages, better housing, and food and other commodities at reasonable prices'.[93]

This was both an accurate description of labourism and a perceptive analysis of the differences between it and socialism. Like all ideologies, labourism was essentially a system of core and adjacent concepts. And as concepts are always situated in certain historical and geographical environments, their meanings are subject to change. This chapter has attempted to demonstrate this process by focusing on two policy proposals: the right to work and labour representation. Uncovering the ideological justification for the right to work has shown how the elevation of the state to a more influential position in labourist morphology altered the meaning of labourism's other concepts. It has also added clarity to the ideological differences between labourism and socialism by determining the precise (and differing) location of concepts in their morphologies. The restrained tone of labourist collectivism marked it off from socialism, but its workerist tone also distinguished it from old and new forms of liberalism.

After establishing the conceptual basis of pre-war labourism, this chapter traced its evolution during the First World War. In doing so, it has suggested that labourism did not undergo a significant transformation during the war years. While wartime developments modified the content of labourist programmes, they did not alter the conceptual framework of labourist ideology. As noted by Slinn, labourists and socialists continued to differ in their attitude to the state and their view on the purpose of collectivist measures. If labourist demands had become more collectivist in tone by 1918, this did not represent the transformation of labourism into socialism. Rather, it demonstrated the contestability of ideological concepts and represented the next stage in an ideological evolution that had begun in the 1880s.

The demand for labour representation on wartime committees also stemmed from pre-war understandings of labourism's core and adjacent concepts. At an abstract level, this demand can be seen as a logical outcome of the relationship between democracy, equality, class, trade unionism, and a set of peripheral concepts including Parliament, the constitution and traditional gender roles. Spatial and temporal contexts, social and political influences, and a whole range of external factors added further nuance to the demand. Thus, in the 1860s, working-class radicals framed it as a way of democratising local Liberal politics. In the 1890s, it was seen by some as a way of defeating organised liberalism both locally and nationally. And during the war years, it was justified as a means to ensure that all sections of the community could play a part in the war effort. While the war temporarily revised the tone of the demand for labour representation, the demand itself, as well as labourist responses to developments such as the Russian Revolution, emanated from a way of thinking that had developed long before the First World War.

Notes

1 The Representation of the People Act of 1918 granted the vote to all men over the age of twenty-one and women over the age of thirty who met a property qualification. For examples of work that emphasises the transformative impact of the First World War, see Joyce, *Visions of the People*, p. 8; Biagini and Reid, 'Introduction', in Biagini and Reid, *Currents of Radicalism*, pp. 16–17. Recent studies have not fundamentally challenged this view. See Worley, *Labour inside the Gate*, pp. 7–8; Pugh, *Speak For*

Britain!, p. 100; Todd, *The People*, p, 30. There are, however, exceptions. See Tanner, *Political Change and the Labour Party*, pp. 351–353.
2 Todd, *The People*, p. 30; Worley, *Labour inside the Gate*, pp. 7–8.
3 Thorpe, *A History of the British Labour Party*, p. 41; McKibbin, *The Evolution of the Labour Party*, p. 105.
4 Harris, 'Labour's political and social thought', p. 16.
5 Tanner, *Political Change and the Labour Party*, p. 429.
6 Freeden, *Ideologies and Political Theory*, pp. 154–155.
7 *Leicester Pioneer*, 8 November 1902.
8 LHA, LP/LRC/13/164, LRC GC, correspondence with Councillor S. Flint (Leicester) with extract from *Eastern Daily Press* (12 January 1904), February 1904.
9 *Norwich Mercury*, 9 January 1904.
10 MRC, MSS.524/4/1/24, TC AR, Ipswich, 1902.
11 *Leicester Pioneer*, 16 December 1905.
12 LSE, LSE, ILP/6/21/4, ILP MEA, Bridge Ward (Ipswich), Edgar Brooks, 1909: emphasis added.
13 LSE, LSE, ILP/6/21/4, ILP MEA, Wyggeston Ward (Leicester), Alfred Hill, 1912: emphasis added.
14 LSE, LSE, ILP/6/21/5, ILP MEA, Catton Ward (Norwich), W. E. Savage, 1912: emphasis added.
15 LSE, FILM 86, BILP M, 16 September 1908; 1 September 1909; University of Bristol Special Collections, Bristol, DM/741/1, Papers of John Gregory, 'New Labour Song', 1902.
16 For examples, see *Western Daily Press*, 28 August 1911; *Western Daily Press*, 27 May 1912; 11 June 1912.
17 LSE, JN1129.L3, LP CR, 1906.
18 M. Taylor, 'Labour and the constitution', pp. 151–156.
19 MacDonald letter to George Banton, leading member of the Leicester LRC, printed in *Leicester Daily Post*, 21 November 1910.
20 *Leicester Daily Post*, 4 January 1910.
21 NFRO, MC 655/4, 790X7, papers of G. H. Roberts MP, Typographical Association circular, February 1910.
22 NCL, 198–781/1910, NEE, 'To the Electors' (J. Gribble and H. Quelch), 1910.
23 G. Dangerfield, *The Strange Death of Liberal England* (London, 1997), p. 192.
24 *Northampton Chronicle and Echo*, 21 September 1911; *Derby Daily Telegraph*, 14 September 1911; LSE, JN1129.L3, LP CR, 1912; *Leicester Daily Post*, 6 September 1911; *Western Daily Press*, 23 August 1911.
25 NHRO, 1977/44/NTC3, NTC M, 21 January 1914.
26 Freeden, *Ideologies and Political Theory*, pp. 200.
27 Freeden, *Ideologies and Political Theory*, pp. 208.
28 Freeden, *Ideologies and Political Theory*, p. 207.
29 Freeden, *Ideologies and Political Theory*, p. 448.
30 Freeden, *Ideologies and Political Theory*, pp. 458–459.

31 *Leicester Pioneer*, 23 August 1902.
32 Letter 'Labourite' to *Leicester Pioneer*, 20 September 1902.
33 *Leicester Pioneer*, 27 September 1902.
34 J. Cronin, *The Politics of State Expansion: War, State and Society in Twentieth-Century Britain* (London, 1991), p. 37.
35 *Western Daily Press*, 4 January 1912.
36 MRC, 547/P/1/16, NUBSO CR, 1900.
37 NHRO, 1977/44/NTC2, NTC M, 16 March 1910.
38 Freeden, *Ideologies and Political Theory*, p. 447.
39 *Leicester Pioneer*, 22 November 1902.
40 Letter 'W. Flanagan' to *Leicester Daily Post*, 9 December 1910.
41 J. Pasiecznik, 'Liberals, Labour and Leicester: The 1913 by-election in local and national perspective', *Transactions of the Leicestershire Archaeological and Historical Society*, 63 (1989), pp. 94–106.
42 *Leicester Daily Post*, 24 June 1913.
43 Roberts claimed that while it reflected their true feelings on the situation, it was not an official party pronouncement. *Leicester Daily Post*, 1 July 1913.
44 *Leicester Daily Post*, 23 June 1913.
45 *Leicester Daily Post*, 28 June 1913.
46 MRC, 547/P/1/18, NUBSO MR, April 1902.
47 For examples of lib–lab dissatisfaction with the Liberal Party, see NHRO, 1977/44/NTC2, NTC M, 20 September 1911; 16 October 1911; 15 November 1911; 19 November 1911; 20 March 1912; 17 April 1912; 16 July 1912; 5 October 1912.
48 NHRO, 1977/44/NTC2, NTC M, 21 September 1910.
49 NHRO, 1977/44/NTC3, NTC M, 1 October 1914; *Socialist Pioneer*, October 1914; June 1915; December 1915; July 1916. For examples of anti-German sentiments in the SDF/BSP, see Ward, *Red Flag and the Union Jack*, pp. 104–105, 117, 121–126.
50 *Northampton Mercury*, 5 July 1918.
51 McKibbin, *The Evolution of the Labour Party*, pp. 33–34; A. Clinton, *The Trade Union Rank and File: Trades Councils in Britain, 1900–40* (Manchester, 1977), p. 64.
52 LSE, ILP/12/1/3, ILP CR, 1915.
53 George Roberts' election address, published in *Eastern Daily Press*, 24 August 1917.
54 *East Anglian Daily Times*, 24 August 1917.
55 *Leicester Daily Post*, 14 October 1914; 15 November 1916. Nevertheless, branch membership of the Leicester ILP doubled between 1916 and 1918. Cox, 'The Labour Party in Leicester', p. 207.
56 Despite the fact that MacDonald was Scottish. *Leicester Daily Post*, 13 December 1918.
57 *Leicester Daily Post*, 16 December 1918. Alderman Chaplin and Councillor Salt, both of whom were expelled from the ILP and the Labour Party in early 1919. *Leicester Daily Post*, 11 November 1919.

Labourism and the challenge of war

58 LSE, ILP/4/1916/69, ILP C, A. Tuck to Francis Johnson (Lincoln). Lincoln Independent Labour Party; seizure of pamphlets, cuttings, 4 May 1916.
59 Pugh, *The Making of Modern British Politics*, p. 200; *Lincolnshire Echo*, 4 December 1918.
60 S. Bryher, *An Account of the Labour and Socialist Movement in Bristol: Part 3* (Bristol, 1931), p. 7; J. Hannam, *Bristol Independent Labour Party: Men, Women and the Opposition to War* (Bristol, 2014); C. Thomas, *Slaughter No Remedy: The Life and Times of Walter Ayles, Bristol Conscientious Objector* (Bristol, 2016); LSE, ILP/6/17/3, *The Bristol Forward*; January 1916; May 1916; June 1916.
61 Lynch, *A Tale of Three Cities*, p. 154; LSE, ILP/5/1916/6, ILP pamphlets and leaflets, 'Defence before the court-martial' by W. H. Ayles, author's defence speech, 1916.
62 Sheppard was due to stand as Labour candidate for Bristol Central but his union, the NUBSO, withdrew their financial support for his candidature due to his stance on the coalition government, *Western Daily Press*, 2 December 1918.
63 Pugh, *Speaking for Britain!*, p. 123.
64 Trade union membership of the party more than doubled between 1910 and 1918. Thorpe, *A History of the British Labour Party*, p. 39.
65 A. Marwick, *The Deluge: British Society and the First World War* (London, 1965), p. 77.
66 NHRO, 1977/44/NTC3, NTC M, 21 April 1915; *NM*, 28 June 1918.
67 *Northampton Daily Echo*, 28 June 1916; *Northampton Mercury*, 30 June 1916; NHRO, 1977/44/NTC3, NTC M, 21 April 1915.
68 Freeden, *Ideologies and Political Theory*, pp. 81, 451.
69 Harris, 'Labour's political and social thought', p. 31.
70 Lawrence, 'Labour and the politics of class', p. 237.
71 NHRO, 1977/44/NTC3, NTC M, 16 June 1915.
72 *Western Daily Press*, 4 December 1918; *Leicester Daily Post*, 13 December 1918; 14 December 1918; *Northampton Daily Echo*, 11 December 1918.
73 Ward, *Red Flag and the Union Jack*, pp. 155–156; B. Jones, *The Russia Complex: The British Labour Party and the Soviet Union* (Manchester, 1977), p. 4.
74 *Western Daily Press*, 2 December 1918; *Leicester Daily Post*, 13 December 1918; 14 December 1918.
75 *Leicester Daily Post*, 28 November 1918; *Western Daily Press*, 6 December 1918: emphasis added.
76 *Lincolnshire Echo*, 17 May 1918.
77 *Western Daily Press*, 24 December 1917.
78 *Northampton Mercury*, 13 December 1918.
79 Arthur Taylor, Labour candidate for Lincoln in 1918. *Lincolnshire Echo*, 26 November 1918. See also Ernest Bevin, Labour candidate for Bristol Central in 1918. *Western Daily Press*, 14 December 1918.
80 For trade unionist responses to these measures, see H. Clegg, A. Fox and A. Thompson, *A History of British Trade Unions since 1889: Volume 2,*

1911–1933 (Oxford, 1985), pp. 153–154; Cronin, *The Politics of State Expansion*, p. 46.

81 For examples, see *Lincolnshire Chronicle*, 4 September 1915; NHRO, 1977/44/NTC3, NTC M, 16 June 1915; BRO, 44562/2, printed political papers, election leaflet for E. Bevin, 1918; BRO, 32080/TC6/2/1, Bristol Labour Party municipal, local and national elections records (hereafter BLP), election leaflet of T. C. Lewis, 1918.

82 LSE, ILP/8/1917/53, Socialist and Labour Thought – ILP pamphlets, H. E. Witard, *The Norwich Trades' Council and Labour Representative Committee and the Right Honourable G. H. Roberts, J. P., M.P*, 1917.

83 Cronin, *The Politics of State Expansion*, p. 45; McKibbin, *The Evolution of the Labour Party*, p. 88.

84 Thorpe, *A History of the British Labour Party*, pp. 41–42.

85 Harris, 'Labour's political and social thought', p. 16.

86 G. D. H. Cole, A History of the Labour Party from 1914 (London, 1948), pp. 44, 55.

87 Worley, *Labour inside the Gate*, p. 13; Harris, 'Labour's political and social thought', p. 13.

88 B. Pimlott, 'The Labour left', in C. Cook and I. Taylor, *The Labour Party: An Introduction to its history, structure and politics* (London), 1980, p. 166.

89 McKibbin, *The Evolution of the Labour Party*, pp. 98–102.

90 L. Minkin, *The Contentious Alliance: Trade Unions and the Labour Party* (London, 1992), p. 10.

91 Thorpe, *A History of the British Labour Party*, p. 45.

92 There was bitter resistance within the NUBSO towards the government's decision to extend unemployment insurance to the boot and shoe trade. Fox, *A History of the NUBSO*, p. 381.

93 *Northampton Daily Echo*, 6 December 1918; MRC, 547/P/1/33, NUBSO MR, June 1917.

8

Old radicalism and the new social order

It is not surprising that so many studies of the Labour Party begin or end in 1918. That year marked not only the end of the First World War but also the moment when Labour announced its intention to become a truly national party. In February 1918, a party conference adopted a new constitution that permitted the establishment of constituency parties with individual membership and committed Labour to pursuing the common ownership of the means of production, distribution and exchange. The aim of these changes was to shift the party's image from that of a trade union pressure group to that of a party capable of forming the official opposition and, eventually, the government. Labour achieved the latter objective in January 1924, by which time the party was on its way to becoming the dominant progressive force in several towns and cities across Britain.

The teleological nature of this narrative belies the chaotic political and industrial atmosphere of the immediate post-war period. The Conservative-dominated coalition government, which had swept to power in a landslide victory in December 1918, had to deal with an unprecedented level of strike action involving textile workers, miners, railwaymen and even the police. The turn from 'boom' economy to recession, which brought a decline in industrial production, a fall in exports, a sharp drop in wholesale and retail prices, and a reduction in wage rates, resulted in a weakening of trade union power and a rise in unemployment. The government's decision to abandon wartime economic controls did little to help matters, and its proposal to hand back control of the mines to colliery owners, who intended to reduce wages and extend working hours, led to a lockout in the industry in early 1921. As the railwaymen and transport workers refused to take action alongside their allies in the 'triple alliance', the miners were defeated and the post-war industrial unrest came to an end.[1]

It was in this context that the Labour Party undertook 'one of the most remarkable transformations in British political history'.[2] Between

1919 and 1922, local Labour parties extended their organisations and made impressive though uneven gains in municipal and parliamentary by-elections.[3] At the 1922 general election, Labour overtook the still-divided Liberal Party to become the official opposition for the first time, and in December 1923, it increased its number of seats from 142 to 191. With the defeat of the Conservative government's protectionist King's Speech, Stanley Baldwin, the prime minister, advised the king to send for Ramsay MacDonald, and the first Labour government was formed with Liberal support.

By this time, there were already signs that Labour was becoming a broad-based, populist party. While the Parliamentary Labour Party (PLP) retained its male trade union bias between 1918 and 1922, the 1922 general election saw the return to Parliament of a new cohort of middle-class intellectuals that included nine public school boys, twenty-one university graduates and twenty-six professionals.[4] Middle-class liberals also found their way into the ILP, which increased its influence in the higher echelons of the Labour Party and the PLP during this period.[5] And in order to accommodate the admission of women to the franchise, Labour appointed a chief women's officer, employed women organisers, encouraged local parties to form or strengthen existing women's sections, and began to make more direct appeals to women in its election literature.[6]

For many activists, these changes were proof that Labour was in the process of becoming a fundamentally different organisation to the one that it had been before the war. But this view exaggerates the extent to which Labour changed after 1918. As Ross McKibbin and others have argued, what was surprising about the post-war party was its 'enduring *ante-bellum* character', the 'continuity of leadership and personnel at all levels' and the 'continuity of organization'.[7] Examining the development of local Labour parties sheds further light on these changes and continuities. Even as Labour presented itself as a national party, it is still more accurate to speak of hundreds of Labour parties, 'all with similarities but all distinctive within their own geographical context'.[8] And for all the transformational impact of the constitutional changes of 1918, individual membership at a local level was largely disappointing and financial support from trade unions remained crucial for the effective functioning of local parties.[9] For McKibbin, most of the reorganised Labour parties were 'not strikingly different, if they were different at all, from the pre-war delegate parties'.[10]

With this in mind, it is not surprising that labourist currents of thought remained active and influential at a local level. As in the pre-war and wartime periods, labourists articulated a vision of the social order and an ideology that set them apart from socialists, liberals and conservatives within and outside the Labour Party. They continued to refer back to historical events in order to present themselves as the direct heirs of older political traditions. In Northampton, Labour candidates and activists frequently mentioned Charles Bradlaugh and what Arthur Henderson described as 'the ideals of militant radicalism which gave Northampton its special place in political history' and which had been 'reincarnated ... in the Labour Party'.[11] During his election campaign in Leicester West in 1918, Ramsay MacDonald spoke fondly of 'the fine old traditions of the Liberal party' and his successor, Frederick Pethick-Lawrence, called himself the 'true heir of the Liberal tradition'.[12] Similarly, during his campaign in Bristol East in 1924, Labour's Walter Baker told voters that 'the Labour movement of today [had] inherited everything that was good in the Radical movement of [his] boyhood'.[13]

Statements of this kind were part of an attempt to win over voters in what were historically radical, Liberal-voting constituencies. But as previous chapters have illustrated, they were also indicative of strong continuities between old and new political traditions and, in particular, between working-class radicalism and labourism. Labourists, like working-class radicals before them, exhibited a strong sense of class while rejecting the theory of the class struggle. As Jon Lawrence has shown, the tone of the interwar Labour Party's radicalism 'often leant more towards workerism than populism', which served to give the party's message 'a distinctly class-inflected dimension'.[14] Even as they came to accept the need to broaden the party's appeal, labourists continued to draw attention to the distinctions between different social classes and intellectual traditions. At the same time, while 'suspicion of middle-class intellectualism was rampant' in the party throughout the interwar period, labourists denied accusations that they sought to stir up class hatred and insisted that they remained committed to treading the path of constitutionalism.[15]

Male labourists clung to many of their restrictive assumptions about groups that had historically been marginalised within the Labour Party, including the long-term unemployed, non-British workers and the undeserving poor. The decision to open up the party to anyone who wished to join was not universally popular, and while centrally produced literature tried to present Labour as the party for all who worked by hand or by brain, 'misconceptions and class prejudices' continued to sour relations 'across the manual/non-manual divide'.[16] Wartime changes in the composition of the workforce also failed to transform male labourist attitudes towards women.[17] As Gail Braybon has found, 'distrust, disparagement and ... amused contempt' were the most common reactions among male workers to women who entered industry during the war years and, despite frequent claims that Labour had become the 'women's party', male party leaders and activists continued to use gendered terms and phrases that reinforced the notion that a woman's place was in the home.[18]

The influx of liberals into the party, the growing internal strength of the ILP, the external influence of the communist movement, and the retirement or death of old lib–lab stalwarts gave Labour a degree of ideological eclecticism that it had lacked before the war.[19] Such diversity enabled the party to highlight or downplay certain aspects of its message depending on the local context. The party's adoption of a socialist constitution proved useful in shoring up support from socialists who may have been tempted to join the nascent Communist Party of Great Britain (CPGB). In former Liberal strongholds, Labour members could present their party as being 'more attentive to Liberal values than the Liberal party itself', while in localities where working-class Conservatism was strong, such as in the West Midlands, the south coast, Lancashire and parts of London, it could play up the 'tory radical' element that had been present in the party since its foundation.[20]

But it is important not to confuse organisational changes with intellectual changes. As numerous studies have shown, many former members of the Liberal Party made the transition into the Labour Party without making any significant adjustment to their ideological perspectives. This was not because Labour was essentially a liberal party, any more than it was a socialist party. It was an ideological broad church that could accommodate intellectual forces that operated within the fluid boundaries laid out (vaguely) in the party's constitution. And while the growing influence of socialists and former Liberals in the upper echelons of the party had the effect of pushing it to a more marginal position in official, national-level Labour discourse, labourism remained an important intellectual current at the grassroots level throughout the interwar period and beyond.

Strengthening the party

For G. D. H. Cole, the main purpose of the 1918 reorganisation proposals was to 'transform the Labour Party from a Federation, able to act only through its affiliated societies, into a nationally organised Party, with a Local Party of its own in every parliamentary constituency'. Local parties were to become 'not so much affiliated societies with a separate life of their own, as subordinate branches of the Labour Party itself'.[21] In theory, then, party leaders were attempting to nationalise the party. To accomplish this, they appointed more organisers and agents, encouraged trades' councils to convert into local Labour parties and compelled parliamentary candidates to give prominence to issues as defined by the national executive and the party programme.[22]

Local studies can be used to assess how successful party leaders were in implementing their plans. Before the war, Leicester was hailed as having one of the best-organised LRCs in the country. The party's strength had been dependent on the local ILP branch, which continued to play a key role in local labour politics after 1918.[23] Although the ILP's stance on the war ensured the defeat of its two candidates at the 1918 general election, it also prompted many to join the party in the immediate post-war period. The influx of members from socially and politically diverse backgrounds diluted the working-class character of the ILP and, to a lesser extent, the local Labour Party. At the 1919 municipal elections, Labour put forward an eclectic mix of candidates that included a masseur, a 'spinster', a cardboard box manufacturer and the customary assortment of trade union officials.[24]

By 1924, Labour could confidently claim to have replaced the Liberals as the main progressive force in Leicester. But initially, electoral progress was intermittent. In contrast to the national trend, Labour candidates did not fare well at the first post-war municipal elections in 1919. According to one local member, this was because Labour candidates faced 'the back-wash of the MacDonald prejudice', but it was also likely that a split in the Labour group on the city council was a contributing factor.[25] Divisions in the party had largely dissipated by March 1922 when the appointment of Gordon Hewart as Lord Chief Justice forced a by-election contest in the industrial constituency of Leicester East.[26] Alderman George Banton, 'the workers' champion', took the seat in a three-way contest on a swing of over 25 per cent, but lost the seat to a National Liberal at the general election eight months later. After winning it back in 1923, Banton narrowly lost the seat again in 1924, this time to a Unionist, before a new candidate captured the seat for Labour in 1929. Labour's advance in Leicester West was more straightforward. After Alfred Hill of the NUBSO avenged MacDonald's defeat by winning the seat in 1922, the Eton-educated Frederick Pethick-Lawrence took over in 1923 and held the seat until 1931.[27] And though Labour failed to capture Leicester South until 1945, it succeeded in replacing the Liberals as the main opposition party in 1924.

The ILP also had a strong influence on labour politics in Bristol. The formation of the Bristol Borough Labour Party, intended as a central co-ordinating body for divisional Labour parties set up in each of Bristol's five parliamentary constituencies, reduced the political influence of the Bristol Trades' Council, which had been at the centre of the political labour movement in the city since the 1880s. This coincided with a growth in strength of the local ILP, which played a crucial role in the organisational development of Bristol labour politics in the interwar period. After serving time in prison as a conscientious objector, Walter Ayles, a member of the ILP's National Administrative Council who had been the party's organiser in Bristol since 1910, became chairman of the Bristol Borough Labour Party and was selected to stand as the Labour candidate for Bristol North. ILP members gained a strong presence in the women's sections of the party and were well represented on the city council, which Labour failed to capture during the interwar period due to the success of a Liberal–Conservative pact. The ILP also saw off challenges to its left, including those from the CPGB and the BSS, the former political home of Ramsay MacDonald and Ernest Bevin that attempted a revival in the early 1920s.[28]

Despite the growing influence of the ILP, there remained a diversity of opinion within the Bristol Labour Party on issues such as the unemployed, whose numbers had swelled to 20,000 in Bristol by September 1921, and the post-war industrial unrest, which saw Bristol dockers, seamen, gasworkers, miners and transport workers engage in strike action.[29] Still, ILPers were well represented among candidates and elected officials. In 1923, Walter Baker, an ILPer and member of the Union of Post Office Workers, became the first Labour MP for Bristol East, a seat that had been in Liberal hands since its creation in 1885. Labour found it more difficult to dislodge the Liberals in Bristol North, where Walter Ayles' brand of 'Socialism, Christian Pacifism and Internationalism' only succeeded when the non-Labour vote was split between two other candidates.[30] Labour was initially unsuccessful in Bristol South, which remained a Liberal seat until 1929, while the party's strategy of running candidates from middle-class backgrounds largely failed in the Unionist strongholds of Bristol Central and Bristol West.

Labour's progress in Lincoln was more consistent with the 'rise of Labour' thesis. Although Labour did not contest the seat before 1918, Robert Arthur Taylor, a locally prominent trade unionist and Labour's candidate at every parliamentary election between 1918 and 1931, drew on a local radical tradition that stretched back centuries. In 1918, Taylor, the son of a village blacksmith and a member of the National Amalgamated Union of Shop Assistants, came second in a three-way parliamentary contest, pushing the sitting Liberal MP into third place. After winning a scholarship to Ruskin College in 1921, Taylor returned to Lincoln to contest the seat at the 1922 and 1923 general elections, failing both times to dislodge the Unionists, before capturing the seat against the national tide in 1924.[31]

The Lincoln Labour Party made slow but steady progress at a municipal level before 1924, when the Liberals and Conservatives joined forces to establish the anti-Labour Citizens' League in order to stop the city from being turned into a 'representative of Russia'.[32] This was an unfair representation of the local Labour Party, which was anything but communist in orientation. In fact, it remained firmly in the hands of moderate trade union officials who had led the Lincoln Trades' and Labour Council in the pre-war period and who continued to stand as municipal candidates after 1918. Between 1919 and 1924, Labour candidates included a painter, a wheelwright and joiner, a fitter, a railway locomotive fireman, a shop steward, the secretary of the local branch of the Amalgamated Society of Engineers, and the president of the local branch of the National Union of Railwaymen ('a doughty son of the proletariat').[33] While Labour did benefit from the exodus of members from the Liberal Party, the deserters who made the most significant impact were former lib–lab trade unionists.[34]

The Northampton Labour Party was also successful at attracting recruits from the divided Liberal Party. This was largely due to the foreign policy pronouncements of the ILP, a party that overtook the successors of the British Socialist Party to become the most influential socialist organisation in Northampton in the post-war period. Beginning in 1918, the ILP used its dominant position in the local party to ensure the selection of ILP-endorsed candidates for parliamentary honours, including at a by-election contest in early 1920. Although she failed to capture the seat, Margaret Bondfield, a prominent ILPer who had held leading posts in the Shop Assistants' Union, the National Union of General Workers and the Women's Trade Union League, improved on Labour's 1918 performance by tapping into voters' anger over high food prices and profiteering.[35] After increasing her share of the vote in 1922, Bondfield became the first Labour MP in Northampton's history and one of the first Labour women elected to Parliament in December 1923.

Though Bondfield lost the seat at the following election, Labour had established itself as the main rival to the Conservative Party in what was a historically Liberal stronghold. Things were rather different at the municipal level, where Labour only succeeded in surpassing the Liberals in 1937. It was also at the municipal level where non-ILP socialists retained an influence in the local party. In 1922, seven out of the party's ten municipal election candidates were either members or former members of the SDF, an organisation that had undergone a series of name changes but which could trace its roots back to the SDF founded in the 1880s.[36] Although the secretary of the local ILP branch insisted that the 'war-mongrels' were a 'very small section' of the local movement, the continued existence of this group and the influence its members exerted over the trade union movement helped to maintain the link between the contemporary Labour Party and older traditions of militant radicalism.[37]

Pro-war socialists had less room to manoeuvre in Norwich, where Labour activists had withdrawn their support from the city's Labour MP, George Roberts, because of his conduct while serving in the wartime government. Roberts topped the poll as a 'Coalition Labour' candidate in 1918, but the newly formed Norwich Labour Party and Industrial Council struck deep roots in the trade union movement and increased its representation on the city council from four councillors and aldermen to nineteen by the end of 1924.[38] The influence of the ILP was again evident in the party's choice of candidates. Between 1918 and 1931, every parliamentary candidate who stood in Norwich was an ILPer, including Walter Smith, an organiser for the NUBSO and honorary president of the National Union of Agricultural Workers, and Dorothy Jewson, a Norwich-born, privately educated teacher and Cambridge graduate who had become a leading figure in the women's section of the National Union of General Workers.[39] A split in the non-Labour vote in 1923 had allowed Smith and Jewson to capture the two parliamentary seats and to take revenge on George Roberts, who had become an anti-socialist member of the Conservative Party.[40] Labour's victory convinced the Conservatives and Liberals to nominate just one candidate each at subsequent elections, which hindered Labour's progress in the city until after the Second World War.

Class party or populist party?

Post-war Labour candidates and activists laced their speeches and literature with terms that demonstrated the survival of older conceptions of the social order. They continued to articulate a strong but non-adversarial sense of class, emphasising Labour's working-class composition while rejecting communist theories of the class war. In Norwich, a handbill produced for G. F. Johnson's and Herbert Witard's campaigns in 1922 advised voters that 'the practical business of the Labour Party in politics' was to fight 'every capitalist attempt to worsen ... the conditions of working-class life, whether in wages, in education, in public health administration, or in any other direction.'[41] Municipal election candidates made similar appeals. At the 1919 elections, Labour candidates in Lincoln placed themselves before the electors 'on the ground that Trade Unionists are under-represented on the City Council'. In Bristol, one of the party's male candidates defended his decision to run against a middle-class female candidate by claiming that he wanted 'women on the City Council who knew the conditions of life amongst the working-class from experience'.[42] In Leicester, one candidate declared that no one could tell 'what the workers wanted better than a man who had lived his life as a worker', while another admitted that 'if elected, he would represent the working man only' because other classes 'had sufficient people to look after their interests already'.[43]

Workerist appeals of this kind were not unique to the towns and cities covered in this study.[44] As in the pre-war period, these appeals also tended to add class inflections not only to seemingly inclusive terms and phrases such as 'the people' but also to visual elements in posters and handbills. In a handbill distributed in Norwich during the 1922 election campaign, one section of text stated that Labour's policy was 'the *People's* Welfare', while the corresponding cartoon depicted the two candidates standing alongside a male factory worker looking towards a rising sun.[45] Similarly, in the run-up to the Northampton by-election in 1920, *The Labour Outlook* published a cartoon that presented 'The Profiteer' as a greedy octopus wearing a top hat who had caught a group of poorly clothed men and women in its tentacles. While the idea of 'the profiteer' was often incorporated into appeals to attract disgruntled middle-class voters, the cartoonist in this case was clear that the profiteer was depicted 'as the workers experience him' (see Figure 3).[46]

Figure 3 'The Profiteer', *The Labour Outlook*, 31 March 1920

Many of these campaigns were conducted during severe social and industrial turmoil that, for Jon Lawrence, served to intensify 'class feeling' in Britain.[47] But class feeling did not necessarily translate into class antagonism. This is an important distinction to make and one that Labour candidates and activists frequently drew attention to. Very often, they were forced into making this distinction by their opponents, who equated Labour's emphasis on the working class with a desire to be unjust to other sections of the community. They were also forced to clarify their views during the post-war industrial unrest, when they attempted to develop an assertive trade union movement without succumbing to the 'direct actionist' ethos that had infected some sections of the movement. This dual emphasis is evident in the recollections of Fred Jex, a member of the NUBSO who became a Labour councillor in Norwich in 1919. While Jex was a staunch trade unionist and an ILPer, he recalled that, at a shoe trade conference in London during the strike wave, he criticised Labour councillors who '[talked] about all sorts of riotous action to force the Government to do something':

> I got on the platform and told them that all they'd been talking about, about riot and disorder could get you nowhere. That won't feed anybody and that won't get anybody a job.[48]

This was a common attitude among Labour leaders and activists who had spent their adult lives in the trade union movement. But after 1918, many in the party wanted to broaden its appeal beyond male trade unionists, which resulted in a shift in the way the party presented its core messages. Though the impact was most pronounced in centrally produced literature, there was a noticeable increase in the use of populist language and phraseology at a local level. ILP members were particularly adept at blending populist and workerist sentiments, perhaps because many of them subscribed to a notion of class relations that was more inclusive than that of their labourist colleagues. ILP-backed Labour candidates such as Margaret Bondfield (Northampton), Luke Bateman (Bristol East), Walter Baker (Bristol East), Walter Ayles (Bristol North), Dorothy Jewson (Norwich) and George Banton (Leicester East) all drew on populist themes in their campaigns, emphasising, among other things, the distinction between small shopkeepers and profiteers, the domination of the coalition government by 'vested interests' and the riches that the prevailing economic system bestowed on the 'idle and useless classes'.[49] Whether consciously or not, these figures were drawing from the linguistic resources of the popular radical and liberal traditions that they were hoping to supplant.

Out of this group of candidates, Walter Ayles was perhaps the most forceful proponent of transforming Labour into an all-encompassing populist party. The inclusive tone of Ayles' rhetoric and his frequent references to non-working-class groups of voters marked a decisive shift from the class-centred ethos of radical and labour politics in Bristol. In *Bristol North Forward*, an election news-sheet issued for the 1922 election contest, the working class was now represented as one of several special interest groups alongside 'The Middle Class' and 'Women Electors'. In late 1921 and early 1922, the news-sheet argued that 'the middle class man [and] woman' were being 'robbed by our "big Capitalist" government', the 'blackcoated worker is as oppressed as the horny-handed one' and the 'Trade Unions [were] powerless to resist wage reductions altogether'. Not only that, but it even suggested that the interests of the workers and of the middle classes were one and the same, a view that directly challenged the old labourist notion that different sections of community, despite being able to work together in tactical political alliances, had distinct experiences, traits and interests. As explained in the December 1921 edition:

> Worker, Tradesman, Blackcoated Clerk and Commercial Traveller, Middle Class Organiser of industry and commerce, your interests are one. The Labour Party is no sectional party. It includes you all. Unite![50]

In a speech delivered in Bristol in July 1924, Ayles also made it clear that he had welcomed the structural changes in the party in 1918 because they served to minimise the influence of 'the great trade unions ... with large funds' and strengthened forces in the party that sought to 'maintain idealism' against 'mere sordid economic interest'.[51]

The ILP's influence in the party apparatus and the PLP certainly gives the impression that the balance of forces between 'idealists' and representatives of the 'sordid economic interest' was shifting in favour of the former. But it is important not to assume that the rise of a relatively small socialist society, which had always wielded an influence in the Labour Party out of proportion to its numerical strength, represented deeper changes in the way the most Labour members thought and spoke about the social order. The post-1918 party was very much an umbrella organisation that could, and did, accommodate multiple political and intellectual tendencies. And while the growing influence of the ILP and of men and women from non-working-class backgrounds served to strengthen previously marginal identities in the party, labourist modes of thought continued to exert a strong influence on the party at a national and a local level.

The survival of the labourist identity was evident in the way male party activists spoke about those who had been marginalised or excluded from pre-war definitions of the working class. Industrial changes brought about by the war appear to have had little impact in shifting the attitudes of male labourists towards those who in many cases had become their work colleagues. As Sarah Boston has noted, the male-dominated trade union movement sought a reversion to the pre-war sexual division of labour that had been 'fundamentally disturbed' by the wartime introduction of women into previously male-dominated areas of industry.[52] This demand conflicted with 'the interests of employers and the hope of women workers', as did the demands put forward by demobilised ex-servicemen who believed that they should have a job to return to after fighting for their country. Not surprisingly, the declaration of peace brought widespread unemployment for women workers, and by 1923 almost all of the industrial gains women had made during the war period were lost.[53]

The extension of the franchise in 1918 encouraged parliamentary and municipal candidates to pay more attention to women's concerns. As well as organising women-only campaign meetings, male candidates and activists began to refer to 'ladies and gentlemen', 'men and women' or, less commonly, 'working-men and working-women'. Some were better at accommodating women voters than others. Herbert Witard, Labour's parliamentary candidate for Norwich in 1918 and 1922, regularly spoke to women voters during and outside election campaigns, on one occasion praising 'those women who battled for women's rights years ago' and applauding 'the excellent work of the women' in changing the 'opinion of the general public'.[54] In July 1921, the Norwich Labour Party and Industrial Council even fought against plans to replace female workers in refreshment rooms on Great Eastern Railway trains with disabled ex-servicemen, contending that 'the Government's duty was to pay salaries to limbless men, not to give them women's jobs'.[55] Not surprisingly, Norwich was one of the first constituencies to elect a woman Labour MP in 1923.

But in other towns and cities, Labour activists continued to marginalise women in a number of ways. Sometimes this took the form of outright exclusion, as in Bristol in 1920 when local party leaders made no serious attempt to intervene when ex-servicemen violently demanded the sacking of women workers.[56] More often, male activists contributed to more subtle forms of marginalisation. In particular, they continued to express their belief that a woman's place, and especially a married woman's place, was in the home.[57] Centrally and locally produced Labour literature often addressed women in this way, and made the assumption that women voters were chiefly concerned with food prices, maternity clinics, widows' pensions, improved milk supply and other domestic issues. A separate-spheres narrative featured in the 1922 election edition of *The New Standard*, a Labour newspaper for Ipswich that included a cartoon and fictional dialogue between a hungry child and her mother:

> Why does Daddie look so sad, and why do you cry so often, Mummie? Is it 'cos Daddy can't get any work? Why don't we have nice things to eat like we see in the shop windows, Mummie?[58]

Gendered assumptions about work and family responsibilities also featured in a section titled 'Why Women Should Vote Labour', in which the author urged women to vote Labour because it cared for 'the welfare of mothers', put 'the needs of children first' and demanded better conditions for 'workers in their workshop and women in their homes'. As Labour was 'the Children's Party' and 'the Peace Party', it was 'Therefore ... the Women's Party'.[59]

By hand or by brain

The war years had also teased out male labourists' attitudes to race, nationality and patriotism. Though the end of the conflict helped to heal some of the divisions that had arisen between anti-war, moderately pro-war and belligerent patriotic sections of the party, developments in the immediate post-war period created new opportunities for activists to express their views on these issues. For example, Labour's decision to leave the coalition government in 1918 and its activities in opposing British involvement in the Russian Civil War opened it up to accusations that it was unpatriotic and anti-British. The party's success in attracting former Liberals also helped Labour to develop a coherent foreign policy agenda, which represented a marked shift from the pre-war period when the party had gained a reputation among continental socialists for being 'hopelessly parochial' and, in the case of some of its members, 'positively jingoistic'.[60]

But again, it is important not to equate the views of a small number of former Liberal intellectuals, however influential they were in developing party policy, with the sentiments of party members as a whole. While labourists regularly reaffirmed their commitment to the internationalist and supposedly anti-militarist ethos of the international workers' movement, they also continued to give expression to basic imperialist and, at times, racist assumptions. The war also accelerated changes in the way urban-based labourists spoke about rural workers. Whereas labourists had once drawn attention to the distinctiveness of rural labourers and their concerns, they now welcomed the 'workers of the land' as part of the working class, praising agricultural trade unions for organising 'labour in our country districts' and describing strikes in rural areas as part of *'working-class* history'.[61] An ILP pamphlet from 1922 which offered advice to speakers planning to deliver lectures in rural districts gives some sense of how far attitudes had come. As well as offering a contemporary take on the old radical notion of the 'Norman Yoke', the leaflet listed reasons why the land should be taken into public ownership:

> [It would] develop ... *workers'* control, and give the agricultural labourer active association with all the problems of management. The improved status of *the worker* in all grades and industries is the most pressing need of to-day. The agricultural labourer must be master in his own house.[62]

This shows how political actors could contribute to extending the definitional boundaries of a term or phrase. This is also evident in the way Labour leaders, thinkers and activists spoke of the 'workers by hand or by brain'. Though the phrase rarely featured in pre-war Labour discourse, it achieved an enhanced status after appearing in both *Labour and the New Social Order* and Clause IV of the 1918 party constitution. From that time on, it became a useful campaign slogan and regularly appeared in election speeches and literature. To some extent, it also accurately described the occupational background of some of the party's new MPs and councillors. Before the war, the Bristol LRC selected its candidates almost exclusively from male-dominated, manual trade unions; its list of candidates between 1909 and 1913 including a stonemason, a carter, a bricklayer, an engineer, a plasterer, a brass finisher, a shoemaker and a carpenter.[63] After the war, however, the Bristol Labour Party drew its candidates from more diverse sources; its slate of candidates between 1919 and 1921 included a photographer, an ex-clergyman, a number of clerks, a 'married woman', a dental mechanic, a shop manager, a 'spinster', a grocer and, of course, an assortment of male trade union officials.[64] Similar changes occurred in Northampton and Leicester, though in Lincoln and Norwich Labour councillors still tended to be drawn from manual working-class occupations.

These changes demonstrate the extent to which previously marginalised groups could prosper in the reorganised Labour Party. Still, this growth was not strong enough to displace pre-existing groups. Rather than seeing Labour as a party that could accommodate *either* class-based or populist forms of politics, it is better to see it as one capable of accommodating one or the other or even both depending on the time or place. Indeed, the organisers of the Bristol Labour Party seemed fully aware of the importance of selecting the most appropriate candidate for a particular constituency. In the socially diverse constituency of Bristol Central, it adopted Brigadier-General Christopher Birdwood Thomson, CBE, a decorated soldier and defector from the Liberals, and J. A. Lovat-Fraser, a Cambridge-educated barrister and defector from the Conservatives, to contest the 1922 and 1924 general elections respectively. In the predominantly working-class and former Liberal stronghold of Bristol East, on the other hand, the party put forward Luke Bateman and Walter Baker, both of whom were trade unionist members of the ILP.[65] Leaders of the Norwich Labour Party also made a conscious effort to win over the 'clerical and small commercial classes' who made up a sizeable proportion of the city's electorate, succeeding in 1923 by offering 'black-coated workers' the chance to vote for the 'solid reliability' of a trade union leader and the 'intellectual brilliance' of a privately educated former teacher.[66]

There were noticeable differences in the way these candidates interpreted and presented Labour's core messages. Middle-class members of the party who had recently defected from the Liberals or the Conservatives were more likely to imbue 'workers by hand or by brain' with a broad meaning. Walter Oram, a cardboard box manufacturer who stood as a Labour municipal election candidate in Leicester in 1919, denied that Labour had a 'selfish, sectional, or class programme', stating that he considered himself one of those whose labour 'whether by hand or brain ... enriched the community'.[67] Christopher Birdwood Thomson's election flyer for the 1922 contest in Bristol Central made similar claims, contending that while Labour 'was originally a party of manual workers', it had been transformed into 'a combination of men and women of goodwill, who desire social progress by constitutional means'.[68] Rhetoric of this kind was not limited to the constituencies covered in this book. The election address of Norman Angell, who contested the Rushcliffe constituency in 1922, denied that Labour stood for 'the special interests of the employed as distinct from those of the employer', rejected claims that Labour was the 'enemy of private property', and even argued that the capital levy, when taken in conjunction with income tax readjustments, would actually make 'possessors of fortunes up to twenty thousand pounds ... better off from an income point of view'.[69]

Conversely, candidates from trade union backgrounds were more likely to use a language of class. Women trade unionists such as Mary Macarthur, founder of the National Federation of Women Workers and

Labour candidate for Stourbridge in 1918, also tended to blend the politics of class with the politics of gender. In her election address, Macarthur made it clear that she stood for 'the WOMAN WHOSE WORK NEVER ENDS', or the woman in the home 'who has been too often neglected or forgotten by politicians'. At the same time, she admitted that if returned to the House of Commons she would 'try to voice in a special sense the aspirations of THE WOMEN WORKERS OF THIS LAND', to whose cause she had devoted so much of her life.[70] Margaret Bondfield made similar appeals in her campaigns in Northampton. In 1923, she provided voters with a succinct summary of the Labour party's mission:

> They were out to help the working classes, not because they wished to perpetuate a class war, but because they believed that the true wealth of the country depends on the health and happiness of the homes of the people, and that no country was rich that had 20 millions of its people on the verge of starvation as we have to-day.[71]

While Bondfield and other trade unionist candidates made explicit appeals to groups outside the working class, they very rarely suggested that the interests of these groups and those of the workers were one and the same. Instead, they tried to convince other groups to join the workers in a tactical alliance of the oppressed. This represented a broadening of the party's appeal, but it was also consistent with an idea deeply rooted in the labourist worldview since the nineteenth century, namely that different social classes could maintain their distinctiveness while working together for specific ends.

Without upheavals and bloodshed

In 1919, the Bristol branch of the ILP published a leaflet outlining some of the key differences between the various sections of the Labour Party. For its author, Labour was composed of three groupings: the trade unions that organised for industrial purposes, the co-operative societies that organised for commercial purposes and the ILP that organised for 'Social and Political purposes'. While the trade unions and co-operative societies supplied Labour with the numbers (and the money), the ILP acted as a political driving force that invested Labour with a sense of purpose and direction.[72]

This view rested on the assumption that Labour members who took an interest in politics were, or should be, members of the ILP. In many ways, this mirrored the view of Labour's critics, who argued that Labour was divided into extremist socialist and moderate trade union wings.[73] But both ILP members and Labour's critics exaggerated the influence of the ILP and the differences between the 'industrial', 'commercial' and 'political' wings of the Labour Party. Their statements also suggest that there remained a large body of labourists who, while committed to the Labour Party, could not bring themselves to join the socialist ILP. As in the pre-war period, labourist responses to social and political issues continued to emanate from the morphology of concepts in labourism. The interrelationship between democracy, class, trade unionism and liberty, combined with historical and cultural assumptions about the English national character and the constitution, helps to account for labourists' rejection of unconstitutional methods of effecting socio-political change. Their commitment to parliamentarianism was severely tested by the growing popularity of 'direct action' and the enhanced prestige of revolutionary politics in the aftermath of the Bolshevik Revolution. On the whole, though, labourists and moderate socialists were united in their desire to keep the Labour Party 'on the path of moderation and of constitutional method', and they were keen to draw a line between their methods and those of the newly formed CPGB.

A preference for constitutional methods united labourists and moderate socialists. During the 1920 by-election campaign in Northampton, Margaret Bondfield, who was adept at blending labourist with socialist themes, reminded voters that they had 'a wonderful political system in this country' which 'the working classes' could take hold of to 'make transformations without upheavals and bloodshed'.[74] For Bondfield, the democratic nature of the British political system meant that it was simply unnecessary for voters to follow the example set by their counterparts in Russia and Germany.[75] Furthermore, for both moderate socialists and labourists, interminable strife between employers and workers would cause as much distress to the latter as it would to the former. Consequently, Labour candidates stressed the expediency of constitutional methods while also arguing that they provided an effective bulwark against 'violent upheaval and class war'.[76]

Labourist statements on Bolshevism were consistent with the views put forward by those who, in the pre-war period, had rejected the revolutionary schemes of small minorities. This view rested on a conviction that the English constitution guaranteed certain rights and liberties to all members of the community. As this was the case, labourists were in no doubt that Labour would be able to form a government if and when the electors willed it.[77] For them, the House of Commons' failure to reflect the social make-up of the country was due not to the actions of political elites but to the inactions of the working class, who, despite forming the majority of the electorate, refused to vote in their own interests. And the fact that the workers chose not to use the political weapon in their hands did not mean that impatient activists should import violent alternatives from abroad.

The idea that revolutionary methods were a foreign import and incompatible with the British sense of fair play was another hangover from the pre-war era. At times, it led activists to express their opposition to communism in xenophobic and anti-Semitic terms. In May 1923, an executive member of the Lincoln Labour Party advocated the deportation of all 'Russian and Polish Jews and disguised Bolshevists' who sought to stir up 'civil war and industrial strife'.[78] But it was more common for labourists and moderate socialists to compare the Bolsheviks' violent tendencies with the British respect for the rule of law and the rights of the individual. As explained by Ethel Snowden, the one-time candidate for Leicester East who had visited Russia with the Labour delegation in 1920, 'Bolshevist methods might be useful [in Russia]' but they were not applicable to Britain, where a strong sense of individuality caused even the most ardent socialist to remain 'an individualist in private affairs'.[79]

Labourists, moderate socialists and liberals in the Labour Party were united in their condemnation of revolutionary violence. Still, there remained important differences in the way members of each tradition articulated and prioritised their demands. One way to identify these differences is to examine the way activists handled the concept of the state. Between 1918 and 1924, Labour election manifestos advocated the nationalisation of the mines, railways and electrical power stations, a 'large programme' of public works, and 'more generous provision' for old-age pensioners.[80] 'Left liberals' who had brought the concepts of equality and the state into closer proximity to the liberal core favoured these proposals as a way of enhancing their notions of individuality and progress.[81] In contrast, ILP socialists tended to interpret them as stepping-stones to a future co-operative commonwealth. As explained in a 1922 election handbill distributed by supporters of the ILP-endorsed Labour candidates for Norwich, Labour's manifesto pledges were 'palliative[s] only' and, as soon as voters returned them to power, Labour intended to 'advance directly to the task of bringing in the new social order' by 'substituting the co-operative commonwealth for the tragic absurdities of capitalism'.[82]

Labourists, on the other hand, believed that the state should assume responsibility only for areas in which fundamental needs were concerned.[83] And because of the relationship between the state, class, democracy, trade unionism and other concepts in labourist morphology, labourists were above all concerned with ensuring that the state protected the rights of the workers. This is not to say that members of the ILP were incapable of expressing similar sentiments, a sign perhaps that the party remained 'both a Labour *and* [a] Socialist party' that could accommodate 'the Labour man' and 'the Socialist'.[84] For example, class-based appeals featured in the campaign literature of Robert Jackson, a former stonemason who contested the Ipswich constituency at every election between 1918 and 1935. Jackson's election address in 1918 was a lucid exposition of the labourist worldview, containing a summary of the working-class credentials of the candidate, a demand that the workers should be represented 'by one who knows their lives', a number of appeals to 'the Workers' rather than to the community as a whole, and proposals for a limited scheme of public ownership. Jackson's 1922 election address removed some of these workerist references but still made no mention of Labour's socialist objective or the ILP's commitment to building a socialist commonwealth. They were also absent from *The New Standard*, the Ipswich Labour Party's election news-sheet through which Jackson expressed his views on political and industrial topics.[85]

In *The New Standard* and his election addresses, Jackson placed a great deal of emphasis on Labour's practical solutions to the problems of the day and the immediate benefits that their enactment would bring to the workers. For instance, in 1922, Jackson condemned the intensification of unemployment for '[playing] havoc with the lives of many of our working people'. He favoured the nationalisation of the mines and railways as a way of improving 'the industrial efficiency of the nation' and the 'precarious condition of the mine workers'. Labour candidates around the country shared Jackson's interpretation of Labour's programme and, like him, gave precedence to the claims of the workers, approached political and social questions from the workers' viewpoint, and frequently drew attention to distinctions between different sections of the community. Even as they came to accept the need to broaden the party's appeal beyond its traditional base, and despite the influx of new members into the party in the post-war period, many Labour candidates and activists refused to abandon their commitment to a class-based rather than populist understanding of the social and political order.[86]

Conclusion

Prior to the formation of its first government in 1924, Labour was in the process of becoming something more than a trade union party. In the aftermath of the constitutional changes of 1918, party leaders encouraged professionals, intellectuals, women and individuals from the public schools and universities to join the party and assist it in replacing the once-dominant Liberal Party. However, it is important not to exaggerate the transformative impact of these organisational changes and the influence that the new members exerted on the party base. Examining the party's post-war development at the local level, it is clear that there remained significant regional variation in the party's composition and focus. Furthermore, for all its attempts to turn itself into a party representing 'the nation', Labour remained, at all levels of its machinery, a party under the influence of the trade union movement.

If this was indeed the case, then it is not surprising that labourism – as both an identity and an ideology – remained a powerful force in local Labour parties in the post-war era. The influx of liberals, socialists and communists into the party, as well as the growing strength of the ILP, added a more populist tone to centrally and locally produced official literature, a change that appeared to minimise the relative power of the labourist tendency. But the arrival of former lib–lab trade unionists, who complemented the existing band of labourist politicians and activists, more than offset these changes. Just as in the pre-war period, labourists continued to promote their distinctive vision of politics and the social order, which, to some extent, could be seen as a middle way between the socially inclusive theories of the liberals and the class-war theories of militant socialists. Labourist candidates and activists exhibited a strong sense of class, appealing directly to working-class voters, emphasising their working-class credentials, privileging the concerns and interests of 'their class', and stressing the importance of working-class representation on local and national governing bodies. And as before the war, they also interpreted certain terms, slogans and party messages such as 'the people' and 'workers by hand and by brain' in a much less inclusive way than their middle-class colleagues.

Post-war political and economic developments forced labourists to consider the lives and conditions of 'other' workers to a greater extent than before. But judging by their attitudes and statements, male labourists continued to hold restrictive assumptions about groups that had traditionally been marginalised within the Labour Party. Most male activists, for example, continued to use highly gendered terms in their political discourse, appealing to women primarily as wives and homemakers rather than as fellow workers. Moreover, while women and other previously marginalised groups such as non-manual workers found more ample space in which to navigate in the post-war party, their increasing prominence did not lead to the displacement of labourist forms of thought and action. This is evident in the sheer variety of Labour messages at a local level, and the divergent ways in which labourists, socialists and liberals within the party interpreted its nature and mission.

Finally, though its voice became less audible in the party after the organisational changes of 1918, labourist ideology remained a significant force in local and national Labour politics. If anything, the ideological concepts that formed the core of pre-war and pre-twentieth-century iterations of labourism remained just as relevant (and perhaps even more so) in the changed political and industrial environment of the post-war era. And while moderate socialists, liberals and labourists agreed on a whole range of policy issues, there remained key differences in the way they understood and prioritised these demands. We can see this clearly in the way representatives of each section discussed Labour's programme of nationalisation, which socialists interpreted in millenarian terms, left liberals as a way of enhancing individuality and progress, and labourists as an effective remedy to age-old problems that would bring immediate benefits to the working class. These differences can be explained by treating socialism, liberalism and labourism as distinct ideologies that, despite similarities and, in some cases, shared origins, were based on contrasting conceptual frameworks. These ideological distinctions continued to cause heated discussions and political splits within the Labour Party throughout the 1920s and beyond.

Notes

1 Clegg, Fox and Thompson, *A History of British Trade Unions since 1889: Volume 2*, pp. 266–275, 312, 568; Worley, *Labour inside the Gate*, p. 35; Thorpe, *A History of the British Labour Party*, p. 50.
2 Pelling, *Popular Politics and Society*, p. 101.
3 D. Tanner, 'Elections, statistics, and the rise of the Labour Party, 1906–1931', *The Historical Journal*, 34:3 (1991), pp. 893–908; Worley, *Labour inside the Gate*, pp. 24, 73; Pugh, *Speak for Britain!*, p. 134.
4 All but eight of the Labour MPs elected in 1918 were sponsored by trade unions. Thorpe, *A History of the British Labour Party*, p. 47.
5 Nearly half of the total number of Labour candidates in 1918 were members of the ILP. LSE, ILP/12/1/4, ILP CR, 1919; Worley, *Labour inside the Gate*, p. 28.
6 By 1924, the party claimed to have a female membership of 150,000. Francis, 'Labour and gender', p. 192.
7 McKibbin, *The Evolution of the Labour Party*, p. 240; C. Wrigley, 'The Labour Party and the impact of the 1918 Reform Act', *Parliamentary History*, 37:1 (2018), pp. 72, 79.
8 Worley, *Labour inside the Gate*, p. 2.
9 Thorpe, *A History of the British Labour Party*, p. 51.
10 McKibbin, *The Evolution of the Labour Party*, pp. 140–141.

11 LSE, ILP/6/20/15, ILP PEA, *The Labour Outlook*, 27 March 1920. See also *Northampton Daily Echo*, 18 November 1918.
12 *Leicester Daily Post* 2 December 1918.
13 *Western Daily Press*, 9 December 1924.
14 Lawrence, 'Labour and the politics of class', pp. 252–253.
15 Worley, *Labour inside the Gate*, p. 44.
16 Lawrence, 'Labour and the politics of class', p. 253.
17 Boston, *Women Workers and the Trade Union Movement*, p. 153
18 G. Braybon, *Women Workers in the First World War* (London, 1981), pp. 68, 72. See also C. A. Culleton, *Working-Class Culture, Women, and Britain, 1914–1921* (Basingstoke, 2000), pp. 52–53; C. Hunt, 'Dancing and days out: The role of social events in British women's trade unionism in the early twentieth century', *Labour History Review*, 76:2 (2011), pp. 104–120.
19 Cole, *A History of the Labour Party from 1914*, p. 54.
20 E. Green and D. Tanner (eds), *The Strange Survival of Liberal England: Political Leaders, Moral Values and the Reception of Economic Debate* (Cambridge, 2007), p. 14.
21 Cole, *A History of the Labour Party from 1914*, pp. 44–45.
22 McKibbin, *The Evolution of the Labour Party*, p. 192.
23 McKibbin, *The Evolution of the Labour Party*, p. 139.
24 *Leicester Daily Post*, 25 October 1919.
25 *Leicester Daily Post*, 5 November 1919; 11 November 1919.
26 *Daily Herald*, 21 March 1922.
27 MacDonald had made a similar appeal in 1918 to no avail. *Leicester Daily Post*, 2 December 1918.
28 *Justice*, 25 January 1923; 29 March 1923; 2 October 1924.
29 Kelly and Richardson, 'The shaping of the Bristol labour movement', p. 219; T. Sinnett, 'The development of the Labour Party in Bristol, 1918–1931' (unpublished doctoral thesis, University of the West of England, 2006), p. 234.
30 LSE, ILP/6/17/3, House Organs, Circulars and Journals, *The Bristol North Forward*, January 1922.
31 *Daily Herald*, 30 August 1921; 1 November 1924; 11 November 1924.
32 *Lincolnshire Echo*, 25 October 1921; *Lincolnshire Chronicle*, 3 November 1923; *Lincolnshire Echo*, 06 October 1924.
33 *Lincolnshire Chronicle*, 18 October 1919; *Lincolnshire Echo*, 2 November 1920; 25 October 1921.
34 *Lincolnshire Chronicle*, 18 October 1919.
35 M. Bondfield, A Life's Work (London, 1948), p. 241.
36 *Justice*, 21 August 1919; 9 November 1922.
37 LSE, ILP/4/1919/48, ILP C, W. H. Austin to J. Ramsay MacDonald (Northampton). Northampton Independent Labour Party questionnaire on local situation, 28 May 1919.
38 *Daily Herald*, 14 October 1920; 20 October 1922; 19 October 1925; NFRO, SO 198/3/1, 937X3, Norwich Labour Party annual reports, 1924.

39 *Daily Herald*, 20 July 1922; 22 November 1923.
40 NFRO, MC 655/4, 790X7, papers of G. H. Roberts MP, 'Labour and Fiscal Issues' leaflet, undated.
41 LSE, ILP/6/20/17, ILP PEA, G. F. Johnson and H. E. Witard (Norwich), 1922.
42 *Lincolnshire Chronicle*, 18 October 1919; *Western Daily Press*, 5 April 1919.
43 *Leicester Daily Post*, 22 October 1919; *Leicester Daily Post* 29 October 1919. See also LSE, ILP/6/21/5, ILP MEA, South Ward (Northampton): W. H. Austin, 1919.
44 Class informed the party's campaigns in Nottingham, Coventry, Horncastle, and localities across the north of England, London, Wales and Scotland. For examples, see P. Wyncoll, The Nottingham Labour Movement 1880–1939 (London, 1985), p. 187; LSE, ILP/6/20/15, ILP PEA, R. C. Wallhead (Coventry), 1918; LSE, ILP/6/20/17, ILP PEA, W. Holmes (Horncastle), 1920.
45 LSE, ILP/6/20/17, ILP PEA, G. F. Johnson and H. E. Witard (Norwich), 1922.
46 See also McKibbin, *Classes and Cultures*, pp. 54–55.
47 Lawrence, 'Labour and the politics of class', p. 238.
48 NFRO, SO 198/5/52, 940X1, Norwich Labour Party historical material, including transcripts of oral history interviews with early Norwich Labour Party members.
49 LSE, ILP/6/20/15, ILP PEA, *The Labour Outlook*, 31 March 1920; *Western Daily Press* 20 August 1923.
50 LSE, ILP/6/17/3, House Organs, Circulars and Journals, *The Bristol North Forward*, December 1921; January 1922.
51 *Daily Herald*, 16 June 1924; *Western Daily Press*, 14 October 1924.
52 Boston, *Women Workers and the Trade Union Movement*, pp. 132–133.
53 Boston, *Women Workers and the Trade Union Movement*, pp. 146–150.
54 *Daily Herald*, 30 September 1920.
55 *Daily Herald*, 15 July 1921.
56 Kelly and Richardson, 'The shaping of the Bristol labour movement', p. 220; *Western Daily Press*, 21 July 1920.
57 Braybon, *Women Workers in the First World War*, pp. 73–74; S. Kent, *Sex and Suffrage in Britain, 1860–1914* (Princeton, NJ, 1987), p. 221; BRO, 32080/TC6/2/1, BLP, election leaflet of T. C. Lewis, 1918.
58 LSE, ILP/6/20/17, ILP PEA, *The New Standard*, 4 November 1922.
59 LSE, ILP/6/20/17, ILP PEA, *The New Standard*, 4 November 1922.
60 Thorpe, *A History of the British Labour Party*, pp. 42–43.
61 *Lincolnshire Chronicle*, 22 July 1916. 'The Burston School Strike' pamphlet, which included a financial appeal written by a member of the Northampton Trades' Council, is attached to NHRO, 1977/44/NTC3, NTC M; emphasis added.
62 LSE, ILP/5/1922/28, ILP pamphlets and leaflets, weekly notes for speakers No. 172, 'The land for the people', 3 August 1922: emphasis added.
63 *Western Daily Press*, 26 October 1909; 25 October 1910; 25 October 1912.
64 *Western Daily Press*, 25 October 1919; 26 October 1920.
65 Sinnett, 'The development of the Labour Party in Bristol', pp. 145–146; *Western Daily Press*, 4 February 1924.

66 *Daily Herald*, 13 October 1924.
67 *Leicester Daily Post* 4 April 1919; 25 October 1919.
68 Quoted in Sinnett, 'The development of the Labour Party in Bristol', p. 146.
69 LSE, ILP/6/20/15, ILP PEA, N. Angell (Rushcliffe Division), 1922. For an example of a middle-class candidate employing a workerist language of class, see LSE, ILP/6/20/15, ILP PEA, Josiah C. Wedgwood (Staffordshire), 1922.
70 LSE, ILP/6/20/15, ILP PEA, M. R. Macarthur (Worcestershire), 1918.
71 *Northampton Chronicle and Echo*, 24 November 1923.
72 LSE, ILP/5/1919/25, ILP pamphlets and leaflets, 'The ILP and the Labour Party. What is the difference?' published by the Bristol Independent Labour Party.
73 For example, see *Northampton Chronicle and Echo*, 31 October 1922.
74 *Northampton Chronicle and Echo*, 25 March 1920.
75 M. A. Hamilton, *Margaret Bondfield* (London, 1924), p. 144.
76 LSE, ILP/6/20/17, ILP PEA, G. F. Johnson and H. E. Witard (Norwich), 1922.
77 Harris, 'Labour's political and social thought', p. 16.
78 *Daily Herald*, 21 May 1923.
79 Ethel Snowden, at one stage the Labour candidate for Leicester East, speaking in Leicester in 1920. *Leicester Daily Post*, 30 August 1920.
80 Dale, *Labour Party General Election Manifestos*, pp. 20–25.
81 Freeden, *Ideologies and Political Theory*, pp. 206–209.
82 LSE, ILP/6/20/17, ILP PEA, G. F. Johnson and H. E. Witard (Norwich), 1922. See also NFRO, HEN 43/104, 561X3, papers of J. F. Henderson, election address of D. Jewson and W. R. Smith (Norwich), October 1924.
83 Freeden, *Ideologies and Political Theory*, p. 200; 447.
84 *Leicester Pioneer*, 23 August 1902: emphasis added.
85 LSE, ILP/6/20/17, ILP PEA, election address of R. Jackson (Ipswich), 'To the Electors of Ipswich', 1918; LSE, ILP/6/20/17, ILP PEA, election address of R. Jackson (Ipswich), 1922; LSE, ILP/6/20/17, ILP PEA, *The New Standard*, 4 November 1922.
86 LSE, ILP/6/20/17, ILP PEA, *The New Standard*, 4 November 1922.

Conclusion

James Hawker was a poacher who lived and worked in the East Midlands as an agricultural labourer, a shoemaker and a soldier between 1836 and 1921. Hawker's journal, compiled during the course of 1904 and 1905, draws attention to the political, discursive and ideological differences that separated radicals from liberals in mid- to late Victorian England. Though Hawker considered 'the Tory' to be his 'Greatest Enemy', he aligned himself politically with radicals who operated on the extreme outer edges of mainstream liberal politics. Like many radicals of his age, Hawker was especially fond of Charles Bradlaugh, the 'Greatest, most fearless of Democrats' who Hawker had cast his first vote for in 1868. For Hawker, Bradlaugh was a 'Poacher on the Privileges of the rich Class', a group that had stolen 'the land from the People' and 'poached upon' the liberty of the people.

Populist radicals would have found little to disagree with in these remarks. However, Hawker often crossed the boundary between populism and class. In his journal, he expressed bitterness not only towards the 'Game-preserving Class' but also to 'all other Employers' who impoverished 'the People'. He viewed the world through the lens of class, venerating the man 'who Toils', the 'Good Honest Workman' and 'The working Class of England', terms which he used interchangeably with 'the people'. And while he believed that the 'Working Men [should] Send their Own Class' to rule over them, he insisted that he was a 'Constitutionalist' who would always bow to the will of the people.[1]

Hawker's journal provides a clear articulation of a distinctly working-class version of radicalism. This book has attempted to rescue this important political tendency from those who have sought to either subsume it within a broader political formation or deny its very existence as an ideologically coherent tradition. As we have seen, working-class radicals articulated a vision of politics and the social order that was distinct from both mainstream liberalism and populist forms of radicalism. Where liberals and populist radicals saw the major division in society as between 'the idle' and 'the industrious', working-class radicals preferred to render political struggles in social terms. Similarly, while liberals and populist radicals emphasised the benefits that their proposals would bring to the community as a whole, working-class radicals were more comfortable in privileging the concerns and demands of the working classes. And contrary to prevailing opinion, working-class radicals also articulated a unique ideology, grounded in an expansive notion of democracy and an exclusivist sense of class, which brought them into conflict with classical liberals and populist radicals. These theoretical and discursive differences may not have been as sharp as those that divided radicals and conservatives, but they were important enough to generate political splits, electoral conflicts, rival campaigns and long-term resentments that proved extremely difficult to overcome.

James Hawker's writings are indicative of a generation of working-class radicals who came to define themselves as labour activists in the final years of the nineteenth century. Indeed, by the early 1900s, Hawker had come to believe that 'every man who [wanted] to Better is [sic] Position' and the position of 'every man who Toils' should vote for candidates representing the Labour Party. If 'very [sic] working man Does his Duty', then Labour, he argued, would 'Rule the world'. For Hawker, Labour was the party of the working class for the working class, a view that was typical among those who supported or sympathised with the party in the first quarter of the twentieth century.

The creation of a national Labour Party was a novel political development. The party's intellectual roots, however, lie in older traditions. Departing from previous studies that have focused on the liberal, socialist and tory roots of the Labour Party, this book has used five case studies to demonstrate the working-class radical influence on the party in its rise to power. It has shown that there were substantial continuities between the working-class radical politics of the mid- to late Victorian era and the 'official' Labour politics of the early twentieth century. During the 1880s and 1890s, working-class radicals established local labour parties that would later evolve into local cells of a national party. These activists added new demands to their political programmes and adopted a more insistent strategy for achieving working-class political representation. They also showed a greater willingness to use the state to improve the lives of the working class and the poor.

But in Bristol, Leicester, Northampton, Norwich and Lincoln, the emergence of labour politics represented the renewal rather than an abandonment of working-class radicalism. Labour activists found much of use in this old political tradition, from a well-developed language of class to an exclusivist yet non-adversarial understanding of social relations.

Labourists, like their political predecessors, were proud of their working-class origins, assiduous in pressing the claims of their class and comfortable with the idea of expressing 'workerist' views in political debates. They also articulated a coherent ideology that, in essence, was a more collectivist version of working-class radicalism. Often overshadowed in the historiography by its more vocal counterparts, labourism, as both an identity and an ideology, deserves to be rescued from the relative obscurity into which it has fallen.

Establishing connections between working-class radicalism and labourism makes it easier to explain why figures such as Hawker could make a seamless transition into the Labour Party. Examining how this transition occurred at a local level also casts fresh light on the nationalisation of British political culture and the Labour Party's role in furthering this process. By forming a small and nominally independent group in the House of Commons, Labour MPs set a valuable example for sympathetic local activists to follow. Even those who expressed disappointment at Labour's close relationship with the Liberals looked to Labour head office to provide guidance and clarity, a development that, whether consciously or not, helped to add a greater degree of consistency to the way labourist messages were presented at a local level. And while there were significant variations in the way labourist and socialist politics was organised at a local level, there were growing signs that local activists – even those who claimed to be critics of the party – considered Labour to be a distinctive political force that deserved workers' sympathy if not their outright support.

By the time of James Hawker's death in 1921, there were signs that Labour was becoming something more than a class party. In opening the party's ranks to the middle class, women and all who worked by hand or by brain, Labour leaders were making a conscious effort to convert the party into a more a socially inclusive body. In many ways, these efforts mirrored the attempts by certain liberals and radicals in the nineteenth century to unite working-class and middle-class reformers in a broad-based political alliance. Much of the language used by middle-class Labour candidates after 1918 also bore a striking resemblance to that used by populist radicals in the nineteenth-century. Like Jeremiah James Colman, Peter Taylor, Jacob Tillett and other middle-class radicals discussed throughout this book, middle-class Labour MPs were essentially *friends* of the workers rather than workers themselves.

For some scholars, this was a sign that Labour was heir to a populist radical tradition that valued an individual's principles rather their class. But seeing radicals, liberals and labour activists as part of the same populist tradition fails to do justice to the complexities that existed both within and between them. Depending on where and when one looks, working-class radicals could be found forming tactical alliances with liberals, opposing liberals in election contests, working closely with middle-class radicals or establishing independent organisations of their own. And just as it is possible to identify divisions in the radical–liberal 'alliance', so it is possible to observe variations in the way different sections of the post-1918 Labour Party interpreted the party's aims and values. When Ramsay MacDonald formed his first government in January 1924, he was at the head of a party that included not only socialists, liberals and even some tories in its ranks, but also a large body of men and women who remained committed to the class-based, moderately collectivist ideology of labourism.

One of the principal aims of this book has been to untangle the different tendencies that together made up – and still make up – the English left. This is not an easy task, mainly because political identities and party labels in one town did not always correspond with those in another. For instance, at various times and in various places, 'labour parties' were independent bodies and sections of cross-class alliances, unorganised tendencies and political organisations in their own right, or parties that contained all local socialists, some local socialists or no socialists at all. Uncovering such variations in popular politics is just one of the benefits of conducting local case studies. As well as addressing the geographical bias of previous scholarship on the subject, a focus on Bristol, Leicester, Northampton, Norwich and Lincoln has also shown how local political activists challenged the views of leading politicians and thinkers and contested the dominant understandings of widely used terms, phrases, concepts and narratives. This being the case, this book has suggested that local studies may be more valuable than purely national studies in tracking changes and continuities in the way people thought about politics, identity and ideology. Of course, this argument can only be tested by conducting further case studies, and re-examining the evidence used to conduct previous case studies, of towns and cities across England, Wales, Scotland and Ireland. Additional analysis of this kind would yield important insights into, among other things, the distinctly English (rather than British) nature of the traditions and the political cultures discussed in this book.[2]

Untangling the various strands of radicalism, liberalism, socialism and labourism is an important task. For one thing, it allows us to develop fresh perspectives on debates about British political history between 1867 and 1924. Drawing attention to continuities within the working-class radical/labourist tradition adds further weight against the once-dominant 'three-stage' account of Britain's political development. But crucially, this book has also offered a novel challenge to the 'continuity thesis', or the view that the revival of socialism, the emergence of labour politics in the 1880s and 1890s and the formation of the Labour Party in 1900 represented a recomposition of a *populist* radical–liberal tradition. By showing that the Labour Party was also rooted in a *working-class* radical tradition whose proponents upheld exclusivist identities and class-centred understandings of society, this book has argued that the continuity thesis exaggerates the sense the unity that prevailed among 'progressives' during the period 1867–1924, and that it has minimised the importance of class as a factor influencing identity and ideology. While the formation of a national Labour Party was undoubtedly an important moment in British political history, identifying the party's roots in a class-based and class-orientated political tradition makes it easier to understand the workerist tone of activists' language and Labour's uneasy relationship with cross-class political forces. The book has also built upon more recent studies that, while also seeking to problematise the continuity thesis, have failed to fully explore intra-radical tensions and have largely focused on establishing links between radical and socialist rather than radical and labour politics.

To disentangle ideological ambiguities between rival progressive traditions, this book has combined Michael Freeden's conceptual approach to ideologies with a study of popular politics in five English towns and cities. Following Freeden, it has treated ideologies as groups of concepts whose meanings are determined by their position in an ideology's 'morphology'. 'Core' concepts, which if removed from their position significantly alter the nature of an ideology, are located at the centre of the morphology. A secondary group of 'adjacent' concepts limit the possible meanings that individuals could assign to the core concepts, while concepts in the 'periphery', which take the form of specific practices, institutions or policy proposals, help to link core and adjacent concepts to their 'real-world' contexts. Crucially, for Freeden, it is not the mere presence of a concept in an ideology that gives it its distinctive meaning, but its proximity to and mutually influential relationship with other core, adjacent and peripheral concepts.

Adopting Freeden's approach has generated several key insights into progressive politics. For instance, it allows us to see radicalism as an ideology in its own right rather than a mere variant of liberalism. Democracy, liberty, individuality, progress and rationality formed the core of radical morphology; concepts such as equality, the general interest and rights comprised its adjacent band; and a range of cultural practices and institutions, from the English constitution and patriotism to Parliament and gendered assumptions about the role of women, formed its perimeter. What set radicalism apart from liberalism and conservatism was not so much the content of its components as the way in which these components were ordered and, ultimately, interpreted. Thus, while liberals and conservatives could also claim to be democrats, radicals articulated a uniquely expansive notion of democracy and a democratic reading of the English constitution that led them to demand a generous extension to the franchise, the reform or abolition of unaccountable institutions such as the House of Lords, a substantial increase in the number of working-class representatives, and a host of other social and political demands that conservatives and many liberals found both impractical and dangerous.

Examining the way in which local activists prioritised and articulated their demands enables us to tease out variations within ideological families. Differences between populist and working-class radicalism, for example, can be explained by acknowledging the presence of class and trade unionism in working-class radicalism's adjacent band but not the adjacent band of populist radicalism, a subtle difference that added a social dimension to intra-radical relations. Freeden's model also helps us to understand the process through which ideologies evolve. As the state migrated to an adjacent position in its morphology, working-class radicalism took on a marked collectivist accent. This was an important intellectual development, which is one of the reasons why this book has used the term 'labourism' to describe this collectivist ideology. Still, the addition of a single concept to an ideology's adjacent band is not enough to significantly alter its internal structure. While it added a collectivist tone to working-class radical/labourist demands, labourism continued to differ in several important respects from the various strands of English socialism. The differences between labourism and socialism, which were widely acknowledged among party leaders and activists, have generated significant debate within the Labour Party throughout its history.

As debates continue to rage about Labour's 'true' values and the social basis of its support, now seems an appropriate time to reconsider just who and what the party originally stood for. The book's focus is especially relevant in this post-Blair, post-Brexit era when the meanings of terms like progressive, socialist, liberal, reform, radical and even democracy are hotly contested by politicians, commentators and voters from across the political spectrum. Has Labour always been a populist party that has sought to build a broad-based coalition of the working class and middle-class progressives? Is it a socialist party that, since 1918, has been officially committed to establishing a socialist commonwealth in Britain? Or was it the product of and the natural successor to the British liberal tradition that needed to find a new political vehicle after the dislocation of the once-great Liberal Party during the First World War?

The geographical diversity of Labour's development means that, to some extent, it has always been all of these things. At a time when the party appears to be in danger of losing its traditional heartlands and becoming an overwhelmingly middle-class party in which ideological liberals and ideological socialists fight for supremacy, it is important to remember that in many industrial towns and cities, Labour was always something more. Rooted in a class-conscious form of radicalism, Labour politics was a democratic politics whose proponents, at least in theory, took the side of the workers against the political and economic establishment. It was a proudly patriotic politics whose supporters expressed pride in the history of the English people and the constitution that they had helped to frame through their struggles against tyranny and injustice. At the centre of this worldview was the working class, a large and sometimes ill-defined social group that underwent a process of change during the period 1867–1924 but which did not lose its place at the core of the labourist analysis. Labourist politics was also associated with a unique ideology – labourism – that deserves to be treated as something more than a weak version of socialism or a class-based form of liberalism. As there is little sign that the rival claims of 'Corbynista' socialists and 'Blairite' liberals will help Labour to re-establish its connection to its traditional supporters, it may be time to look again at a much-abused ideology that was radical in its intentions and which privileged the concerns of the very people the Labour Party was created to represent.

Notes

1 Hawker, *A Victorian Poacher*, pp. 12–13, 20, 23, 62, 76–78, 103.
2 Lloyd-Jones and Scull, 'A New Plea for an Old Subject?', pp. 10–11.

Bibliography

Primary Sources

Archival material
Bristol Records Office, Bristol
Bristol ILP records
Bristol Labour Party records
Bristol Trades' Council records
Papers of Alderman Frank Sheppard
Papers of John Wall

British Library, London
Northampton LRC annual reports

British Library of Political and Economic Science, London
Bristol ILP general secretary monthly reports
Bristol ILP minutes books
Francis Johnson correspondence files
ILP conference reports
ILP election ephemera
ILP municipal election addresses
ILP pamphlets and leaflets
ILP parliamentary election addresses
Labour Party conference reports
Labour Party National Executive Committee minutes
Papers of Arthur Ebenezer Cooke

Labour History Archive and Study Centre, Manchester
J. R. MacDonald office correspondence files
Labour Party general correspondence files
Labour Representation Committee general correspondence files

Modern Records Centre, Warwick
Dock, Wharf, Riverside and General Workers' Union annual reports

Labour and Socialist pamphlets
National Union of Gasworkers and General Labourers annual reports
NUBSO monthly and conference reports
Trades' councils annual reports

Norfolk Record Office, Norwich
Election ephemera
Norwich Labour Party records
Norwich Trades' Council records
Papers of G. H. Roberts
Papers of J. F. Henderson

Northamptonshire Central Library, Northampton
Election ephemera

Northamptonshire Record Office, Northampton
Northampton Trades' Council records

Record Office for Leicestershire, Leicester and Rutland, Wigston
Election ephemera
Leicester Amalgamated Hosiery Union records
Leicester Liberal Association records
Poems by Joseph Green
Trade union ephemera

University of Bristol Special Collections, Bristol
Election ephemera
Papers of John Gregory

University of Leicester Special Collections, Leicester
Papers of Archibald Gorrie

Journals and newspapers
Bellshill Speaker
Beverley and East Riding Recorder
Bristol Forward
Bristol Guardian
Bristol Labour Herald
Bristol Mercury
Bristol North Forward
Bristol Observer
Bristol Times & Mirror
Bristol Weekly Mercury
Crewe Guardian

Daily Herald
Derby Daily Telegraph
Dundee Courier
East Anglian Daily Times
Eastern Daily Press
Eastern Evening News
Justice
Lancashire Evening Post
Leeds Times
Leicester Chronicle
Leicester Daily Mercury
Leicester Daily Post
Leicester Journal
Leicester Pioneer
Lincoln, Rutland and Stamford Mercury
Lincolnshire Chronicle
Lincolnshire Echo
London Evening Standard
Manchester Evening News
Norfolk Chronicle
Norfolk News
Northampton Chronicle and Echo
Northampton Daily Echo
Northampton Independent
Northampton Mercury
Northampton Socialist
Northern Daily Telegraph
Norwich Mercury
Pall Mall Gazette
Reynolds's Newspaper
The Scotsman
Sheffield Independent
Socialist Pioneer
Southern Echo
Western Daily Press
Western Morning News
Wigan Observer and District Advertiser
Workington Star

Contemporary works

Adkins, W., *The Position of Northampton in English History* (Northampton, 1897).

Hamilton, M. A., *Margaret Bondfield* (London, 1924).

Labour and the New Social Order: A Report on Reconstruction (London, 1918).

MacDonald, J. R., *The New Unemployed Bill of the Labour Party* (London, 1907).

The Policy of Labour. Reprinted from the 'Labour Elector,' and issued by The Executive Committee of the National Labour Electoral Association (London, 1889).
Robertson, J. M., *Practical Radicalism* (London, 1892).
Saxton, J. H., *Recollections of William Arnold* (Northampton, 1915).
Smith, C. M., *The Working-Man's Way in the World: Being the Autobiography of a Journeyman Printer* (London, 1853).
A Speech Delivered by Mr. William Newton, President of the Labour Representation League, at the Corn Exchange, Ipswich, on the 18th of December, 1875 (London, 1875).
Tovey, R. G., *The Dock Question; or, the Way the Money Goes: Being a Paper Read before the Trades Council* (Bristol, 1886).
Young, W. W., *Robert Weare of Bristol, Liverpool and Wallasey, Born: 1858, Died: 1920: An Appreciation, and Four of His Essays* (Manchester, 1921).

Secondary Sources

Published books and articles

Anderson, P., 'Origins of the present crisis', *New Left Review*, I:23 (1964), pp. 26–53.
Arnstein, W., *The Bradlaugh Case: A Study in Late Victorian Opinion and Politics* (Oxford, 1965).
Ashcraft, R., 'Liberal political theory and working-class radicalism in nineteenth-century England', *Political Theory*, 21:2 (1993), pp. 249–272.
Auerbach, S., *Race, Law, and 'The Chinese Puzzle' in Imperial Britain* (Basingstoke, 2009).
Barnes, J., 'The British women's suffrage movement and the ancient constitution, 1867–1909', *Historical Research*, 91:253 (2018), p. 505–527.
Barrow, L., *Independent Spirits: Spiritualism and English Plebeians, 1850–1910* (London, 1986).
Barrow, L. and Bullock, I., *Democratic Ideas and the British Labour Movement, 1880–1914* (Cambridge, 1996).
Beers, L., *Your Britain: Media and the Making of the Labour Party* (London, 2010).
Belchem, J., *Popular Radicalism in Nineteenth-Century Britain* (New York, 1996).
Belchem, J. and Kirk, N. (eds), *Languages of Labour* (Aldershot, 1997).
Bernstein, G., 'Liberalism and the progressive alliance in the constituencies, 1900–1914: Three Case Studies', *The Historical Journal*, 26:3 (1983), pp. 617–640.
Bevir, M., 'The British Social Democratic Federation 1880–1885: From O'Brienism to Marxism', *International Review of Social History*, 37:2 (1992), pp. 207–229.
Bevir, M., *The Making of British Socialism* (Princeton, NJ, 2011).
Biagini, E. F., *Liberty, Retrenchment and Reform: Popular Liberalism in the Age of Gladstone, 1860–1880* (Cambridge, 1992).

Biagini, E. F. and Reid, A. J. (eds), *Currents of Radicalism: Popular Radicalism, Organised Labour and Party Politics in Britain, 1850–1914* (Cambridge, 1991).

Bild, I. (ed.), *Bristol's Other History* (Bristol, 1983).

Blaxill, L., 'Elections', in D. Brown, R. Crowcroft and G. Pentland (eds), *The Oxford Handbook of Modern British Political History, 1880–2000* (Oxford, 2018), pp. 400–416.

Bondfield, M., *A Life's Work* (London, 1948).

Boston, S., *Women Workers and the Trade Union Movement* (London, 1980).

Braybon, G., *Women Workers in the First World War* (London, 1981).

Briggs, A. and Saville, J. (eds), *Essays in Labour History, 1886–1923* (London, 1971).

Brown, K. (ed.), *Essays in Anti-Labour History: Responses to the Rise of Labour in Britain* (London, 1974).

Brown, K., 'The Labour Party and the unemployment question, 1906–1910', *The Historical Journal*, 14:3 (1971), pp. 599–616.

Bryher, S., *An Account of the Labour and Socialist Movement in Bristol: Part 1* (Bristol, 1929).

Bryher, S., *An Account of the Labour and Socialist Movement in Bristol: Part 2* (Bristol, 1931).

Bryher, S., *An Account of the Labour and Socialist Movement in Bristol: Part 3* (Bristol, 1931).

Bullock, A., *The Life and Times of Ernest Bevin, Volume One: Trade Union Leader, 1881–1940* (London, 1960).

Callaghan, J., Fielding, S. and Ludlam, S. (eds), *Interpreting the Labour Party: Approaches to Labour Politics and History* (Manchester, 2003)

Cannon, J., *The Chartists in Bristol* (Bristol, 1964).

Caramani, D., *The Nationalization of Politics: The Formation of National Electorates and Party Systems in Western Europe* (Cambridge, 2004).

Cash, A. C., *John Wilkes: The Scandalous Father of Civil Liberty* (London, 2006).

Chase, M., 'George Howell, the Webbs and the political culture of early labour history', in K. Laybourn and J. Shepherd (eds), *Labour and Working-Class Lives: Essays to Celebrate the Life and Work of Chris Wrigley* (Manchester, 2017), pp. 13–30.

Cherry, S., *Doing Different? Politics and the Labour Movement in Norwich, 1880–1914* (Hunstanton, 1989).

Childs, M., 'Labour grows up: The electoral system, political generations, and British politics 1890–1929', *Twentieth Century British History*, 6:2 (1995), pp. 123–144.

Clark, D., *Colne Valley, Radicalism to Socialism: The Portrait of a Northern Constituency in the Formative Years of the Labour Party 1890–1910* (London, 1981).

Clarke, P., *Lancashire and the New Liberalism* (Cambridge, 1971).

Clarke, P., 'The social democratic theory of the class struggle', in J. Winter (ed.), *The Working Class in Modern British History: Essays in Honour of Henry Pelling* (Cambridge, 1983), pp. 3–18.

Clegg, H., Fox, A. and Thompson, A., *A History of British Trade Unions since 1889: Volume 1, 1889–1910* (Oxford, 1977).
Clegg, H., Fox, A. and Thompson, A., *A History of British Trade Unions since 1889: Volume 2, 1911–1933* (Oxford, 1985).
Clinton, A., *The Trade Union Rank and File: Trades Councils in Britain, 1900–40* (Manchester, 1977).
Cole, G. D. H., *British Working Class Politics, 1832–1914* (London, 1965).
Cole, G. D. H., *A History of the Labour Party from 1914* (London, 1948).
Collins, H., 'The Marxism of the Social Democratic Federation', in A. Briggs and J. Saville (eds), *Essays in Labour History, 1886–1923* (London, 1971), pp. 47–69.
Cornford, J., 'The transformation of conservatism in the late nineteenth century', *Victorian Studies*, 7:1 (1963), pp. 35–66.
Cox, D., 'The Labour Party in Leicester: A study in branch development', *International Review of Social History*, 6:2 (1961), pp. 197–211.
Cox, G. W., 'The development of a party-orientated electorate in England, 1832–1918', *British Journal of Political Science*, 16:2 (1986), pp. 187–216.
Crick, M., *The History of the Social-Democratic Federation* (Keele, 1994).
Cronin, J., *The Politics of State Expansion: War, State and Society in Twentieth-Century Britain* (London, 1991).
Culleton, C. A., *Working-Class Culture, Women, and Britain, 1914–1921* (Basingstoke, 2000).
Cunningham, H., 'The language of patriotism, 1750–1914', *History Workshop*, 12:1 (1981), pp. 8–33.
Dale, I. (ed.), *Labour Party General Election Manifestos, 1900–1997* (London, 2000).
Dangerfield, G., *The Strange Death of Liberal England* (London, 1997).
Davis, M., '"Labourism" and the new left', in J. Callaghan, S. Fielding and S. Ludlam (eds), *Interpreting the Labour Party: Approaches to Labour Politics and History* (Manchester, 2003), pp. 39–56.
Drake, B., *Women in Trade Unions* (London, 1984).
Dresser, M. (ed.), *Women and the City: Bristol 1373–2000* (Bristol, 2016).
Dresser, M. and Ollerenshaw, P. (eds), *The Making of Modern Bristol* (Tiverton, 1996).
Emy, H., *Liberals, Radicals and Social Politics, 1892–1914* (Cambridge, 1973).
Epstein, J., '"Our real constitution": Trial defence and radical memory in the Age of Revolution', in J. Vernon (ed.), *Re-reading the Constitution: New Narratives in the Political History of England's Long Nineteenth Century* (Cambridge, 1996), pp. 22–51.
Epstein, J., 'Understanding the cap of liberty: Symbolic practice and social conflict in early nineteenth-century England', *Past and Present*, 122 (1989), pp. 75–118.
Feldman, D. and Lawrence, J. (eds), *Structures and Transformations in Modern British History* (Cambridge, 2011).

Finn, M., *After Chartism: Class and Nation in English Radical Politics, 1848–1874* (Cambridge, 1993).
Fleming, P., 'The emergence of modern Bristol', in M. Dresser and P. Ollerenshaw (eds), *The Making of Modern Bristol* (Tiverton, 1996), pp. 1–24.
Foote, G., *The Labour Party's Political Thought* (Beckenham, 1986).
Fox, A., *A History of the National Union of Boot and Shoe Operatives 1874–1957* (Oxford, 1958).
Francis, M., 'Labour and gender', in D. Tanner, P. Thane and N. Tiratsoo (eds), *Labour's First Century* (Cambridge, 2000), pp. 191–220.
Freeden, M., *Ideologies and Political Theory: A Conceptual Approach* (Oxford, 1998).
Freeden, M., *Liberalism Divided: A Study in British Political Thought, 1914–1939* (Oxford, 1986).
Freeden, M., *The New Liberalism: An Ideology of Social Reform* (Oxford, 1978).
Freeden, M., Sargent, L. T. and Stears, M. (eds), *The Oxford Handbook of Political Ideologies* (Oxford, 2013).
Freeman, M., *Social Investigation and Rural England, 1870–1914* (Woodbridge, 2003).
Gibbons, I., 'Labour and Irish revolution: From investigation to deportation', in L. Marley (ed.), *The British Labour Party and Twentieth-Century Ireland: The Cause of Ireland, the Cause of Labour* (Manchester, 2016).
Green, E. and Tanner, D. (eds), *The Strange Survival of Liberal England: Political Leaders, Moral Values and the Reception of Economic Debate* (Cambridge, 2007).
Griffin, B., *The Politics of Gender in Victorian Britain: Masculinity, Political Culture and the Struggle for Women's Rights* (Cambridge, 2012).
Griffiths, C., *Labour and the Countryside: The Politics of Rural Britain, 1918–1939* (Oxford, 2007).
Groves, R., *Sharpen the Sickle! The History of the Farm Workers' Union* (London, 1981).
Hall, C., McClelland, K. and Rendall, J. (eds), *Defining the Victorian Nation: Class, Race, Gender and the British Reform Act of 1867* (Cambridge, 2000).
Hanham, H., *Elections and Party Management: Politics in the Time of Disraeli and Gladstone* (London, 1959).
Hannam, J., *Bristol Independent Labour Party: Men, Women and the Opposition to War* (Bristol, 2014).
Hannam, J. and Martin, M., 'Women in Bristol 1835–1914', in M. Dresser (ed.), *Women and the City* (Bristol, 2016), pp. 92–135.
Harris, J., 'Labour's political and social thought', in D. Tanner, P. Thane and N. Tiratsoo (eds), *Labour's First Century* (Cambridge, 2000), pp. 8–45.
Harrison, R., *Before the Socialists: Studies in Labour and Politics, 1861–1881* (London, 1965).
Hatley, V., *Shoemakers in Northamptonshire 1762–1911: A Statistical Survey* (Northampton, 1971).
Hawker, J., *A Victorian Poacher: James Hawker's Journal* (Oxford, 1978).

Hill, F., *Victorian Lincoln* (Cambridge, 1974).
Hobsbawm, E., 'The "new unionism" reconsidered', in W. Mommsen and H. Husung (eds), *The Development of Trade Unionism in Great Britain and Germany, 1880–1914* (London, 1985), pp. 13–31.
Hobsbawm, E., *Worlds of Labour: Further Studies in the History of Labour* (London, 1984).
Hobsbawm, E. and Scott, J. W., 'Political shoemakers', in E. Hobsbawm, *Worlds of Labour: Further Studies in the History of Labour* (London, 1984), pp. 103–130.
Holton, B., *British Syndicalism 1900–1914: Myths and Realities* (London, 1976).
Howarth, J., 'The Liberal revival in Northamptonshire, 1880–1895: A case study in late nineteenth century elections', *The Historical Journal*, 12:1 (1969), pp. 78–118.
Howe, S., 'Labour and international affairs', in D. Tanner, P. Thane and N. Tiratsoo (eds), *Labour's First Century* (Cambridge, 2000), pp. 119–150.
Howell, D., *British Workers and the Independent Labour Party, 1888–1906* (Manchester, 1983).
Howkins, A., *Poor Labouring Men: Rural Radicalism in Norfolk 1870–1923* (London, 1985).
Hunt, C., 'Dancing and days out: The role of social events in British women's trade unionism in the early twentieth century', *Labour History Review*, 76:2 (2011), pp. 104–120.
Hyslop, J., 'The imperial working class makes itself "white": White labourism in Britain, Australia, and South Africa before the First World War', *Journal of Historical Sociology*, 12:4 (1999), pp. 398–421.
Jackson, B., *Equality and the British Left: A Study in Progressive Political Thought, 1900–64* (Manchester, 2007).
Jackson, D., *Popular Opposition to Irish Home Rule in Edwardian Britain* (Liverpool, 2009).
Johnson, N., *Reshaping the British Constitution: Essays in Political Interpretation* (Basingstoke, 2004).
Jones, B., *The Russia Complex: The British Labour Party and the Soviet Union* (Manchester, 1977).
Joyce, P., 'The constitution and the narrative structure of Victorian politics', in J. Vernon (ed.), *Re-reading the Constitution: New Narratives in the Political History of England's Long Nineteenth Century* (Cambridge, 1996), pp. 179–203.
Joyce, P. 'The imaginary discontents of social history: A note of response to Mayfield and Thorne, and Lawrence and Taylor', *Social History*, 18:1 (1993), pp. 81–85.
Joyce, P., *Visions of the People: Industrial England and the Question of Class, 1840–1914* (Cambridge, 1991).
Joyce, P., *Work, Society and Politics: The Culture of the Factory in Later Victorian England* (Aldershot, 1991).

Kaarsholm, P., 'Pro-Boers', in R. Samuel (ed.), *Patriotism: The Making and Unmaking of British National Identity, Volume I: History and Politics* (London, 1989), pp. 110–126.

Kelly, K. and Richardson, M., 'The shaping of the Bristol labour movement, 1885–1985', in M. Dresser and P. Ollerenshaw (eds), *The Making of Modern Bristol* (Tiverton, 1996), pp. 210–236.

Kent, S., *Sex and Suffrage in Britain, 1860–1914* (Princeton, NJ, 1987).

Kirk, N., *Change, Continuity and Class: Labour in British Society, 1850–1920* (Manchester, 1998).

Kirk, N., 'Class and the "linguistic turn" in Chartist and post-Chartist historiography', in N. Kirk (ed.), *Social Class and Marxism: Defences and Challenges* (Aldershot, 1996), pp. 87–134.

Kirk, N., 'Decline and fall, resilience and regeneration: A review essay on social class', *International Labor and Working-Class History*, 57 (2000), pp. 88–102.

Lancaster, B., *Radicalism, Cooperation and Socialism: Leicester Working-Class Politics 1860–1906* (Leicester, 1987).

Large, D., *The Municipal Government of Bristol 1851–1901* (Bristol, 1999).

Large, D., *Radicalism in Bristol in the Nineteenth Century* (Bristol, 1981).

Large, D. and Whitfield, R., *The Bristol Trades Council, 1873–1973* (Bristol, 1973).

Lawrence, J., 'The British sense of class', *Journal of Contemporary History*, 35:2 (2000), pp. 307–318.

Lawrence, J., 'The dynamics of urban politics, 1867–1914', in J. Lawrence and M. Taylor (eds), *Party, State and Society: Electoral Behaviour in Britain since 1820* (Aldershot, 1997), pp. 79–105.

Lawrence, J., 'Labour and the politics of class, 1900–1940', in D. Feldman and J. Lawrence (eds), Structures and Transformations in Modern British History (Cambridge, 2011), pp. 237–260.

Lawrence, J., 'Popular politics and the limitations of party: Wolverhampton, 1867–1900', in E. F. Biagini and A. J. Reid (eds), *Currents of Radicalism: Popular Radicalism, Organised Labour and Party Politics in Britain 1850–1914* (Cambridge, 1991), pp. 65–85.

Lawrence, J., 'Popular radicalism and the socialist revival in Britain', *Journal of British Studies*, 31:2 (1992), pp. 163–186.

Lawrence, J., *Speaking for the People: Party, Language and Popular Politics in England, 1867–1914* (Cambridge, 1998).

Lawrence, J. and Taylor, M., 'British historians and political sociology', *Politix*, 81 (2008), pp. 13–39.

Laybourn, K. and Reynolds, J., *Liberalism and the Rise of Labour, 1890–1918* (London, 1984).

Laybourn, K. and Shepherd, J., *Labour and Working-Class Lives: Essays to Celebrate the Life and Work of Chris Wrigley* (Manchester, 2017).

Lloyd-Jones, N. and Scull, M. M., 'A new plea for an old subject? Four nations' history for the modern period', in N. Lloyd-Jones and M. M. Scull, *Four*

Nations' Approaches to Modern "British" History: A (Dis)United Kingdom? (London, 2018).
Lunn, K., 'Immigrants and strikes: Some British case studies 1870–1914', in K. Lunn (ed.), *Race and Labour in Twentieth-Century Britain* (London, 1985), pp. 30–42.
Lynch, J., *A Tale of Three Cities: Comparative Studies in Working-Class Life* (London, 1998).
Malos, E., 'Bristol women in Action, 1839–1919', in I. Bild (ed.), *Bristol's Other History* (Bristol, 1983), pp. 97–128.
Marley, L (ed.), *The British Labour Party and Twentieth-Century Ireland: The Cause of Ireland, the Cause of Labour* (Manchester, 2016).
Marley, L., 'Introduction', in L. Marley (ed.), *The British Labour Party and Twentieth-Century Ireland: The Cause of Ireland, the Cause of Labour* (Manchester, 2016), pp. 1–13.
Marwick, A., *The Deluge: British Society and the First World War* (London, 1965).
May, J. P., 'The Chinese in Britain, 1860–1914', in C. Holmes (ed.), *Immigrants and Minorities in British Society* (London, 1978), pp. 111–124.
McClelland, K., '"England's greatness, the working man"', in C. Hall, K. McClelland and J. Rendall (eds), *Defining the Victorian Nation: Class, Race, Gender and the British Reform Act of 1867* (Cambridge, 2000), pp. 71–118.
McKibbin, R., *Classes and Cultures: England 1918–1951* (Oxford, 2000).
McKibbin, R., *The Evolution of the Labour Party 1910–1924* (Oxford, 1983).
McKibbin, R., *The Ideologies of Class: Social Relations in Britain, 1880–1950* (Oxford, 1991).
McWilliam, R., 'Liberalism lite?', *Victorian Studies*, 48:1 (2005), pp. 103–111.
McWilliam, R., *The Tichborne Claimant: A Victorian Sensation* (London, 2007).
Meisel, J., *Public Speech and the Culture of Public Life in the Age of Gladstone* (New York, 2001).
Meisel, J., 'Words by the numbers: A quantitative analysis and comparison of the oratorical careers of William Ewart Gladstone and Winston Spencer Churchill', *Historical Research*, 73:182 (2000), pp. 262–295.
Miliband, R., 'Socialist advance in Britain', *The Socialist Register*, 20 (1983), pp. 103–120.
Minkin, L., *The Contentious Alliance: Trade Unions and the Labour Party* (London, 1992).
Moore, J. R., 'Progressive pioneers: Manchester liberalism, the Independent Labour Party, and local politics in the 1890s', *The Historical Journal*, 44:4 (2001), pp. 989–1013.
Morgan, K., 'The new liberalism and the challenge of labour: The Welsh experience, 1885–1929', in K. Brown (ed.), *Essays in Anti-Labour History: Responses to the Rise of Labour in Britain* (London, 1974), pp. 159–182.
Mullen, S., 'The Bristol Socialist Society 1885–1914', in I. Bild (ed.), *Bristol's Other History* (Bristol, 1983), pp. 36–67.

Niblett, B., *Dare to Stand Alone: The Story of Charles Bradlaugh, Atheist and Republican* (Oxford, 2011).
O'Connor, E., 'British Labour, Belfast and Home Rule, 1900–14', in L. Marley (ed.), *The British Labour Party and Twentieth-Century Ireland: The Cause of Ireland, the Cause of Labour* (Manchester, 2016), pp. 55–66.
O'Gorman, F., 'Campaign rituals and ceremonies: The social meaning of elections in England, 1780–1860', *Past and Present*, 135 (1992), pp. 79–115.
O'Gorman, F., *Voters, Patrons and Parties: The Unreformed Electoral System of Hanoverian England 1734–1832* (Oxford, 1989).
Otte, T. G. and Readman, P. (eds), *By-Elections in British Politics, 1832–1914* (Woodbridge, 2013).
Ó Tuathaigh, G., 'A tangled legacy: The Irish "inheritance" of British Labour', in L. Marley (ed.), *The British Labour Party and Twentieth-Century Ireland: The Cause of Ireland, the Cause of Labour* (Manchester, 2016), pp. 17–30.
Owen, J., *Labour and the Caucus: Working-Class Radicalism and Organised Liberalism in England, 1868–88* (Liverpool, 2014).
Parry, J., 'The impact of Napoleon III on British politics, 1851–1880', *Transactions of the Royal Historical Society*, 11 (2001), pp. 147–175.
Parry, J., *The Politics of Patriotism: English Liberalism, National Identity and Europe, 1830–1886* (Cambridge, 2006).
Parry, J., *The Rise and Fall of Liberal Government in Victorian Britain* (London, 1993).
Pasiecznik, J., 'Liberals, Labour and Leicester: The 1913 by-election in local and national perspective', *Transactions of the Leicestershire Archaeological and Historical Society*, 63 (1989), pp. 94–106.
Pearson, H., *Labby: The Life and Character of Henry Labouchère* (London, 1948).
Pelling, H., *A History of British Trade Unionism* (Middlesex, 1967).
Pelling, H., *Popular Politics and Society in Late Victorian Britain* (London, 1968).
Pelling, H., *Social Geography of British Elections 1885–1910* (London, 1967).
Pentland, G., 'Parliamentary reform', in D. Brown, R. Crowcroft and G. Pentland (eds), *The Oxford Handbook of Modern British Political History, 1880–2000* (Oxford, 2018).
Phillips, J. A. and Wetherell, C., 'The Great Reform Bill of 1832 and the rise of partisanship', *Journal of Modern History*, 63:4 (1991), pp. 621–646.
Pierson, S., *British Socialists: The Journey from Fantasy to Politics* (London, 1979).
Pierson, S., *Marxism and the Origins of British Socialism: The Struggle for a New Consciousness* (London, 1973).
Pimlott, B., 'The Labour left', in C. Cook and I. Taylor, *The Labour Party: An Introduction to its history, structure and politics* (London), 1980, pp. 163–188.
Pugh, M., *The Making of Modern British Politics, 1867–1939* (Oxford, 1982).
Pugh, M., *Speak for Britain! A New History of the Labour Party* (London, 2010).
Randall, N., 'Understanding Labour's ideological trajectory', in J. Callaghan, S. Fielding and S. Ludlam (eds), *Interpreting the Labour Party: Approaches to Labour Politics and History* (Manchester, 2003), pp. 8–22.

Readman, P., 'The 1895 general election and political change in late Victorian Britain', The *Historical Journal*, 42:2 (1999), pp. 467–493.
Readman, P., *Land and Nation in England: Patriotism, National Identity, and the Politics of Land, 1880–1914* (Woodbridge, 2008).
Readman, P., 'The Liberal Party and patriotism in early twentieth century Britain', *Twentieth Century British History*, 12:3 (2001), pp. 269–302.
Reid, A., 'Old Unionism reconsidered: The radicalism of Robert Knight, 1870–1900', in E. Biagini and A. Reid (eds), *Currents of Radicalism: Popular Radicalism, Organised Labour and Party Politics in Britain 1850–1914* (Cambridge, 1991), pp. 214–243.
Reid, A., *United We Stand: A History of Britain's Trade Unions* (London, 2004).
Reid, F., 'Keir Hardie's conversion to Socialism', in A. Briggs and J. Saville (eds), *Essays in Labour History, 1886–1923* (London, 1971), pp. 17–46.
Rendall, J. (ed.), *Equal or Different: Women's Politics 1800–1914* (Oxford, 1987).
Richardson, M., 'Bristol and the labour unrest of 1910–14', in D. Backwith, R. Ball, S. E. Hunt and M. Richardson (eds), *Strikers, Hobblers, Conchies and Reds: A Radical History of Bristol 1880–1939* (Newton Abbott, 2014), pp. 197–238.
Rix, K., *Parties, Agents and Electoral Culture in England, 1880–1910* (Woodbridge, 2016).
Roberts, M., '"Villa Toryism" and popular conservatism in Leeds, 1885–1902', *Historical Journal*, 49 (2006), pp. 217–246.
Roberts, S., 'Thomas Cooper in Leicester, 1840–1843', *Transactions of Leicestershire Archaeological and Historical Society*, 61 (1987), pp. 62–76.
Robinson, E., *The Language of Progressive Politics in Modern Britain* (London, 2017).
Rowbotham, S., *Rebel Crossings: New Women, Free Lovers, and Radicals in Britain and the United States* (London, 2016).
Royle, E., *Radicals, Secularists and Republicans: Popular Freethought in Britain, 1866–1915* (Manchester, 1980).
Saunders, R., 'Parliament and people: The British constitution in the long nineteenth century', *Journal of Modern European History*, 6:1 (2008), pp. 72–87.
Savage, M., *The Dynamics of Working-Class Politics: The Labour Movement in Preston, 1880–1940* (Cambridge, 1987).
Stedman Jones, G., 'The determinist fix: Some obstacles to the further development of the linguistic approach to history in the 1990s', *History Workshop Journal*, 42 (1996), pp. 19–35.
Stedman Jones, G., *Languages of Class: Studies in English Working Class History, 1832–1982* (Cambridge, 1983).
Tabili, L., *'We Ask for British Justice': Workers and Racial Difference in Late Imperial Britain* (London, 1994).
Tanner, D., 'Class voting and radical politics: The Liberal and Labour parties, 1910–31', in J. Lawrence and M. Taylor (eds), *Party, State and Society: Electoral Behaviour in Britain since 1820* (Aldershot, 1997), pp. 106–130.

Tanner, D., 'The development of British socialism, 1900–1918', *Parliamentary History*, 16:1 (1997), pp. 48–66.

Tanner, D., 'Elections, statistics, and the rise of the Labour Party, 1906–1931', *The Historical Journal*, 34:3 (1991), pp. 893–908.

Tanner, D., *Political Change and the Labour Party, 1900–1918* (Cambridge, 1990).

Tanner, D., Thane, P. and Tiratsoo N. (eds), *Labour's First Century* (Cambridge, 2000).

Taylor, A., '"The glamour of independence": By-elections and radicalism during the liberal meridian, 1869–83', in T. Otte and P. Readman (eds), *By-Elections in British Politics, 1832–1914* (Woodbridge, 2013), pp. 99–120.

Taylor, A., '"The Old Chartist": Radical veterans on the late nineteenth- and early twentieth-century political platform', *History*, 95:4 (2010), pp. 458–476.

Taylor, I., 'Ideology and policy', in C. Cook and I. Taylor (eds), *The Labour Party: An Introduction to Its History, Structure and Politics* (London, 1980), pp. 1–32.

Taylor, M., *The Decline of British Radicalism, 1847–1860* (Oxford, 1995).

Taylor, M., 'Labour and the constitution', in D. Tanner, P. Thane and N. Tiratsoo (eds), *Labour's First Century* (Cambridge, 2000), pp. 151–180.

Thane, P., 'Labour and welfare', in D. Tanner, P. Thane and N. Tiratsoo (eds), *Labour's First Century* (Cambridge, 2000), pp. 80–118.

Tholfsen, T., *Working Class Radicalism in Mid-Victorian England* (London, 1976).

Thomas, C., *Slaughter No Remedy: The Life and Times of Walter Ayles, Bristol Conscientious Objector* (Bristol, 2016).

Thompson, E. P., *The Making of the English Working Class* (Aylesbury, 1968).

Thompson, J., 'After the fall: Class and political language in Britain, 1780–1900', *Historical Journal*, 39:2 (1996), pp. 785–806.

Thompson, P., *Socialists, Liberals and Labour: The Struggle for London, 1885–1914* (London, 1967).

Thorpe, A., *A History of the British Labour Party* (London, 1997).

Tichelar, M., 'Socialists, Labour and the land: The response of the Labour Party to the land campaign of Lloyd George before the First World War', *Twentieth Century British History*, 8:2 (1997), pp. 127–144.

Tillett, B., *Memories and Reflections* (London, 1931).

Todd, S., *The People: The Rise and Fall of the Working Class, 1910–2010* (London, 2014).

Tuckett, A., *Our Enid: The Life and Work of Enid Stacy, 1868–1903* (Salford, 2016).

Vernon, J., *Politics and the People: A Study in the English Political Culture, c. 1815–1867* (Cambridge, 1993).

Walker, A., 'The development of the provincial press in England c. 1780–1914', *Journalism Studies*, 7:3 (2006), pp. 373–386.

Ward, P., *Red Flag and the Union Jack: Englishness, Patriotism and the British Left, 1881–1924* (Woodbridge, 1998).

Ward, P., 'Socialists and "true" patriotism in Britain in the late 19th and early 20th centuries', *National Identities*, 1:2 (1999), pp. 179–194.

Webb, S. and Webb, B., *The History of Trade Unionism, 1666–1920* (London, 1920).
Whitfield, R., 'Trade unionism in Bristol, 1910–1926', in I. Bild (ed.), *Bristol's Other History* (Bristol, 1983), pp. 68–96.
Wolfe, W., *From Radicalism to Socialism: Men and Ideas in the Formation of Fabian Socialist Doctrines, 1881–1889* (London, 1975).
Woollacott, A., *On Her Their Lives Depend: Munitions Workers in the Great War* (London, 1994).
Worley, M., 'Building the Party: Labour Party activism in five British counties between the wars', *Labour History Review*, 70:1 (2005), pp. 73–95.
Worley, M. (ed.), *The Foundations of the British Labour Party: Identities, Cultures and Perspectives, 1900–39* (Farnham, 2009).
Worley, M., *Labour inside the Gate: A History of the British Labour Party between the Wars* (London, 2005).
Wrigley, C. (ed.), *A History of British Industrial Relations, 1875–1914* (Brighton, 1982).
Wrigley, C., 'The Labour Party and the impact of the 1918 Reform Act', *Parliamentary History*, 37:1 (2018), pp. 64–80.
Wyncoll, P., *The Nottingham Labour Movement 1880–1939* (London, 1985).
Yeo, E., 'Language and contestation: The case of "the People", 1832 to present', in J. Belchem and N. Kirk (eds), *Languages of Labour* (Aldershot, 1997), pp. 44–64.

Unpublished theses
Atkinson, B., 'The Bristol labour movement, 1868–1906' (doctoral thesis, University of Oxford, 1969).
Buckell, J., 'The early socialists in Northampton 1886–1924' (MA thesis, University of Leicester, 1977).
D'Arcy, F. A., 'Charles Bradlaugh and the world of popular radicalism, 1833–1891' (doctoral thesis, University of Hull, 1978).
Dickie, M., 'The ideology of the Northampton Labour Party in the interwar years' (MA thesis, University of Warwick, 1982).
Dickie, M., 'Town patriotism and the rise of Labour: Northampton 1918–1939' (doctoral thesis, University of Warwick, 1987).
Harding, E., 'Conceptualising horizontal politics' (doctoral thesis, University of Nottingham, 2012).
Sinnett, T., 'The development of the Labour Party in Bristol, 1918–1931' (doctoral thesis, University of the West of England, 2006).
Young, D. M., 'People, place and party: The Social Democratic Federation 1884–1911' (doctoral thesis, University of Durham, 2003).

Index

agricultural labourers 20, 59–60, 66, 71–73, 134, 154–155, 165–170, 213–214
ancient constitution 8, 48, 64–66, 75, 89
anti-semitism 114, 169, 218
aristocracy 31, 35, 40, 48, 61, 71, 110, 192, 225
Ayles, Walter 190, 206, 210–211

Baker, Walter 203, 206, 210, 215
Banton, George 186, 192, 205, 210
Bevin, Ernest 165, 192–193, 206
Boer War 136, 140, 168
Bondfield, Margaret 163, 207, 210, 216–217
Bradlaugh, Charles 19, 37–38, 41–43, 55–76, 85–87, 91–93, 106–108, 140–141, 193, 203, 225
Bristol
   Conservative politics in 114, 206
   ILP (Independent Labour Party) 114–117, 135–136, 157, 161, 190–191, 205–206, 210–211, 215–216
   Labour Party (and LRC) 135–136, 146, 156–157, 160–161, 166, 190–192, 203–216
   labour politics (pre-Labour Party) in 81–94, 105–106, 113–117, 123
   Liberal Association 33–34, 62, 67–69, 105, 113–116, 136, 143, 157, 206
   local economy 59, 72, 113, 162, 169, 206
   radical politics in 33–34, 39, 47–49, 62, 65, 67–71, 89, 93, 113
   radical traditions in (pre-1867) 8, 32, 34
   Socialist Society 113–117, 136, 157, 161, 206
   trade unionism in 34, 48, 71–72, 86–92, 113, 160, 162, 166, 169, 190–191, 206, 212, 214
   Trades' Council 34, 72, 136, 160–161, 190–191, 205–206
British Socialist Party 141, 157, 161, 185–191, 207
Broadhurst, Henry 93, 155

Chartism 8–9, 29, 32, 65, 141
Chinese slavery 144, 158, 168
class
   exclusivist conception of 4–6, 14, 18–21, 30–59, 70–73, 76, 81, 83, 87–101, 107, 110–112, 119–122, 135, 152–171, 177–180, 191–193, 203, 216–220, 225–230
   politics of 17, 42–43, 70, 75–76, 110, 130, 135, 144–146, 152–163, 170, 178–180, 186–187, 192, 203, 208–210, 213–220, 226–227
   war, theory of 6, 21, 30, 46, 81, 86, 89, 91–94, 100, 108–111, 116, 120, 152–153, 157, 160–162, 168, 170, 182–187, 192, 203, 208–210, 217–220, 226
collectivism 15, 19, 80–84, 88, 95–98, 111–112, 116, 194–196, 230
   see also state, the

Communist Party of Great Britain *see* CPGB
Conservative politics 32–37, 42, 57, 60, 62, 69, 70, 75–76, 88, 105, 113–114, 117–123, 133, 190, 204–208
constitution, the
  in labourism 15, 83, 88–89, 94, 112, 120–121, 153, 168, 178–183, 191–193, 203, 217–218
  in radicalism 11–14, 48–50, 57–58, 63–69, 74–75
  in working-class radicalism 49
continuity thesis 3–5, 28–30, 55–56, 60, 81–82, 101, 106–107, 152, 176, 227–229
CPGB (Communist Party of Great Britain) 204, 206, 217

democracy
  in labourism 83–84, 87, 97, 111–112, 117, 170–171, 178–182, 191, 217
  in radicalism 11–12, 31–33, 45, 48, 58, 65–67, 75
  in working-class radicalism 14, 47–48, 226
Diggers 12, 65

elections *see* general elections
empire, imperialism 13, 115, 143, 154, 168–169, 181, 213
English Civil War 8, 12, 32, 65
equality, concept of 11–12, 31, 45, 47–48, 58, 65, 67, 83, 97, 111–112, 178–179, 192

Fabian Society 16, 122, 170, 185
First World War
  conscientious objectors 190, 192, 206
  evolution in attitudes to the state 20, 176–177, 193–196
  and Labour Party 20–21, 176–178, 188–192
  and women 203–204, 212
franchise, suffrage 11, 31, 35, 40, 45, 47, 58, 61, 65–66, 87, 138, 141, 154, 163, 176, 181, 212

Freeden, Michael 9–10, 58, 66, 75, 94–95, 112, 183–184, 229

general elections
  (1868) 35–38, 40, 42, 70, 143, 225
  (1874) 36, 38, 43, 143
  (1880) 36, 38, 42, 56, 60, 63, 70, 143
  (1885) 56, 60, 63, 143
  (1886) 56, 60, 89, 143
  (1892) 93, 117–118, 143
  (1895) 19, 101, 105–127, 143
  (1900) 134–135
  (1906) 130–134, 141, 155, 158–160, 166
  (1910, January) 136, 141, 146, 157, 159, 161, 166, 168, 181
  (1910, December) 133, 181
  (1918) 189–194, 201, 205–208, 212
  (1922) 202, 205–209, 211–212, 215, 219
  (1923) 205–208
  (1924) 205–208
Gladstone, William Ewart 28–29, 35, 37, 49, 51, 56, 115, 143
Gore, Hugh Holmes 114–117, 123
'Great Labour Unrest' 136, 153, 160, 164, 181–183, 188

Hardie, Keir 9, 114, 116–117, 134, 145, 156
Harris, Jose 10, 16, 192, 194
history, politicisation of 8, 13–14, 48, 58, 64–68, 75, 88–89, 105, 120, 140–142, 165, 181, 203
hours of work 80, 86–87, 95–96, 98, 111–112, 116, 140, 143, 167
House of Lords 11, 13, 31, 47, 110–111, 143, 146, 180–181, 193
Hyndman, Henry 84–85, 95–96, 186, 189

ideology 9–18, 67, 82–84, 87, 95
  local articulations of 7–10, 16–17, 21, 30, 56, 82–84, 122–123, 160, 185–187, 228
  see also Freeden, Michael

ILP (Independent Labour Party) 4, 92–93, 97, 105, 114–123, 133–144, 155–157, 161–163, 166, 184–191, 204–208, 210–220
Inskip, William 90, 93, 98–99, 108
Ipswich 92, 180, 192, 213, 219
Irish Home Rule 11, 31, 111, 114–116, 129, 143, 146

Jewson, Dorothy 208, 210
Joyce, Patrick 3, 152–153, 159

Labouchère, Henry 36, 38, 62, 95–96, 107, 109–112
Labour and the New Social Order 21, 194–195, 214
Labour Party (and LRC)
  early growth 128–151, 152–175
  head office-constituency relations 7, 20, 129–132, 135, 142–148, 186, 189, 227
  historiography of 6
  ideology 10, 11, 16–17, 192–194, 203–204, 208–209
  rise of 2–3, 6, 20, 92, 128–129, 176–177, 191, 201, 206
  literature 131, 147–148, 152, 159–160
  MPs 7, 20, 130–131, 137–140, 142, 145–147, 227
  and politics of class 17, 130, 135, 144–146, 152–162, 170, 178–180, 192, 203, 208–209, 213–220, 226–227
  and politics of populism 152–162, 202, 210–211, 214–220, 227
  referring to radical traditions 1, 141, 181–182, 203, 206, 226
  and women members 21, 202, 207, 215–216, 219, 227
  and women voters 202–206, 212–216, 227
  see also Bristol; labourism; labour politics (pre-Labour Party); Leicester; Lincoln; Northampton; Norwich
labour politics (pre-Labour Party) 1–5, 80–91, 97–101, 105, 226

liberal politics, relationship with 81–82, 89–91, 105–122, 143
  see also Bristol; Leicester; Lincoln; Northampton; Norwich
labourism
  class, exclusivist conception of 5–6, 20–21, 81, 83, 87–94, 96–97, 100–101, 107, 110–112, 119–122, 135, 152–171, 177–180, 191–193, 203, 208–210, 216–220, 226–228
  conceptual framework of 10, 15–21, 80, 83–84, 87–89, 94–100, 107, 111–112, 117, 120–122, 153–155, 168–171, 176–185, 191–196, 203, 213, 217–221, 227
  distinctiveness from socialism 80–81, 85–87, 94–100, 107, 114, 120–122, 183–187, 194–196, 217–221, 230
  hostility to 'class war' 6, 21, 81, 86, 91–94, 100, 111, 120, 153, 160–161, 168–170, 182, 187, 192, 203, 208–210, 217–220, 226
  see also Labour Party (and LRC); labour politics (pre-Labour Party)
land question 13, 73, 154, 165–167, 213–214
Lawrence, Jon 4, 154, 203, 210
Leicester
  Conservative politics in 35, 105, 190, 205
  ILP (Independent Labour Party) in 93, 105, 134, 138–144, 157, 184–185, 205
  Labour Party (and LRC) 32, 134–135, 142–145, 155–160, 171, 180, 186–192, 203, 205, 209, 214–215, 218
  labour politics (pre-Labour Party) 81–82, 86–87, 89–93
  Liberal Association 34–35, 63, 90, 93, 105, 135, 144, 158–159, 178, 186–190
  local economy 34, 72–73
  radical politics in 34–35, 39, 44–45, 63, 70

Index

radical traditions in (pre-1867) 32, 141–142
Social Democratic Federation (and British Socialist Party) in 185–187
Socialist League in 140
trade unionism in 34–35, 39, 44–46, 63, 66, 72–73, 86–87, 92–93, 98, 134, 138, 156, 162, 164, 189–190
Trades' Council 93, 134, 140, 142, 144, 155, 159, 167, 186
Leicester Pioneer 12, 17, 140–145, 156–158, 160, 167, 169, 179, 184–185, 190
Levellers 9, 65
Liberal Party *see* liberal politics
liberal politics
  and radical politics 4, 18, 28–39, 43, 47–51, 56–57, 60–69, 74–75, 226
  see also Bristol; Leicester, Lib-Lab politics; Lincoln; Northampton; Norwich
Liberal Unionists 105, 115, 143
liberalism 9–12, 31, 66–67, 218, 221
  see also new liberalism
liberty, concept of 11, 31, 45, 48, 83, 96, 111, 180–182, 193, 217
Lib-Lab politics 16, 82, 89–90, 93, 105–111, 116–121, 130, 133–139, 155, 158–161, 182, 187–188, 204, 207, 220
Lincoln
  Conservative politics in 32, 206–207
  ILP (Independent Labour Party) in 157, 190
  Labour Party (and LRC) 190, 193, 206–208, 214, 218
  labour politics (pre-Labour Party) 82, 89–90, 93
  Liberal Association 35–36, 82, 90, 93, 105, 190, 206–207
  radical politics in 35–36, 47
  radical traditions in (pre-1867) 32, 206
  Socialist League in 91–92
  trade unionism in 36, 92, 190, 206–208
  Trades' and Labour Council 190, 207
Lloyd George, David 181, 191

MacDonald, James Ramsay 116, 132–135, 140–144, 155, 158–162, 166, 185–186, 189–206, 228
McKibbin, Ross 6, 16, 59, 194, 202
migration
  'alien' 59, 168–169, 203
  rural 59, 165–166
Mill, John Stuart 28, 139, 141
Morley, Samuel 41, 62, 67–69
Morris, William 84, 121, 139, 141, 185

National Secular Society 38, 55
National Socialist Party 189, 207
nationalisation, collective ownership 10, 13, 84, 86, 95–99, 111–112, 116, 121, 144, 165–166, 181, 185, 194–195, 218–219
  see also state, the
nationalisation of politics 128–130, 143
  Labour's contribution to 7, 20, 106, 128–151, 186, 204–205, 227
new liberalism 123, 170, 183, 187
new unionism 15, 80–82, 91–94, 110, 113, 137
  see also strikes and lockouts
nonconformity 32, 61–62, 66, 114
Norfolk 8, 32, 134, 165–166
'Norman Yoke' 8, 48, 214
Northampton
  British Socialist Party in 141, 157, 207
  Conservative politics in 42, 60, 62, 75–76, 105, 113, 207
  ILP (Independent Labour Party) in 188–189, 207–208, 217
  Labour Party (and LRC) 136, 156, 188–191, 195, 203, 207–209, 214–217
  labour politics (pre-Labour Party) 82, 85–93, 97–98, 105–113, 136–137, 186, 188
  liberal politics in (pre-1880) 38, 42–43, 62, 68–69, 74–76, 82, 90
  Liberal and Radical Union/Association 90, 93, 105, 107–111, 136–137, 188, 207
  local economy 37–38, 41, 72–73, 107–108, 162

radical politics in 37–38, 41–44, 55, 58–65, 68–70, 74–76, 85, 95–96, 109–112, 115
radical traditions in (pre-1867) 8–9, 32, 37
Social Democratic Federation/Party in 85, 95–96, 105–112, 136–138, 141, 145, 157, 161–163, 182, 186, 188–181, 207–208
trade unionism in 17, 41–42, 73, 76, 87, 90–92, 98, 107–111, 136–138, 162, 166, 182, 186, 188, 207–208
Trades' Council 87, 136–137, 166, 182, 188
Northamptonshire 73–74, 92, 98, 165–166, 186
Norwich
 Conservative politics in 37, 117–120
 ILP (Independent Labour Party) in 117–123, 133–134, 141, 144, 155, 157, 161, 166, 189, 208, 210, 218
 Labour Party (and LRC) 133–134, 144, 155, 158–161, 166, 178–179, 182, 187, 189, 193–194, 208–212, 214–215, 218
 labour politics (pre-Labour Party) 82, 90, 93–94, 106, 117–123
 Liberal Association 82, 90, 93, 105, 117–123, 133–134, 158, 178–179, 187, 208
 liberal politics in (pre-1880) 37, 63
 local economy 59, 73, 119, 134
 radical politics in 36–37, 39–40, 46, 49, 63, 70, 72, 117, 119–121
 radical traditions in (pre-1867) 8, 32, 141
 Social Democratic Federation/Party in 118, 120–121
 Socialist League in 118, 120–121
 trade unionism in 46, 72–73, 92–94, 106, 118–122, 133, 165–166, 189, 208, 210, 212
 Trades' Council 93, 118–122, 133, 189

Odger, George 34, 49

Palmer, John Hinde 35–36
patriotism
 and labourism 20, 88–89, 154–155, 168–169, 181, 192, 203, 213, 217–218
 and radicalism 13–14, 48–49
 and socialism 88, 168–169
 and working-class radicalism 73, 74
payment of MPs 45, 87, 130, 180
Peasants' Revolt 8, 65, 92
pensions, old-age 13, 80, 83, 95, 111, 130, 137, 181, 185, 218
'the people' 29–32, 38, 40, 44, 153, 158–162, 180, 209, 220
 see also populism
Peterloo Massacre 8
popular radicalism 3–4, 14–19, 29–32, 38–41, 44, 50, 55, 82–83, 95–96, 100, 106, 109–112, 119–120, 152, 210, 225–226
populism 2–5, 18–19, 29, 32, 44–46, 82, 88–89, 100–101, 106–110, 152–175, 176, 187, 202–203, 208, 210–211, 214, 227–230
poverty, the poor 60, 71, 122, 154, 167, 170, 203
profiteers 192, 207, 209–210

race, politics of 59, 60, 71, 154–155, 168–169, 192, 213, 218
radical politics
 and class see working-class radicalism
 liberal politics, relationship with 4, 18, 28–39, 43, 47–51, 56–57, 60–69, 74–75, 226
 see also Bristol; Leicester; Lincoln; Northampton; Norwich
radicalism
 conceptual framework of 11–14, 18, 30–33, 44–46, 48–50, 57–58, 63–69, 74–75, 82–83, 85, 96, 111–112, 229–230
 distinctiveness from liberalism 11–12, 18–19, 28–32, 44–45, 49–51, 57–58, 66–69, 75, 225–226, 229–230
religious liberty 56–57, 61–62, 64, 66, 69, 75

Representation of the People Act (1867) 18, 34–35, 40, 42, 48, 49
Representation of the People Act (1884) 66
Representation of the People Act (1918) 176
republicanism 32, 35, 38, 47, 55, 61, 63
right to work 15, 84, 86, 95, 154, 166–167, 183–185, 195
'rights of labour' 15, 46, 51, 83, 109
Roberts, George Henry 133–134, 141, 144, 155, 158–159, 161, 165–166, 168, 178–179, 182, 186, 189, 191, 193, 208
Russian Revolution 192–193, 196, 207, 213, 217–218

secularism 32, 34–35, 38, 55, 61, 68
'separate spheres' 48, 72, 154, 163, 181, 212–213
see also women
Sheppard, Frank 136, 146, 157, 165–166, 191
Social Democratic Federation/Party 4, 84, 85, 95–97, 105–117, 136–138, 141, 145, 157, 161–163, 182, 185–187, 206–208
socialism 95, 100, 184
  Christian 114, 190, 206
  and labourism 80–81, 85–87, 94–100, 107, 114, 120–122, 183–187, 194–196, 217–221, 230
  revival in 1880s 1–3, 15, 19, 80, 82–84, 105, 185
  Tory 16, 106, 114–117, 204
Socialist League 84, 91–92, 118, 120–121, 140
Somerset 165
stagist account of history 2–3, 28–30, 60, 81, 92, 100, 176, 228
state, the
  in labourism 10, 19, 83–84, 86–87, 95–99, 107, 121–122, 176–178, 183–185, 193–196, 218–221
  in radicalism 11–12, 31, 50, 82–83, 85, 96, 111–112
  in socialism 10, 86–87, 95, 97, 111, 183–185, 194–195, 218

in working-class radicalism 1–2, 15, 19, 83–84, 87, 97, 100, 226
Stedman Jones, Gareth 3, 14, 16, 29
strikes and lockouts
  boot and shoe lockout (1895) 107–108, 111
  'Great Labour Unrest' (1910–1914) 136, 153, 160, 164, 181–183, 188
  new unionism 15, 80–82, 91–94, 110, 113, 137
  post-war militancy 201, 206, 210
  'rural rebellion' (1910–1914) 165

Taff Vale case (1901) 142, 179, 184
Tanner, Duncan 6, 16, 129, 136, 178
Taylor, Peter Alfred 35, 63, 142, 227
Taylor, Robert Arthur 190, 193, 206
Thompson, E. P. 5
Tichborne campaign 29
Tillett, Jacob Henry 36–37, 40, 63, 227
Todd, Selina 177
Tory socialism 16, 106, 114–117, 204
trade unions
  Amalgamated Society of Engineers 207
  Amalgamated Society of Railway Servants 107, 110
  Dockers' Union 92, 206
  evolution of literature 137–139, 147, 163
  Gasworkers' Union 92, 206
  General Railway Workers' Union 93
  Independent National Union of Boot and Shoe Women Workers 164
  National Agricultural Labourers' and Rural Workers' Union 134, 165–166, 208
  National Amalgamated Union of Shop Assistants 206–207
  National Federation of Women Workers 164, 215
  National Sailors' and Firemen's Union 59, 92, 168–169, 206
  National Union of Boot and Shoe Rivetters and Finishers/Operatives 17, 41, 66, 71, 90–93, 97–99, 107–108, 111–113, 134–139, 146, 155, 161–165, 186–188, 205, 208, 210

National Union of Clerks 168
National Union of General Workers 207–208
National Union of Railwaymen 189, 207
Typographical Association 189
Union of Post Office Workers 206
women in 72, 138, 153–154, 162–164, 203–204, 212, 215–216
Women's Trade Union League 207
Workers' Union 165
see also new unionism; strikes and lockouts
trades' councils *see* Bristol; Leicester; Lincoln; Northampton; Norwich
triennial parliaments 11, 31, 47, 180

unemployment, the unemployed 20, 59–60, 71–72, 80, 83, 86, 91, 95–96, 98, 112, 116, 122, 130, 137, 144, 146, 154, 160, 165–167, 170, 185, 203, 206, 212

Union of Democratic Control 190

Wilkes, John 65
Winstanley, Gerrard 12
Witard, Herbert 193–194, 208, 212
women 72–73, 153–154, 162–165, 170, 203–204, 212, 220
and Labour Party 21, 202–207, 212–216, 219, 227
see also 'separate spheres'
working-class radicalism
class, exclusivist conception of 4–6, 14, 18, 30–35, 38–42, 45–51, 59, 70–73, 76, 100–101, 225–226, 230
conceptual framework of 1–4, 14–15, 18–19, 30–31, 33–35, 38, 41–42, 45–50, 71–72, 83–84, 87, 97, 100, 144, 183, 225–226
hostility to 'class war' 30, 46
Worley, Matthew 11, 177, 194